# FILMMAKING
## The Collaborative Art

The American Film Institute Series

Editor of *Filmmaking: The Collaborative Art*
James Powers for The American Film Institute

Richard Leacock and Fellows of The American Film Institute Center for Advanced
Film Studies at a seminar.

# FILMMAKING
## The Collaborative Art

by
## DONALD CHASE
For The American Film Institute

Little, Brown and Company / Boston / Toronto

FIRST EDITION

T 02/75

Chase, Donald.
    Filmmaking:    the collaborative art.

    (The American Film Institute series)
    Contains interviews with various filmmakers.
    1.   Moving-picture industry.   I.   Title.   II.   Series:   American Film Insti-
tute.   The American Film Institute series.
PN1994.C3434      338.4'7'79143      74-19371
ISBN 0-316-13819-3

Designed by Milly Robinson

*Published simultaneously in Canada
by Little, Brown & Company (Canada) Limited*

# Foreword

An aspiring architect, musician, or writer can find at any great university a library containing the accumulated wisdom of men and women who have distinguished themselves in these fields of endeavor. An aspiring filmmaker has few places to turn in search of specific information and knowledge about the many creative crafts which comprise the filmmaking arts. For the most part, this knowledge has not been printed or recorded even though the motion picture medium has been a part of our lives for three quarters of a century.

We decided at The American Film Institute that one of our continuing objectives would be to seek out, collect and publish ideas and experiences of people of significant accomplishment in the fields which use the moving image and sound. We do this primarily in seminars with leading filmmakers at our conservatory, the Center for Advanced Film Studies, in Beverly Hills.

We invite film artists whose accomplishments are considerable and through the seminars gain insights into the creative processes that make filmmaking the successful collaborative art that it is. Too, we invite lawyers, agents and business affairs people who can explain the financial and legal processes which attend every endeavor in the film medium and make it a most complex art-industry.

Since we opened the Center for Advanced Film Studies in September 1969, 187 seminars have taken place with individual creators and teams of motion picture and television professionals. This book is one step forward transmitting that knowledge to a wide readership. We are indebted to Little, Brown and Company for their interest and help in bringing these ideas to the public. We hope that someday there will be libraries containing the accumulated knowledge of what we consider the most exciting art form and means of communication yet devised by man.

George Stevens, Jr.

September, 1974

# Preface

The phenomenon of diverse talents coming together for a specified time to fashion an entertainment — possibly, a work of art — is not peculiar to the film medium, but the pooling of specialists that results in movies has its own distinct characteristics, generates its own special excitements and despairs. Like the collaborations that result in other types of "theater," it takes place in the most pressured of circumstances, with time and money always at a premium, and is open to invasion by the vagaries of chance. The unknown quantities are myriad; so many things can go wrong — or right — unexpectedly. To the extent that movie artists and technicians are free of many of the formal constraints that limit their counterparts who work on various kinds of "live" entertainment, their sense of the possible is greater and more exhilarating. Yet with the film workers' freedom comes a terrible responsibility, for the flexibility of the medium is finite.

Once a movie is put together and released, it's usually unalterable. It's also relatively available for any number of re-viewings; the contributions of its makers are, in a sense, never exempt from judgment.

The permanence and accessibility of movies, along with the belated recognition of film as *the* twentieth-century art form, are among the more convincing explanations offered for the burgeoning of curiosity, over the last two decades, about how movies are made, and why certain movies were made as they were. It is both inevitable and just that the first serious attempts to satisfy this curiosity focused on the director.

The director is, or should be, at the center of the filmmaking process, and the failure of the many critics to take this into account was behind the formulation, by the editors of the French film publication *Cahiers du Cinéma,* of *la politique des auteurs,* or the *auteur* theory as it is called in America. Writer-director Eric Rohmer, a former contributor to *Cahiers du Cinéma,* has said: "The other [non-*auteur*] critics didn't even know who was responsible for the direction, and they only wanted to deal with the work by itself," that is, exclusive of its place in the body of a director's work — his *oeuvre.*

The *auteur* critics' wagering but unwavering insistence that certain directors are the "authors" of their films (regardless of whether they wrote the screenplays), and their tendency to look at a film as the work of *only* its director, just naturally triggered questions about other contributors to film — speculations on their roles and functions, musings on whether the director, even the writer-director, might be aided by one or more coauthors. I, for one, questioned and speculated and mused, but mostly randomly and privately until the time, in 1973, when The American Film Institute invited me to base a study of filmmaking as a collaborative art on its collection of transcripts of seminars with various categories of movie personnel.

The professional recollections and opinions of movie personnel I selected for inclusion here argue, by turns, for a theory of film stressing the centrality of the writer, the art director, the editor, and so on, and in sum for a *politique des collaborateurs.* Yet it should be clear that the drawing of definite conclusions to set forth any theory of film is somehow untrue to the nature of filmmaking, which changes from director to director, collaborator to collaborator, day to day.

The occasional biases this study admits of stem both from the representatives of the areas of filmmaking whose comments comprise the bulk of each chapter — they see things from their own perspectives, of course — and this writer, who chose a format which allows them to speak for themselves and, at times, interprets their remarks from their perspectives. I once heard a disillusioned Brandeis University student, whose first experience of moviemaking was three days' work as an extra in *Love Story,* say of filmmaking personnel: "I mean, these people are into *power games.*" Simplistic but true, like many observations couched in the locutions associated with Consciousness III. If I seem to transfer my allegiances from one faction in the moviemaking coalition to another, advocating a strong producer here, a strong composer there, I do so provisionally and with the knowledge that a single situation in which everybody is strong would be a nightmare — especially for the director.

It should be apparent that the paucity of statements by directors is intentional, a preconception if you will. Another preconception was discarded as a result of the statements made by the director's collaborators. Originally, I had intended to investigate only their working relationships with directors. It was after I reviewed the material the collaborators provided that I decided that it was both pertinent and necessary to devote at least as much attention to their working relationships with one another.

An attempt was made to record as broad a spectrum of experience as possible in each chapter. The careers of the artists and technicians quoted have peaked at various times and against different backgrounds. The film workers interviewed especially for this study were encouraged to speak about those situations in which they didn't feel a sense of full participation, didn't, for one reason or another, contribute all they might have, as well as about those in which they did. It is understandable that many of their remarks on relatively noncollaborative or otherwise unpleasant working experiences were unprintable, or brief and unspecific, and that they chose to expound on assignments that challenged them or relied heavily on their contributions. It is unfortunate, however, that some of the films and directors the collaborators remembered fondly and elected to discuss in depth are not as creditable as those they dismissed with a few words. One could argue that in the context of this investigation it doesn't matter if a film is good or a director is exceptionally gifted as long as the filmmaking experience involved is illustrative, but it does matter, of course. With few exceptions, I think, the films that are considered here at any length, or from more than one point of view, are good or interesting or the work of talented directors or, at the very least, outstanding in the area from which they are approached.

The order of the chapters corresponds, in a rough way, to the order in which the director's collaborators enter, or figure most importantly in, the filmmaking process. To a significant degree, the personnel dealt with in the core of the book — from the chapter on the actor through the chapter on the editor — begin and continue their work simultaneously, so the ordering of this section may strike some readers as arbitrary. But the producer and the screenwriter usually function most tellingly before a film goes into production, and the composer does all or the greater part of his work after filming is complete. Where practical, the work of the collaborator under discussion in any given chapter is approached along chronological lines, that is, traced from his entry into the filmmaking fray to the completion of his assignment.

There are slights and omissions. A writer cites the influence of Darryl F. Zanuck's story-editor "advisors," the importance of the sound crew's contribution should be apparent from the chapters on the composer and the editor, a script supervisor recalls a situation in which an assistant director was a pivotal figure. It is hoped that future studies along the lines of this one will devote more space to the activities of the story editor, the sound crew and the assistant director, among others, and investigate the province of the stunt coordinator, who is often responsible for a large part of the "direction" of action sequences.

With the exception of extracts from previously published studies cited in the text, the quoted material in this book derives primarily from the transcripts of tape-recorded seminars and discussions held at or under the auspices of The American Film Institute's Center for Advanced Film Studies. I am indebted to the guest speakers at these gatherings, for generously sharing their time and their knowledge; to the AFI's Fellows and staff members, for their provocative and intelligent questioning of the guest speakers, and to the American Society of Cinematographers and International Photographers Local 659, for their cooperation in arranging the seminars with cinematographers. The seminar and discussion-group speakers are: Gene Allen, Hal Ashby, Jack Benny, Pandro S. Berman, Elmer Bernstein, Ray Bradbury, Lynn Carlin, Leslie Caron, John Cassavetes, Robert Christiansen, the late Merian C. Cooper, Roger Corman, Linwood Dunn, Lonne Elder III, Howard Estabrook, Peter Falk, Nina Foch, Henry Fonda, John Green, Conrad Hall, Edith Head, Charlton Heston, Winton Hoch, Harry Horner, James Wong Howe, Frank Keller, the late Hal Mohr, Alex North, Rick Rosenberg, Joseph Ruttenberg, Hannah Scheel, Budd Schulberg, Leonard Spigelgass, Robert Stephens, Ingrid Thulin, Liv Ullmann, Jon Voight, Haskell Wexler, and the directors Federico Fellini, Miloš Forman, Howard Hawks, Irvin Kershner, and Jean Renoir.

The material from seminars and discussions was supplemented by the results of investigations sponsored by the Louis B. Mayer Film History Program, first under the auspices of the University of California at Los Angeles, then under The American Film Institute, and by personal interviews. Material from the Mayer program's oral histories of the following people is reproduced with all due acknowledgment to both the oral history subjects and their interrogators: Pandro S. Berman, Mike Steen; Nunnally Johnson, Thomas R. Stempel; Daniel Mandell, Barry Steinberg; Joseph Ruttenberg, Bill Gleason; John F. Seitz, James Ursini, and Donald Ogden Stewart; Max Wilk. The following were kind enough to communicate their experiences and reflections during the course of personal interviews: Peter Bart, Leigh Brackett, David Bretherton, Jerry Goldsmith, Laszlo Kovacs, Polly Platt, W. D. Richter, Albert S. Ruddy, Alvin Sargent, Hannah Scheel, Fredric Steinkamp, Jean-Louis Trintignant, Theadora Van Runkle, Gordon Willis and Karen Wookey.

My gratitude extends to Richard McDonough, of Little, Brown and Company, and James Powers, Director of Publications, Center for Advanced Film Studies, for their confidence and guidance; Rochelle Reed and Jean Poling, of Jim's office, and the staff of the Institute's Charles K. Feldman Library, for their patient assistance; Genevieve Rathman, for her astute translation of Jean-Louis

Trintignant's remarks; Neil Koenigsberg, for his general helpful-
ness during the months this project took shape, and to Helen
Cieszynski, Victoria Chase and Ellyn Jaffe, for their sympathetic
indulgence during an earlier period.

— Donald Chase

Los Angeles, California

# Contents

# FILMMAKING
## The Collaborative Art

# ONE

## The Producer

The producer — one of the director's collaborators, or his prime antagonist?

In the silent days, D. W. Griffith and other important directors were often their own producers and, as such, were responsible for the fiscal as well as the artistic aspects of filmmaking. When there was a separate producer, he performed the traditional function of his European counterpart — he put up the money and stood back, permitting the director to make the film. The producer's influence was likely to be felt before or after the film was shot because, as Kevin Brownlow asserts in *The Parade's Gone By* . . . , "the front office knew little about production methods."

As the studio system evolved and moviemaking in America developed along corporate-industrial lines, studio heads, in an effort to brake what they considered directorial extravagance, instituted a system of supervision which was in general use by the late 1920s.

3

PANDRO S. BERMAN: The title supervisor was used to refer to a man who was assigned by the head of the studio to work on individual pictures but who didn't have any great authority in matters such as purchasing [story] material or casting. He was more or less expected to carry out the policy laid down by the head of the studio. . . . It was the first job that really started to strip away some of the authority of the director.

As the supervisors gained in power and influence, they gradually became known as producers. Without denying the important role played by Irving Thalberg, the legendary second-in-command of Metro-Goldwyn-Mayer production from 1924 until the mid-30s, Berman credits Louis B. Mayer with initiating the "producer system" at the studio and making it work.

PANDRO S. BERMAN: He made producers responsible for finding the properties and watching over the development of the screenplay. . . . I always considered that my job as a producer was to find the material, be intelligent in the selection of a writer, and work closely with the writer to get a screenplay.

Berman notes, however, that at MGM "social and political restrictions" precluded the acquisition of certain properties. "Louis Mayer wouldn't make a picture like *Born Yesterday* because it insulted Congress; Nick Schenck wouldn't make a picture like *Picnic* because he thought it was a dirty play." *From Here to Eternity* was thought potentially offensive to the army, *The Caine Mutiny* to the navy, and so forth. Furthermore, when Berman joined MGM in 1940, he, like all Metro producers, was assigned a special executive who was supposed to "service" him, but whose effective function was a supervisory one.

PANDRO S. BERMAN: This supervision by the executive was . . . purely a financial one. It had nothing to do with anything except how much you paid for your property, your writer, your actors, and so on. . . . In addition to this setup, they also had a group of so-called editors. Script editors, as opposed to film editors. The editors would swoop down on every script that was finished, read it, and come bursting in to tell you what was wrong with it. On my very first picture [at MGM], after going through the usual discussions with the [story] editors and more or less winning my way in spite of everything through the early stages and the shooting, I suddenly found that Bernie Hyman and Margaret Booth, who was his [film] editorial assistant, were down in the projection room looking at my film, making suggestions on the film. I went in to my executive, Sam Katz, and told him he could have the job and I was leaving. Pretty soon, Louis Mayer made an edict that they would leave me alone, that they wouldn't interfere with the postproduction editing of my pictures. I was particularly adamant about this because I had been a film editor and felt so much better qualified to edit my films than anybody else.

Berman came to MGM after many years as a producer at RKO, where he had also been a studio executive for two brief periods. Armed with less imposing credentials, Berman's resignation might have been accepted. "There were at least twenty producers at Metro," he says, "of which fifteen were under [the studio executives'] domination completely. And there were twenty-five directors, of which twenty were under their domination completely."

ALBERT S. RUDDY: Under the old studio system, where decisions were in effect made by the giants — Goldwyn, Cohn, Louis B. Mayer — the producer's job, basically, was to watch the money. That is not how it works today. The industry has, in a sense, given such a mystique to the director because many producers and money men [didn't and still] don't understand the technology of moviemaking and are intimidated when they see it in operation.

Berman's knowledge of editing obviously made him less susceptible to intimidation than many of his contemporaries. "It was much nicer in those days," he says, "because there were no unions. A fellow who wanted to learn the business could switch around. I was an assistant director [in the 1920s] and I wasn't learning too much. I got a job as an assistant cutter." Ironically, Berman's unhappy experience as producer of 1969's *Justine*, on which he functioned more or less like one of the studio-dominated employee producers of his early MGM days, helped hasten his retirement.

PANDRO S. BERMAN: It became the first picture in my experience where I did not really make the decisions and stand or fall by my own decisions. There were two or three directors I wanted very, very badly for *Justine*. And I also wanted very, very much to use Sophia Loren in *Justine*. Well, the company [Twentieth Century-Fox] decided not to use Sophia. To use Anouk Aimée. The company decided to use Joe Strick [who was later replaced by George Cukor]. And that's where I made my fatal error, by allowing it to happen. And that's when I decided I was not for motion pictures anymore. Because once I had gotten to the point, after forty-five years, of having to let someone else upstairs make the decisions, I no longer thought of myself as the producer. . . . The producer today is beginning to look like the European producer. He's the guy who goes around and scrounges up a deal to get the picture financed. Larry Turman [*The Graduate*] said to me that he felt his job as a producer was to get Mike Nichols to make a picture and then run away. . . . I guess the present-day producer is an agent. He is a packager.

ALBERT S. RUDDY: There are producers, mostly ex-agents . . . I'm not a dealmaker. I mean, I can make a deal as good as any guy in this business can, but it's not all I do. It depends on where you see yourself fitting in and what kind of work you like. I like to be involved in the creative end — I've worked as a writer — I like being involved in casting, I like the filmmaking process, and I like the postproduction work. I've learned the job, I've learned the craft of being a producer. If a cameraman tried to give me some crap about not being able to do a shot, I could tell him why he could do it — it's happened to me a couple of times, even on *The Godfather*. I can sit down with a production man [e.g., a unit production manager, or someone else concerned with the "practical" day-to-day logistical problems of film production] and talk about how to move the slots on the board [used to make up a shooting schedule by combining personnel and locations in the most expeditious — economical — way possible] with equal facility — that's basically logic. I can go over a budget and an audit and find out where we may be getting sandbagged on Teamster charges or things along those lines. Not that there's any great secret to it, or that I'm a genius, it's just that very few producers get involved on that level.

To conclude that the producer who wanted, in Ruddy's words, his "creativity or point of view or coloring to be a factor in the film" had to establish his authority in terms of the studio in the 1930s through the 1960s and in terms of the director in the years since would leave one open to charges of simplism. As far back as the first decade of the sound era there were directors to whom producers had to defer, and the fact that since the 1960s the major studios have functioned more as financing and distribution than as production companies hasn't decreased the producer's accountability to them.

PANDRO S. BERMAN (Speaking of the time when he was affiliated with RKO): It was very simple. You would give directors as much help as you thought they would accept. Otherwise you would leave them alone. I was able to work with George Stevens much better than I was able to with John Ford. Still, I was giving Stevens his creative freedom because he was deserving of it. Ford is an absolute autocrat. He did everything his own way. The only contribution that I could make to *The Informer* was to supply him with $15,000 to buy the story. He would bring his own writer in, Dudley Nichols. He did everything in his own way. He was always the boss.

ALBERT S. RUDDY: Ultimately, this business will only continue to exist if we make money; we cannot constantly make films that lose money and think that when motion picture people go to Wall Street, or the pool of available capital in this country, they won't give it to General Motors or Du Pont, who guarantee a certain rate of return, instead of the motion picture industry. . . . The studio, in a sense, represents the investor, or the money — whatever you want to call that entity that provides the lubricant for the intermeshing of all the different talents — the writer, the producer, the director, the cutter. Not that the creative people involved in the making of a film hope to ever let it get to that point, but if a situation becomes extremely polarized, it is not a rare instance where the studio becomes a final arbiter, siding with the director against the producer or the producer against the director.

PANDRO S. BERMAN: I know how they operate today at Universal. There are X number of dollars allotted by Lew Wasserman [board chairman of MCA, Universal's parent company] for a project, and that's that. And you make it for that price or else everybody gets off the picture. I can't say that I think they would be any more open than Fox was in the case of *Justine* about letting me or any other producer make decisions. Sometimes it's important to go over budget or over schedule a day in order to get a great sequence, you know. . . . In general, I think that they're more oriented today toward allowing the decisions to be made, if by anyone other than themselves, by a director rather than a producer.

Bob Christiansen and Rick Rosenberg, who as a team produce feature-length movies for television, report that they must get approval on a piece of material they want to produce both from Tomorrow Entertainment, the production company to which they are under contract, and the television network that will eventually air the film.

BOB CHRISTIANSEN: There are probably two people at our company that we have to satisfy. In most situations, you also have two network people to satisfy before you get a final okay on a project and can go ahead and film it. Now, those two network people have talked to God-only-knows how many others. They have talked to readers. They have talked to attorneys. They have talked to Publicity. They have talked to sponsors.

Yet, sometime-director Merian C. Cooper, who was John Ford's producer on a number of films, exercised what Berman considers one of the producer's most important prerogatives by working with Ford and writer Frank S. Nugent in the preparation of the script for *Fort Apache*, and a number of contemporary producers involve themselves in the development of their properties.

MERIAN C. COOPER: On all my pictures I always write the history of each character from birth to death. If you do this, when you get someone playing the characters you know all about them: What country they came from, what their lives had been, what they ate, how they slept, whom they loved, whom they hated, how they died. There were eighteen characters, I think, in *Fort Apache* that Jack and I did that way. Ford did more than me, I guess. And then we hired Frank Nugent, who'd never done a script before. Nugent would go and write, and we'd all three meet for lunch. Then he'd go back and write again. That's the way we usually worked.

ALBERT S. RUDDY: I'm involved in a film now called *The Longest Yard*. I developed the script [from my own story idea] with [screenwriter] Tracy Keenan Wynn, I've hired Burt Reynolds, and now I'm going to hire a director. [Robert Aldrich was Ruddy's eventual choice. — D.C.] There are many producers who find a book, hire a director, and then think the director's going to do everything: work with the writer to get the script, do the casting, deliver all the other creative personnel.

BOB CHRISTIANSEN: [Rick Rosenberg and I] like to work with writers and we like to talk with them. We like to talk about the points that we don't like and the points that we do like. We like to keep the writers involved throughout the entire production — if they want to be. They can be involved in casting discussions, they can even be involved in the selection of the director. We took Tracy Keenan Wynn with us to the location of *The Glass House*. He literally went into the prison where we were shooting, and because Salt Lake City isn't the most exciting town at night and we could all get together and rap . . . he wrote maybe twenty-five percent [of the version of the script that was shot] during the production period.

Producer Roger Corman backed the first films of directors Peter Bogdanovich, Irvin Kershner, Francis Ford Coppola and Monte Hellman.

ROGER CORMAN: Generally, on the films I back, I pick the subject matter. I'll say, "Okay, now, I think we would like to go with the bike picture" or, "I think we would like to have a contemporary horror story." Then I'll turn it over to the filmmaker, who, as likely as not, is writer and editor as well as director of the film, to see what he can come up with within that framework. And, generally, there's not even a treatment. A lot of these things are just talk at the start. You just throw the ideas back and forth. . . . I'd rather start from scratch and have something designed specifically for the type of movie that I'm interested in.

It should be apparent by now that the function of the producer is inextricably involved with money: he secures it from a studio or extra-industry source on the one hand, and dispenses it to the director on the other.

ROGER CORMAN: I feel that any script can be made for any budget, but the result will be somewhat different. You can make *Doctor Zhivago* in six days for $50,000 but it's going to look somewhat different [from the version MGM made over several months at a multimillion-dollar cost]. I feel that you're better off not trying to make a spectacle on a low budget. You're better off trying to work in-depth on a subject that lends itself to the amount of money you have to spend. Otherwise, your concentration is given to making something small look big rather than taking something small and making it look good.

ALBERT S. RUDDY: I try to find in every film I do what I call the optimum point, i.e., knowing exactly the quality that you want, that you *need*, but not spending a penny more than is necessary to get it. You can do it cheaper, but it won't be what you want; you can spend more money, but you won't get any more than you wanted. As you acquire expertise as a producer you develop

a facility for finding that optimum point, which is the cutoff
point to the penny, it's where you stop.

PANDRO S. BERMAN: I think the general tendency of a producer is
to bring the picture in under budget, and the general tendency
of the majority of directors is to bring the picture in — period.
The greatest friction I ever experienced, and perhaps the greatest friction producers have experienced with directors over the
years, resulted from something other than a matter of script
changes or casting. It dealt with cost. Basically, the times I got
into hot water with directors were generally in arguments about
cost and time, how many more extras he could get in a scene . . .

ALBERT S. RUDDY: I feel that my reputation as a creative person
rides on every film I do and my fiscal responsibility rides on
every film I do. And the director is in exactly the same situation,
whether or not he wants to acknowledge it. His reputation as
an artist certainly rides on every film and, as for the other part
of it — well, there's an endlessly long list of good directors
studios will not deal with because they don't trust them to
bring a film in at a stated figure. So, the producer and the director share exactly the same responsibilities in my way of thinking, and I see no basic conflict between their positions.

As to the optimum point that I mentioned, I believe that the
director and the producer must both be looking for it. I firmly
believe that, had we spent a million dollars less on *The Godfather* we would not have had as good a movie, but I'm just as
convinced that, had we spent a million dollars more we would
not have had a better movie. Coppola's very good at helping
to determine the film's optimum point; he is very dollar conscious because of his early experience in making small films.

You get very specific when you hire a director. You say,
"We're going to do this movie in forty-two days or forty-eight
days or sixty-five days, for so much money, and we have three
days to do this scene, one day for that." If the director tells you,
"I can't do that scene in a day, and in my opinion it doesn't take
sixty days but seventy-five . . ." Now that's a twenty-five percent
increase, and with that in mind I make my decision about
whether to hire this particular director. But he must be honest.

If a guy tells you sixty days and in his own mind plans to go seventy-five — I find that utterly reprehensible. I think that kind of duplicity is a reflection of that traditional way of thinking which says that the director and the producer are necessarily working at cross purposes.

PANDRO S. BERMAN: It's up to the director and producer to keep the picture at a cost that will insure its profitability if it succeeds in reaching that special audience or audiences it is intended for. Those special audiences that exist today, as compared with the mass general audience of the past.

In the halcyon days of the studio system, the length of the director's involvement with a specific project was likely to be much shorter than it is currently. According to Pandro S. Berman, it was not uncommon for a director to be assigned to a film two weeks prior to the start of principal photography. Berman says that at the time of the director's entry, "months of labor were generally behind us." The "us" in Berman's case consisted of himself, the writer or writers and, possibly, the principal performers. (Katharine Hepburn, for instance, was not only set to star in Berman's production of *Alice Adams* before George Stevens was set to direct it, but also played an important part in selecting Stevens for the assignment.) Berman says, however, that "any good director would come in with ideas of his own and any intelligent producer would welcome them. But for the most part they were things that could be done in a short period of time." The genesis of *The Longest Yard* — as noted, producer Albert S. Ruddy worked on the screenplay with writer Tracy Keenan Wynn and engaged star Burt Reynolds before a director became involved with the film — seems something of a throwback to earlier times.

ALBERT S. RUDDY: A lot depends on the point at which the director comes on. Hopefully, in concept, *The Longest Yard* has been crystallized enough so that a director who would be interested in it is obviously seeing it in a certain way. He's not only seeing an idea, he's seeing something far more specific: a shooting script, a flesh-and-blood person playing a part. That is not to say that a director couldn't come in and say, "I've got a great idea about selling this particular point, taking another moment here, putting in another scene there, telescoping these scenes." You operate under the assumption that there's no such thing as a perfect script. Obviously you're open to ideas, and you're a fool not to encourage them. But if a director is not seeing a film as I see it, if we're not thinking of the same film, then we have a big problem. And it's very advisable, at the point when that becomes apparent, either to find yourself a new director or to abdicate from the film. When two people tear away at a piece of material on a day-to-day basis, you end up with the worst, not the best.

In a conversation with Delfina Ratazzi reproduced in the January 1973 issue of *Interview* magazine, Dino De Laurentiis distinguishes what he calls "author films" from "production films." Author films, he says,

> rely on the imagination, intelligence and creativity of one man, of one director or one writer, and the producer puts all his energy to the task of helping this author. . . . Then there is the production film . . . where the producer has a more important role. . . . There are never any problems because I make myself clear from the beginning. If I hire Fellini, I let him do what he wants. If I hire somebody else, he does what I want him to do.

Though the John Ford productions Pandro S. Berman was involved with seem to call for classification as author films (as, possibly, do certain of the films Roger Corman has backed), and Berman's production of *Ivanhoe* seems to fit the production film definition, the majority of American movies probably fall somewhere along a continuum between De Laurentiis's mutually exclusive categories.

PANDRO S. BERMAN: *Ivanhoe* is a perfect example of the producer's picture. For whatever it is, good or bad, I take the full responsibility.

I brought the picture to Metro. I brought the subject to Metro. I didn't purchase the rights to the Sir Walter Scott novel, because it was in public domain. What I did purchase, with funds approved by MGM for this purpose, was a little treatment that a man by the name of Aeneas MacKenzie had written. He had written the treatment for Paramount, and they sold it to RKO after several attempts at developing a script from it. RKO subsequently abandoned it, and I bought it for a small sum of money. We could have started with the book; as a matter of fact, we did go back to the book. But we thought it would be wise to clear all of those rights pertaining to the treatment before we started, so there wouldn't be any danger of law suits. And we got that little treatment as a basis to go on.

The next step was to develop it into a screenplay. A staff writer named Marguerite Roberts and I worked out a first and then a second draft of the screenplay. The script was pretty good from the standpoint of story construction — form. But Marguerite was incapable of writing it in the vernacular of the period. So, just before I started production I engaged an Englishman by the name of Noel Langley who, in eight or nine days, revised the dialogue to suit the period. He really didn't contribute very much to the construction of the overall story or of individual scenes.

I picked Richard Thorpe to direct the film before I had any cast. I picked him for a very specific reason. I knew this was going to be a tough picture to make physically. At that time he was the most efficient, fast-moving, competent action director that we had at Metro. He was also a director who was perfectly willing to let the producer develop the script, cast the film, edit the film — all of that. He just wanted to be there on the set. He was also willing, as some men are, to allow the producer to break up the thing into units. Maybe half of this picture was done by the second unit, under the direction of Yakima Canutt. He did all of the big battle scenes, the tournaments, and so forth. We shot with both units going simultaneously; while Thorpe was making the interiors, Yakima was making the exteriors. The costumes of the period — the helmets particularly — made it easy to double the principals.

As it was, we made the picture quite economically. I think that on the Metro books you would find the film's cost listed as $3,800,000. Actually, we spent $1,800,000. After the film was released and [the studio] saw it was a hit, they immediately added two million dollars in overhead charges. Most of that

$1,800,000 was below the line. Marguerite Roberts got very
little; she probably got five or six hundred dollars a week. Noel
Langley only worked a week or two. Dick Thorpe was a contract director, so he didn't get much. Robert Taylor was a
contract player and wasn't getting a lot of money. Under the
contract system, actors were paid on a weekly basis, and if you
used them you got them ridiculously cheap. I paid as little as
forty thousand dollars for Clark Gable on a picture.

At that time [1953] at MGM, the director was usually taken
off the film at the end of the shooting. He had nothing more to
do with it. He would come to the preview and see it. I always
thought that editing was among my principal functions, because
I had been a cutter all my life.

ROGER CORMAN: On most of the films I've backed [the directorial
débuts of Coppola, Bogdanovich *et al.*], the filmmaker's deal
called for him to write, direct and cut. Quite frankly, he did
not get a great deal of money for doing this. The reason was:
I was giving him an opportunity to make his first film on the
basis, hopefully, that I would make a profit and, hopefully, his
career would take off. It's an even trade: he gets a small
amount of money and makes his film; I get the profit from
the film.

On projects like these most of my controls are before the
shooting and afterwards. For instance, I'll check out everything
very carefully beforehand — the script, the production staff,
the casting and so forth. During the actual shooting, on most
of the films I've backed, I never even go to the set. I really feel
it's best to work this way on the basis that I've made a decision
to back this man as a director and he should have the opportunity to simply go and direct his film. I don't think any producer
can have a great deal of control during the shooting unless he
just comes in and takes over. In general, the only time I'll step
in is when I see something in the rushes that really causes me
to jump out of my chair or when the director falls a great deal
behind schedule. But if the work looks even somewhere near
what I would consider to be acceptable commercial standards
and he's near his schedule and budget, I prefer, frankly, not
even to talk to him. After completion, I'll generally look at the

director's second or third cut in the projection room and tell him my thoughts on it. That would be on a film that's gone smoothly. On others, when I think we have problems, I'll go into the cutting room with him. However, I'd say that with the majority of films I've backed, I've never been on the set and I've never been in the cutting room.

RICK ROSENBERG: During production, a lot of producers will sit in their offices. They will look at the dailies and attend to business. [Bob Christiansen and I] like to be on the set. In fact, we have been accused of hiring directors who are malleable and will tolerate us on the set. There are directors, however, who seem to like the kind of support and assurance that a physically present producer can give: "This is great. Fantastic!" Tom Gries directed *The Glass House* for us. We had discussed another project with him about a year and a half prior to *The Glass House*. It was an adaptation of a novel. He saw in it what we had seen in it. We felt, This is a man we would eventually like to work with. After sitting and chatting with him about *The Glass House*, we knew it would probably work. We worked very, very closely with Tom because we felt that he wanted and, maybe, needed for us to do so.

BOB CHRISTIANSEN: If you are there all the time, rapping and keeping [Tom Gries] up, he is more likely to get great things for you, especially from the actors. He is very good with actors.

RICK ROSENBERG: There is another director in this town — if he doesn't have that kind of support, he will go to sleep on you. Really.

Very seldom will we interrupt a director in his work and say, "Hey! . . ." If we do see something we try to pick an opportune time and be as tactful as possible.

BOB CHRISTIANSEN: The director has to realize that the only contribution you are trying to make is to make a better picture.

We only saw one rehearsal of a key scene between Cloris Leachman and Mildred Dunnock in *A Brand New Life*. We had to leave to look at the rushes of the previous day's shoot-

ing. After we looked at them we called Sam O'Steen, the director, on the phone and told him, "The dailies look great." We
asked him how the shooting went, and he said, "Fine," and that
he did the scene in one take.

We got really nervous, only because we weren't sure that we
weren't going to need a couple of close shots of the two actresses. So we said, "Goddammit, Sam, why didn't you shoot a
couple of close-ups of this? What's going on?" He said, "You
know, I'm nervous about it too. But what would have happened
if I had tried to do close-ups?"

The way the scene was shot, down a long corridor, he would
have had to use three cameras, one for the long shot and two
for the close-ups. We had only two cameras on the unit we were
using. And then one of the cameras went bad and it was getting late into the day. And Cloris had shot her wad with the
scene; it was a rough one, with crying. She did it in rehearsal
and she did it on that one take.

Then Sam said he thought there was a way he could get some
close-ups of the scene, optically. Sam was the cutter on *Catch-
22*. There are a lot of close-ups in [*Catch 22*] that were done
optically — the camera did not go in at all. Still, Rick and I
looked at each other and said, "Optically, yeah, here we go."
Then we saw the scene in dailies and it was fine. He didn't
need any close-ups.

PANDRO S. BERMAN: Gregory LaCava was a difficult man to work
with, and a very rewarding man to work with. The difficulty
came as a result of his intense desire never to crystallize on
anything, to keep everything fluid to the degree that no script
was ever a script in his mind until a scene had been photographed. Our procedure in making a film was that we had a
kind of guideline script and then we would hire the actors.
Now LaCava was able to really function. Because he was capable, more than anybody else I ever met in this business, of
exploiting the personality of an actor. There was never improvisation by the actors themselves during the shooting. There
was improvisation by Gregory LaCava each morning when he
would come in and rewrite the scene that was to be shot that
day based on his knowledge of the actors' talents from previous

days. So that the mornings were spent writing scenes and the afternoons in photographing. I remember one of his favorite expressions was "Don't worry about the dialogue. I can always spit that out at the last minute." As long as he knew generally what the subject matter was and in what general direction the story was going, he was capable of improvising good scenes daily.

I feel I was constructive and helpful in the early stages of development of material with LaCava . . . to the degree of getting a story line, situations — a framework on which he could hang his scenes. So, I was able to make some contribution to the film itself as well as to the general production side. My biggest job with LaCava, really, was to get him to shoot a scene because, as I say, he was always anxious to keep it fluid, thinking that something better would come along tomorrow.

In general, with the pictures I produced, I would visit the set every day. Maybe twice a day. Morning and afternoon. But they were strictly visits. They'd be courtesy visits, or they'd be in connection with some business that came up, decisions that had to be made on things like casting. Or they'd be, occasionally, to tell [a director] how good or bad his dailies looked to me! I never believed in sitting around on the set or in attempting to help a director direct a picture. I felt my function was to get a good director and provide him with a script, provide him with a cast. Help him whenever he needed help. Keep him from going too far with expenses and edit for him when he was through. But leave him strictly alone when he was making a scene.

Vincente Minnelli could work economically and very fast and often did. He was also a man who had a tendency to lose himself in one big sequence in almost every picture. There would be one sequence, like the waltz in *Madame Bovary,* that he would fall in love with and develop, perhaps a little too much for the budget. I managed to overcome that in my pictures with him by having my associate, Jane Loring, go down on the set and stay there with him. She was able to get him to make decisions, in advance, on sets and dressings of sets and so forth. So that they would be ready for him when he moved in to work on them. Whereas, if he had been left to his own devices, he wouldn't have tackled these problems that far in advance. He would have moved into the set and then started changing the set and the dressings. Vincente Minnelli was the most agreeable man about letting you put his picture in shape for him. Vincente Minnelli would ask me to edit the picture. Then he would come and look at it with me and make a few suggestions. But he didn't want to go through that labor. He was more involved with the whole concept [including the editing] of the musicals which Arthur Freed produced.

Richard Brooks came into the business a little later, and as a result of that and the fact that he was also a writer, was not part of the Metro system under which a director was assigned to a picture a short time before production and taken off of it a short time after. Richard was with it from its inception to its finish. He was very much responsible for everything that happened, but it was still a collaboration between us when we worked together. I always believed that a director should be permitted to show his film to me exactly the way he wanted to show it. I was only too happy when a man like Richard Brooks was eager to do that kind of work and really buckle down in the cutting room rather than just let an editor do it for him. Then I could enter at the final editing stage and make suggestions, talk him into changes, or be talked out of them. Other directors would be delighted to avoid the work of editing and, once I assigned an editor, would be away from the picture until the editor and I had put it together for them. Then they would come in and make a few suggestions of their own. Brooks would sit in the cutting room by himself for three months before he would even let me look at the first cut.

When a director is nominally his own producer (nominally, because an executive, associate or coproducer often takes on the responsibility of the practical aspects of production), he assumes a greater portion, or all, of the fiscal responsibility that Albert S. Ruddy says he normally shares equally with a separate producer. In dealing with a producer-director, the studio, represented either by an absentee employee executive or by one or more members of the producer-director's practical production staff, may, in what seems like a return to the practices of the late-silent and

early-sound eras, function in a supervisory way. And despite the
increased freedom of the director since the 1960s and the con-
comitant rise in the number of directors who are full or partial
producers of their films, the studio or studio executive may perform some of the traditional functions of the "strong" or "creative" producer. In successive positions as Paramount's vice president in charge of creative affairs and that company's vice
president of production, Peter Bart has functioned in both supervisory and strong-creative producer capacities.

PETER BART: What I've tended to do is, say, twice a year, take
   projects that really interest me and work on them with a writer
   alone, functioning basically as a producer does. The writer and
   I will try to figure out the construction of the story, figure out,
   most importantly, what story we want to tell. I optioned a
   novel called *Addie Pray,* by Joe David Brown, and worked on
   the screenplay with a writer named Alvin Sargent. We had a
   book which told about ten stories, and we just decided which
   three or four of those ten we'd use. We ended up leaving out
   more than half of the book — it's a selection process. When we
   finished our third draft we gave it to Peter Bogdanovich, who
   then directed it for The Directors Company [as *Paper Moon*].
   He did some work on the script with Alvin, but, basically, he
   shot the script that was developed by the studio. In effect, this
   particular picture originated as a house project, which is somewhat ironic in view of the idea behind The Directors Company. It became a Directors Company picture after Peter Bogdanovich entered and it was cast with our advice and consent,
   though Paramount's agreement with The Directors Company
   gives him basic autonomy as to the casting of his picture and,
   in general, making it as he sees fit.
      As an example of the front office functioning in a supervisory
   way, as opposed to making a creative contribution, take the
   case of *The Parallax View.* The picture was behind schedule
   and over budget when an issue pertaining to going on location
   came up. It was a question of whether to shoot a certain scene
   at Lake Powell, an interesting and good backdrop in terms of
   the scene. Having seen the dailies, and being close to
   [producer-director] Alan Pakula, the script and so forth, the

question that I as a studio functionary have to answer is, Do you spend the extra couple hundred thousand dollars to go to Lake Powell when you're running behind already, or do you shoot the scene around Los Angeles at a considerably lower cost? You sit down with [Alan Pakula] . . . and you really ulcerate over the decision. How much would that location add to the picture, is it worth an additional overage? In this case, Alan and I agreed that we should not go to that location.

In dollar terms, *The Godfather* is the most successful movie ever made. It's also one of the few immensely popular movies that is also a very good one; not many of the films listed in *Variety*'s annual compilation of "All-Time Boxoffice Champs" as having earned, let us say, twenty million dollars in domestic film rentals pleased as broad a spectrum of the critics as *The Godfather* did. An odd amalgam of circumstances and sensibilities was involved in the genesis of *The Godfather* both before and after the entry of director Francis Ford Coppola. Yet, against what would seem insuperable odds — its origin and development as a film project within the confines of a studio, the studio's substantial monetary investment, the presence of a forceful and opinionated producer, etc. — the film is very much the work of its director. Peter Bart and Albert S. Ruddy tell the story of *The Godfather* (some details of which have been included in previously published accounts of the making of the film) from the standpoints of the studio executive and the producer, respectively. The contradictions in their recollections of events that took place two to three years earlier are especially ironic in that Bart and Ruddy were the only two people interrogated expressly for this study with an opportunity to reconcile each other's stories. It was Ruddy who solicited and facilitated the setting up of an appointment to interview Bart. Ruddy, incidentally, has admitted elsewhere to occasional "personality clashes" with Coppola.

PETER BART: [Paramount] bought the rights to *The Godfather* after seeing fifty or sixty manuscript pages and an outline of the rest of the book. That was a case where one took a piece of material which, at the beginning, a lot of people were very unsure about and seeing it through the various stages over a

period of years, seeing it through the obstacles. I was responsible for optioning the basic material, I worked on the screenplay with Mario Puzo, I brought in Al Ruddy as producer, and
later, Al and I brought Francis Ford Coppola in as director.
Mario Puzo was always going to do our first-draft screenplay.
The basic decision we faced in terms of developing the screenplay was whether to make a relatively inexpensive action-
gangster picture, or whether to tell it from the point of view of
a family chronicle. It was the decision of all of us to try for the
bigger, more substantial film, not just a rip-off Mafia picture.

ALBERT S. RUDDY: Because of the disastrous returns on *The
Brotherhood* and a general lack of faith in doing another film
dealing with the same subject matter, Paramount kind of enter-
tained some very staggering offers from people who wanted to
buy the rights to the book. Because the book topped the best-
seller list for about sixty-five weeks, they decided to make the
movie. [The relationship between cause and effect may be
more ambiguous than Ruddy suggests. It has been rumored
that Paramount, with a vested interest in *The Godfather*,
underwrote some portion of the book's promotional costs, was,
in effect, at least partially responsible for its best-seller list
tenure. — D.C.] When we started out conceptually, when I was
hired by Paramount, before any script had been written or any
actors hired, Paramount felt more comfortable thinking of *The
Godfather* as a three-million-dollar movie. Before I got there,
they went to a number of big producer-directors of the ilk of
Richard Brooks, who for one reason or another didn't want to
do *The Godfather*. They thought it was just a big commercial
thing about gangsters and didn't see it as a film with redeeming
social or any other value. There's no question [Paramount]
would have preferred to do *The Godfather* with Fred Zinnemann or Elia Kazan than with Francis Ford Coppola. And
they probably would have preferred to do it with Sam Spiegel
than with Al Ruddy.

I was the first person on *The Godfather*. I then hired Mario
Puzo and worked with Mario, I would say, about three months,
developing the script. It was imperative, I thought, from a

commercial standpoint, to keep Mario Puzo locked into the project because . . . he *was The Godfather.*

PETER BART: In choosing a director, first you look at the list of available directors and you moan and groan over the fact that there aren't more directors you'd want to hire. Then you experience some guilt feelings about why isn't the company doing more to train new directors. And after you get through that phase you go down the list again and try to cast a director. I believe that directors should be cast like actors. The error the town makes is thinking that if a director made a picture that was a success, no matter what kind of picture you have you're wise to put him in it. I thought Francis Ford Coppola was perfect casting for *The Godfather.* (On the other hand, if we were making a Western I think Francis would be a terrible choice.) Yes, absolutely, the suggestion [to use Coppola] originated with me. I fought like hell to get Coppola in *The Godfather.* Objections? Little details like he had never done a successful picture, he wasn't disciplined enough, not experienced enough.

ALBERT S. RUDDY: Mario Puzo had never done a screenplay before. One of the biggest attractions that Francis Ford Coppola held for me, aside from the fact that he was a fine director and understood production problems, was that he was a very gifted writer. It became a very easy transition at that point to have the director and not another writer work with Puzo. Not that Mario Puzo's screenplay needed that much help, because it was, basically, very good. But it wasn't in perfect screenplay form. When Francis was hired for the film he went to work immediately with Mario and really slicked it up, brought it up to shooting form. Although, in fact, many of the bones, the architecture of the script, had been settled by Mario when we had worked together.

PETER BART: Francis contributed greatly to the refinement of the screenplay, but the credit for *The Godfather* as a piece of material should all be Mario Puzo's. And Francis is the first to admit it.

ALBERT S. RUDDY: Francis read the script, we had our discussions, we both realized where it was at, and he started working with Mario on the final rewrite. There was very little supervision; nor was any required at that point. It would be pretentious of me, I would be lying if I said that I had to supervise Francis and Mario at that stage. We were in an enormous time press — Francis came on about five months before shooting started — and there were many other things that required attention; big political problems originating with certain pressure groups that didn't want to see *The Godfather* made were starting to brew.

PETER BART: Francis and I stayed very close during the casting of the picture. [Paramount's vice-president in charge of production] Bob Evans and I conferred a lot about casting, but the decisions about casting were ultimately Francis's and they were brilliant decisions.

ALBERT S. RUDDY: The initial concept was to do it as a small contemporary film and try to ride the title. And it was only after we really got into it, especially the inclusion of Marlon Brando — I must say that it was Francis who fought for the period idea — it suddenly became a meld of a lot of ideas and different elements that started bringing it to a bigger, more expensive film.

PETER BART: A lot of the idea for making it a family chronicle came from discussions that I had early on with Francis. It wasn't any brilliant brainstorm I had; it grew out of our discussions. . . . That idea of doing the film as a period piece was Al's, it was Evans's, it was mine, it was Francis's. When the decision was made to do it as a substantial picture, to spend the money on it, then we decided to make it a period rather than a contemporary film. . . . Once the picture started shooting, it was very much Francis's ball game.

ALBERT S. RUDDY: . . . There is a moment when the director takes it over. And that is why you've got to hire the right director.

You must build a wall around him so that he can address the greatest possible amount of his creative energies to the execution of the film and not be concerned with a lot of the other pressures. However, that must always be within the framework of sharing. As I share, in a sense, his job in that his reputation is riding on the film, so I insist that he have a concern for my job and my reputation. In the case of *The Godfather,* there were areas where the creative judgment had to be placed against or counterpointed to the dollars we had to spend, making for problems that Francis and I had to solve together on a moment-to-moment basis. That's the area where the two jobs overlap and you both share the same concern. If we're shooting on Fifth Avenue, as Michael [Al Pacino] and Kay [Diane Keaton] come out of Best & Co., I want to have enough period cars on the street so that it looks real and Francis wants enough. But the budgetary demands may restrict how many cars you can have.

I would say that the movie was very tightly controlled as to how the money was spent. There were a lot of bright, young people who worked on it in a production capacity, in assisting Francis, in assisting the production designer, Dean Tavoularis, who really made great contributions. They did research and got certain things that were critical to the film — secured certain locations — and it was not done by dint of a lot of money. "I don't care what you want for this place, we'll pay you!" — it was never done that way.

When production started the budget was locked at somewhere between $5.4 and $5.5 million. The film came in at $6.1 million, but the film never slipped. It was things we had no control over: Al Pacino got hurt, it started snowing. Filming in New York in the winter, with a $5.5 million budget, the expenditure of an additional half million or so does not represent a slide. A real slide on a film on that scale could bring it up to, maybe, eleven million. That's because the cost of making a film, at certain points, increases not arithmetically but geometrically. You have the various departments — camera, sound, wardrobe, Teamsters — and if you lose, or start sliding, in one department it affects every other department. If the set you've constructed is not staying up, then you can't proceed with set dressing; and everybody else is not working, literally, but is being paid nevertheless.

PETER BART: I would say that the front office does not make, despite allegations to the contrary, creative contributions while a film is before the cameras.

ALBERT S. RUDDY: As the film started to generate an enormous amount of publicity and the dailies indicated to the studio that there was quality . . . there arose a very expansive feeling about the potential success of *The Godfather*. We were going to do the scene where Jimmy Caan is killed at the tollbooth — in one day, on a real highway out near Jones Beach. Paramount said, "Don't worry about the money, do a spectacular job." So, we went out to a deserted airstrip at Floyd Bennett Field which would be much easier to control than an actual location, and dressed it up to look like a highway. Dean Tavoularis designed two tollbooths, and we shot there almost three days. I would say that scene cost $100,000, but that was a conscious choice. It reflected the feeling of all of us that we could keep reaching for a little more quality — at moments — and that every dollar we spent would be money well spent both in terms of the creative return on the film and the financial return on the film.

I worked on the various stages of the editing and I was in on the mixing from the first minute to the last minute. Francis has a facility in San Francisco — American Zoetrope — and a wife and kids and a house in San Francisco. When we wrapped in Sicily he had been gone from San Francisco for about eight or nine months. He wanted to do the first assembly of the film in San Francisco at American Zoetrope, and I thought it was not only fair, but I felt that we would probably get through that maze much more rapidly by letting Francis live at home and work at his own facility. We had two cutters up there with him, I went up once a week, but, basically, the first assembly of the film was done in San Francisco by Francis. Then we started refining, taking out certain things, Francis came down here, we moved the cutters down here, and we worked in Los Angeles. Francis and I worked on the first cut basically without anyone from Paramount looking in. When we finished our cut it ran two hours and fifty-five minutes, we showed it to Bob Evans and — as a result of our anxiety, because we knew that Paramount wanted a two-hour-and-twenty-five-minute movie — we cut it down to two-twenty-five.

PETER BART: . . . In postproduction, there have been instances where the front offices of the different studios have been extraordinarily astute. Bob Evans makes very insightful suggestions at the postproduction stage. I think that many directors are extremely shortsighted in that they aren't open to ideas when they're editing. If you go to people you respect and solicit their advice, you might get, out of ten ideas or suggestions, one that really makes it better.

ALBERT S. RUDDY: I must say, to Bob Evans's credit, and Paramount's, he said, "It's better at two-fifty-five, it played faster at two-fifty-five." And so, again, you had a corporation that was going against what you'd call standard studio procedure.

In my opinion, there is not another director in the world who could have made *The Godfather*. I totally believe that, for a lot of different reasons. Francis Coppola is as bright a person as I've met — as a writer, as a director, and as a producer.

PETER BART: Francis's conceptualizing was brilliant, his casting was brilliant, his sense of production was brilliant, his direction was brilliant.

✸

ROGER CORMAN: As a director I want to do pictures that I'm personally interested in; as a producer it's a different thing. As a producer you normally function in what is essentially a businesslike manner, although on some films the personal vision can be there as well.

PANDRO S. BERMAN: I was emotionally involved in many of my films: the excitement that came with knowing and feeling that you were getting something very good, and the terrible depression that came with knowing you were getting something that wasn't good.

ALBERT S. RUDDY: I would like to feel that any movie I make would make money. You are assuming that obligation in the motion picture business when you are spending that kind of money. Otherwise, do a painting or write a book, where your initial investment in executing your idea is much less. But there's nobody I know in this business, whom I respect, who is in it just to make money. Emotionally, that's not what it's about. I think you'd find that the median income of film producers over the years is surprisingly low. That's partially because so many producers do only three or four movies and then get lost somewhere. But there are guys who continue in the field though they may wait two years to do a movie that goes nowhere, wait another two years to do a movie that goes nowhere. There are a lot of producers who have made very comfortable livings, but they haven't come out of it with as much money as a good doctor makes. For *The Wild Seed,* the first film I produced, I got $2,500, and it took a year and a half to get it made. There's a whole different reason as to why people stay in it.

To me, it's a profession and it's something that's got to be learned and it takes a great talent with all that knowledge. The great talent consists in the ability to be a combination of an idealist and a politician. You must know what you want and have a sense of integrity about it, and be enough of a politician to get it when no one wants to give it to you.

# TWO

## The Screenwriter

LEONARD SPIGELGASS: The advent of the film changed the whole relationship between the creator of the work of art, of the drama, and the implementer of the work of art, of the drama. Up until the motion picture, there was really no such thing as a director. A director was a man who directed traffic on the stage so that the actors didn't bump into each other. There was never the signature of the director on a play.

Spigelgass, a past president of the Writers Guild, may overstate the case a bit. (Surely Stanislavsky, Meyerhold, Reinhardt and Granville-Barker put their signatures on the plays they staged, as Peter Brook does today.) But there's a large germ of truth in his statement, and, significantly, an echo of the masochistic, melancholy resentment that infects many contemporary screenwriters' meditations on their lot.

In the silent period, when the medium was essentially visual, and directors wrote their own scripts or developed them from a writer's scenario — an outline detailing the sequence of events and significant action in a film, the "story," basically — the second-class status of the writer seems to have been taken more or less for granted. Still, writers with reputations in other media — Elinor Glyn, Michael Arlen and Maurice Maeterlinck, for example — were sufficiently intrigued by the potentialities they saw in the medium or lured by the money offered them by producers to write silent scenarios. And silent-film title-card writers, who may or may not have authored the scenarios of the films they narrated and dialogued, actually attained some measure of recognition and celebrity. In *The Parade's Gone By . . .* Kevin Brownlow quotes the January 1929 issue of *Photoplay*: "A Hollywood theater announces, in electric lights, 'Titles by Ralph Spence,' being the first time on record a title writer rated billing."

With the introduction of sound came the necessity of fully written, predialogued scripts and the importation, primarily from the East, of large numbers of playwrights and novelists to supply them. Accustomed to functioning with relative autonomy, and, in the case of the playwrights, under the protection of the Dramatists Guild rule that prohibited unauthorized alterations to their work, the emigrant screenwriters found themselves in the position of factory employees whose output could be revamped to suit the specifications of the studio, the producer, the director, or the star. "You had to learn," says Donald Ogden Stewart, "the first thing you had to learn was not to let them break your heart."

The importation of *auteur* criticism to the United States in the 1960s broke many veteran writers' hearts more painfully than earlier infringements on their creative freedom ever did. The writers read that various of their films had been "authored" to one degree or another by the men who directed them. Parenthetically, Nunnally Johnson complains that as early as the thirties, critics, writing mostly from a distance of three thousand miles and unsure as to who did what on a film, were prone to attribute to the director contributions from other sources.

In the sixties, roughly concurrent with the critics' minimization of the historical role played by the writer in American films, the actual independence and control permitted the American director increased. The director, even the run-of-the-mill director, became involved with a film at an earlier stage than previously and had more of a hand in shaping the script. Whether the average Hollywood director today plays a more decisive role in shaping a script of a film than the producer (or studio) for, or with, whom the writer worked primarily in the past is a moot point. The writer's contention seems to consist in the fact that the director-as-author theory about the past, dismissed as bogus, has become a reality in the present.

One sympathizes with the writer's feeling of neglect, and recognizes the legitimacy of his bid for a share, at least, of the possessory credit for a film. On the other hand, the more militant advocates of "writer power" appear to have overlooked the potential advantages of working *with* the director: a longer, closer, more productive involvement with a film project that may extend into the shooting and editing stages. The screenwriter seems increasingly to be asked to collaborate with the director, not just to provide him (or a producer or studio) with a piece of material and hope for the best. One suspects that the chapter dealing with the screenwriter in a volume of this sort written ten years from now will devote a proportionately greater number of pages to his relationship with the director simply because the available material on the writer-director relationship will have grown substantially by that time.

Though a large number, perhaps a majority, of screenwriters insist that they are craftsmen (Nunnally Johnson calls himself a "cabinetmaker"), the author of an original screenplay can claim, with some justification, the status of artist or creator. In the paragraphs that follow, Budd Schulberg, Nunnally Johnson and Alvin Sargent describe the wellsprings of three original screenplays. The basis of Schulberg's *A Face in the Crowd*, Sargent's *Love and Pain and the Whole Damn Thing* in personal experience suggests that the novelist's inspiration and the screenwriter's are not as dissimilar as is often assumed.

BUDD SCHULBERG: [The prototype for the central figure in *A Face in the Crowd*] could have been Arthur Godfrey, but it wasn't meant to be him. The seed of the story was planted by Will

Rogers, Jr. He was a close friend of mine, way back. One night
we were sitting and talking about his father. Actually, we were
talking about both of our fathers, and he was saying, "You
know, it was just a myth about my old man. He had a big
house and he loved to have big shots around. He was no more
with the common people than . . ." And I think that was where
the idea started. But then I saw others. And from a Godfrey, I
began to see the sense of power that we [confer upon certain
entertainment-world figures]. . . . A *Face in the Crowd*, Elia
Kazan and I started it together. We talked about it, planned it,
thought it out, and I was on the set every day. We worked as
closely as two people could, as closely as we did with *On the
Waterfront*.

NUNNALLY JOHNSON (With reference to *The Prisoner of Shark
Island*): Zanuck called me in one morning and showed me a
clipping out of *Time* which had something to do with Dr.
Mudd, who had served for a long period in a prison in the Dry
Tortugas. He was arrested after the assassination of Lincoln.
Zanuck said, "Does this sound like a picture to you?" I said, "It
might." I had never heard of Dr. Mudd. I knew that there was
a conspiracy and I knew that Mrs. Suratt had been hanged and
I knew this, that, and the other about it. Zanuck said, "Well,
why don't you look into it and see if we can get something?"
There was a book by Lloyd Lewis called *Myths After Lincoln*,
which I had read some years before. It was a very interesting
book, and among the author's stories was one about whatever
became of John Wilkes Booth, whether he was actually killed
in that barn. . . . I finally got from Washington the transcript
of the trial of the conspirators. Although Mudd was a Southern
sympathizer and had been at Mrs. Suratt's boardinghouse on
one or two occasions, it was far from certain that he had had
any part in the conspiracy. From what research I could do, I
came to the conclusion that we were equally justified in saying
that he was innocent. So I went to work on the story on the
basis that Mudd was a man who was accidentally brought into
this thing and the trial verdict was in effect saying, like a Scot-
tish verdict, "Not proven, but just for the hell of it, we'll give
him six years for being around there." . . . Abraham Lincoln's

request, in the opening sequence of the film, that "Dixie" be played is true in the sense that that was in Lloyd Lewis's book. I didn't make it up.

ALVIN SARGENT: Alan Pakula and I were having a drink together after having seen the final print of *The Sterile Cuckoo* at Paramount, and I proposed an idea. In 1953 I was in Hawaii. I saw a woman, I just saw her face — that's all. I saw her through glass; I was looking through a window and she was on the other side. She had the most self-conscious manner I'd ever seen. Her ears turned red when she caught my glance. I was uncomfortable, I was alone, she was alone. She looked like a schoolteacher from Ohio, I suppose, and she walked away and that was it. But I never forgot her face. One day, almost twenty years later, I started thinking, What if I had gone up and introduced myself, and then a story began to take form. I imagined what if somehow or other we came together, and I imagined our having some kind of relationship that turned to romance and that I married her and she died and I left Hawaii a widower. I had arrived a totally unpulled-together kid, I left a widower, and what would happen to my life? That's the story I started out to tell; it was called *The Widower* [a title it retained until just before its release as *Love and Pain and the Whole Damn Thing*]. Alan said, "Why not just do this story up to the point where they get married: how do you bring these two 'turtles' together?" That's how it started. From there we played around with it, I sat down and worked a few drafts, and I had a lot of trouble, but I think, finally, it came together — for me — because it really talked about something of great importance. You just can't get through life happily without experiencing some degree of both love and pain and . . . how we're all closed up in certain areas. That theme is something I could deal with forever.

The disappointing critical and financial returns on screen translations of successful plays and novels in recent years has resulted in an increase in the number of films based on original material. However, the bulk of the screenwriter's work still consists of adapting works conceived for another medium.

NUNNALLY JOHNSON: I have learned to look for the backbone, the skeleton of a novel, what this fellow was setting out to tell, so that actually he could have told it in a nightletter. Almost. John Steinbeck wanted to tell, in *The Grapes of Wrath*, what an act of nature did to a great segment of helpless people and how they reacted. Not only that, because that would just be a tract, but he created human beings — Ma and Pa and Grampa and Preacher and Rosasharn. That's a tremendously impressive thing to think of, [and] I had to read the book two or three times before it all became clear to me, like an X-ray photograph. You know, the bones became visible.

RAY BRADBURY: After being offered the job of adapting *Moby Dick*, I took *Moby Dick* home, and how did I read it? Do I start at the beginning? Like hell I do. I open it and I find the thing about the spirits. I read all about the fountains of Versailles that have somehow gone to sea late at night to sprinkle the deeps with diamonds and jewels. I turned to another section and I found the becalmment. Then I found the section on the whiteness of the whale. I read that. Then I came to the last section, where Ahab says, "It's a mild, mild day and a mild-looking sky." I turned back to the opening of the book and I read, "Call me Ishmael." I went back to John Huston the next day, and I said, "Wow. It's the right time in my life. I'm old enough."

One reason why I refuse to adapt anyone else's novel from here on in is that it takes roughly six months of reading somebody else's novel to get it into your bloodstream. While I was working on the adaptation of *Moby Dick* in Dublin, I suffered severe depressions. I was going through a process of reading that book nine times over. I was having a hell of a lot of trouble, and Huston wasn't much help, because we are both essentially intuitive people and not intellectuals. But a beautiful thing happened along about the seventh month. I got out of bed one morning, looked in the mirror, and said, "I am Herman Melville." In one day, eight hours, I rewrote the last forty pages. It took me six or seven months of getting Melville into my bloodstream so he could finally come out of my fingers. Before this, he was self-conscious. "How do I use this ship? Where do I put

that captain? What do I do with this lorry?" That is all functioning stuff. It's data collecting and sorting out. It finally has
to be struck with lightning. There are a lot of damn good things
in that film, but the last forty minutes of it have a fantastic
flow. They have an inevitable flow. The rhythm is gorgeous
because of that one day. We never changed any of those pages.
I never rewrote or revised any of that. I wish I could have done
that with the whole screenplay. The thing that happened was
that I found ways of using symbols to enclose symbols, metaphors to enclose metaphors.

When you adapt another person's book, it's got to get into
your bloodstream so completely that it can come out on an
emotional level and be recreated. It has to be recreated through
your emotions and not rethought. Your emotions will do the
rethinking for you. . . . In doing a thing like *Moby Dick* you
have to outline. [The scenario on which the screenplay was
based is the result of "at least twenty-five outlines," Bradbury
says. — D.C.] I would much rather have done that screenplay
all the way through ten times emotionally and done it wrong
so that I would come to it the eleventh and right time emotionally. Most of those outlines got us nowhere.

LONNE ELDER III: The novel *Sounder* had a kind of atmosphere
about it that was conducive to making a picture out of it, but
there were a number of elements I didn't like. I felt that,
basically, there were some subterranean or subliminal elements
that I thought were basically against black people. I didn't
think the author of the book consciously did it. I just thought
they were subconscious, the elements of racism. One of them
being that the focus on a dog in a story like that tends to
[nullify] the whole essence of the everyday struggle for sur-
vival. The focus was on the dog and the family's efforts to keep
the dog alive. It's almost absurd that a black sharecropper
family in the South in the 1930s — their basic drive and function would be toward self-survival of the family. When I met
with the producer I told him that's the way I would have to
approach it. I would have to approach it basically dealing with
the elements of family life. We had a long session and he
agreed with me and we approached it from that angle.

NUNNALLY JOHNSON: I wasn't as experienced in screenwriting at the time of *The Grapes of Wrath* as I am now, and also I wasn't sure how much I could tamper with a book of quality, very well known, and so I talked it over with Pare Lorentz. Pare was a very good friend of mine and, as a matter of fact, I think he introduced me to Steinbeck. He said, in effect, "Look. If it doesn't violate the book, do whatever you want. I'll promise you that John won't object, because he knows enough to know that this is another medium." I didn't hesitate, after that, to switch things around, or switch speeches around.

Steinbeck had those intermediate chapters about a turtle crossing the road, or this, that, and the other. It was a piece of magnificent journalism, really. [Events and characters from the novel's rhapsodic interchapters, which attempt to comment on and universalize the vicissitudes of the Joad family, the focal characters, become part of the Joad family's experience in the film. Also, the government camp episode comes at an earlier point in the novel than it does in the film. — D.C.] The placement of the government camp episode seemed to me dramatically right. . . .

In Jack Kirkland's stage version of Erskine Caldwell's *Tobacco Road* [which Johnson adapted for the screen], there were things Kirkland had either overlooked or hadn't thought well of or that didn't fit in with his pattern but fit with mine. I don't think I went back to the book, except that I read the book and I'd mark something I'd remember, "I hope I can use this," and then find a place for it. . . . The screenwriter's duty, his loyalty, is not to the book. Whenever I work on adaptations, my eye is on the audience, not on the author. If, afterwards, the author chooses not to like it, but the audience did, all I can say is, "Well, there it is. That's my business. Pleasing an audience. Not pleasing an author."

RAY BRADBURY: I had to realign everything in *Moby Dick*. You had to weigh every single encounter and see by the ounce which weighed the most. The lighter elements had to go at the beginning.

I took a little thing which in the novel was a small throwaway scene — the calm at sea. There is no drama in that in the novel.

I took the calm. Then I borrowed a scene from another section of *Moby Dick* where a sailor fell from the mast. I put that incident with the sailor before the calm. They were in Moby Dick's waters. If the sailor fell from the mast and hit the sea and was never seen again, that would be a bad omen. The calm came right after that and, therefore, it was another warning. In the middle of the calm they see the coin on the mast. The Manxman looks up and says, "Lad, pull that gold coin off the mast. Throw it into the sea. Pay the fates back, and maybe the calm will get out of these waters." That coin is in another part of the novel too. In the middle of all this Queequeg begins to throw the bones and see his future. He sees his death and he orders the coffinmaker to build his coffin. This, again, is in another part of the novel. Ishmael speaks to him and says, "If you go on this way and kill yourself, I will never speak to you again." In the novel this is sort of thrown away. You never really find out what brings Queequeg out of his deathlike trance. But on the screen I thought that if his best friend, his beloved mate Ishmael, is threatened with death, that would be enough to bring him out of his trance. On top of that there would be the arrival of Moby Dick on the scene for the first time. In the novel Moby Dick arrives earlier, but in a screenplay you have to save these things and pay them out. So you have the sequence with the coin, the trance, the silence of night, the threat to the young person Ishmael, and the arrival of Moby Dick. This is an example of taking separate elements that are strewn all through the book and making one huge scene in the center of the screenplay. It plays beautifully.

There are no jokes in all of *Moby Dick*. It is one of the few films ever made where there is no release of tension through jokes. When I sat down to write *Moby Dick* I said to Huston, "The first thing that we do is eliminate Parcy Fedallah or we're going to have a comedy. You've got to find other ways of breaking tension." Huston immediately agreed. We threw Fedallah out and he's never been missed. Instead of Fedallah being taken down on the whale and being brought back up again, it was Ahab. Who else? Why shouldn't he be? It's Ahab's will. It's Ahab's fate. It's much more beautiful. That was a real stroke of luck that I thought of getting rid of Fedallah. Then I

could bring Ahab up at the end and have him wave to his men
and bring them on to their doom.

*Moby Dick* is an action novel but is poetical and Shakespeare-
influenced, with lots of asides. You can't put all of those asides
on the screen. You've got to pick and choose. You build your
tension to a moment of silence and then give a moment of truth.
Then you can have a Shakespearean aside. You can have a
dialogue between Captain Ahab and Starbuck. Or you can
have an encounter with the captain of a passing ship.

I think that in some areas of *Moby Dick* we could go back
and do some simplification. But I think I would still go with
the soliloquies. I think you have to. In the chart scene down in
the cabin, you have the benefit of a number of visual things to
work with. You have more of an exchange when Ahab says,
"Here are the charts. Here is where the sperm whales go." He
had something to point to when he was talking. In the scene
between Queequeg and Ishmael, where they were talking about
whaling, I put in the book so you would have a picture of the
whale and the Tower of London. I always tried to find something that was visual.

LONNE ELDER III: In the novel *Sounder* the people have no names;
in fact they're older people — the boy is an old man. They're
really not people; they're not characters. The series of events
that conclude the novel would be easy to accept in this context,
in this kind of symbolic parable. The father comes home from
prison a vegetable; his whole body is caved in on one side; he
droops, with his head down; he can hardly walk. The dog then
returns almost in the same fashion, with the sockets of his eyes
empty, half of his leg is off. The father dies, and two or three
days later the animal dies. It was easy to accept the way the
story is written — as a fantasy, a legend. It would have become
a downer for the kind of picture I was doing. It just wouldn't
have worked. When I came to that particular section in the
first draft, I went to the producer's office to talk to [him] about
it. I said to [him], "I don't think this should happen; I think we
can take a different course. [He] didn't fight that, as I recall.
Keeping Nathan Lee alive wasn't very hard.

In addition to eliminating, telescoping and shuffling individual scenes and characters from the source material, and refocusing it as a whole, invention — the creation of entirely new scenes or parts of scenes — is an option open to the adapter.

ALVIN SARGENT: The scene in the café in *Paper Moon* is invention. There is no scene that corresponds to the hill scene in the book.

Interestingly, Peter Bogdanovich has said that the café and hill scenes are what attracted him to *Paper Moon* and caused him to see the possibilities inherent in a source — Joe David Brown's novel *Addie Pray* — that, otherwise, would have been without much interest.

W. D. RICHTER: The novel *Deadfall,* from which *Fat Chance* was taken, relied much more on style than it did on story. A lot of people met in various rooms and had elaborate conversations that would become tedious in a film, so I had to invent a lot of action that could carry the thing through. I created most of the action sequences completely when I wrote the first draft. In one of them, two hit men — two assassins — are trying to escape the detective hero after they've tried to kill him and failed. And, looking at it as an avenue of escape, they get on a freeway ramp at dusk and find that there's bumper-to-bumper traffic. You're going to have the feeling of a high-speed chase coming up, and suddenly it's three miles per hour and cars sliding back and forth and looking through several panes of glass to find where everybody is and what their relationship to each other is. There's a feeling of creeping around in an old dark house, but the rooms are on wheels and are changing the relationships of the people within. The assassins have silencers, and you're involving a lot of motorists who have no direct role in the action. It has the potentiality of being a really stupid or a really horrifying sequence.

Alvin Sargent's remark about screenwriting, "It's hard, I hate it!" suggests a strong emotional investment in his work, which has

consisted primarily of adaptations. Sargent recalls the writing of
the crucial telephone scene in his adaptation of John Nichols's
novel *The Sterile Cuckoo*.

ALVIN SARGENT: I had no idea how that girl [Pookie Adams,
played by Liza Minnelli] was ever going to get her boyfriend to
invite her to visit him during Easter vacation. I was in agony,
as she was, trying to get him to invite her. The problem became
enormous, and then it became a game: you know there's an
answer, there's always a way. I think I got stumped in the
middle — she didn't know what to do and I didn't know what
to do — so I had those people come into the room. And her
frustration, when she screams "Get out of here, you goony
virgins!" was the writer's frustration. The line surprised me,
and then I hoped it would surprise an audience. I'm always the
first audience, and I need surprises. He invited her, finally. We
wore him down — by we, I mean Pookie Adams and myself —
we wore that poor guy down.

One of the marks of an *auteur* director is a distinguishable
thematic and/or stylistic consistency that makes his *oeuvre* all of
a piece, identifiably the product of a single sensibility. A director's
repetition of themes or "touches" seen in his earlier films (or his
prefiguration of idiosyncrasies in later ones) suffice as evidence
of a consistent line, as certification of the director's "authorship."
Though the screenwriter, historically, has probably had less freedom to select his themes than the director and, usually, nothing
to say about how his work is interpreted, there are bodies of
writers' work (which include adaptations) evincing an *auteur-
istique* consistency.

LEONARD SPIGELGASS: Isobel Lennart worked with many directors
and she always put her signature on the picture. Whatever picture she made, there was always a preoccupation with humanity
and the fact that people had to be nice to other people. Whatever she did, it was done with this in it. She did pictures with
all kinds of actors, all kinds of styles . . . but they are Isobel
Lennart's pictures.

NUNNALLY JOHNSON (In response to a question about the "significance" of the relatively large number of married heroes in the
body of his work): I guess it goes back to my choice of the
picture or the story, and it also has something to do with my
taste and my awareness of my inadequacy at telling a purely
romantic story. I think that there's a certain grace of mind necessary for romantic scenes, which I lack. I can't think of what
to have them say. I can have a love scene between a husband
and a wife, and I've done it time and time again. To me, it's
the truest kind of love I can feel, I can understand. I think it's
the best kind. But picking up the handkerchief and meeting
her and swinging through the wheat field and all that kind of
stuff — it just isn't in me. . . .

LEIGH BRACKETT (With reference to the independent, seemingly
tarnished but pure-hearted heroine who recurs in the films Jules
Furthman wrote for Howard Hawks and figures also in the
films Furthman wrote for von Sternberg): Mr. Hawks does not
like conventional heroines. He does not like "nice" girls; he
finds them exceedingly dull. It's probably a matter of Hawks
and Furthman sharing the same attitude. They like that type
of heroine and do well with it, and therefore it kept cropping
up in the films they did together. My taste in heroines is somewhat similar to theirs, so I was able to work well within the
framework of the character of Feathers [Angie Dickinson] in
*Rio Bravo*, on which I collaborated with Furthman.

ALVIN SARGENT: You look for where people are vulnerable and you
must never try to "get them." I don't go after people, but you
do look for that part of a person that can really be reached,
touched. I mean, I will never write anyone who stutters —
unless you're going to understand him and care about him and
feel close to him — because I know that there must be people
in the audience who stutter, and how are they going to feel?
I don't like gags about people's infirmities, I think they're hostile and cruel. Trixie Delight [Madeline Kahn] in *Paper Moon*,
with her big tits and the fact she was a carny dancer. I began
to feel so unfair to that character, it would be exploiting her to

write her as the straight stereotyped cartoon that she was in the book on which the film was based. I felt, there's something in this girl I want to know about, I want to feel for. I want to know what's going on in that girl. I want to care about her. So I wrote the scene on the hill, and that did the trick.

There's a soft spot in all of us somewhere. So you take Pookie Adams in *The Sterile Cuckoo* and you put her on a bus and she comes on really strong. But she's a wreck. I don't think I ever found out where the boy, I can't even remember his name — Paine, Jerry Paine [Wendell Burton] — I don't think I ever dealt with that part of him that was in trouble. I'm not sure what made him tick. But *Love and Pain* — two very obvious wrecks.

I like to take each character and deal with him alone. Not for the script necessarily, but just as an exercise. I put them in a restaurant, a restroom, at home, in bed at night, lost in Alaska. In *Paper Moon*, Addie [Tatum O'Neal] goes into the bathroom and starts doing all that stuff in the mirror. That's not in the book, but I just wanted to see her alone. We all do things in front of the mirror that we don't do in front of other people. Every character should go to the powder room once, if only as an exercise for the writer.

When a director is not known to have written or collaborated on the script of a film, his performance is evaluated in terms of how he has translated a piece of writing into visual terms; just about everything that is visible is likely to be attributed to him.

NUNNALLY JOHNSON: I don't think John Ford ever claimed anything that wasn't his, but John has been the beneficiary of more gifts by critics than any man I know of. He's aware of it, or he was aware of it when he was working. The first time I met him, at some gathering, was after I had done a script called *The Man Who Broke the Bank at Monte Carlo*. I had handed it in [to Darryl F. Zanuck]. I didn't know it had been offered to Ford. I didn't know whom it had been offered to. Somebody began talking about directorial touches, which was a favorite cliché of critics who hadn't the faintest idea what they were talking about. John said he'd read a script he liked very much, but he said, "I'll tell you a thing that would be attributed to the director." Without looking at me, complete deadpan, he described a scene I had written. I only remember that it had something to do with a wagon wheel passing over a flower. I recognized it, and then he looked at me and grinned. He said, "Don't you think that's true, Mr. Johnson?" I said, "I don't know whom it's going to be attributed to, but I wrote it." He said, "I know it."

RAY BRADBURY: I got the best advice in my life when I started *Moby Dick* from Peter Viertel. He said, "Write a silent motion picture." *Moby Dick* has more silent moments than talking moments. . . . If I can find visual metaphors to act out the truths for me, to begin scenes and end them, then I do it. . . . When Queequeg signed in, it was my idea to have him sign with the picture of the whale.

NUNNALLY JOHNSON: When a man writes the script, he directs it at the same time.

ALVIN SARGENT: I write a lot of detail, a lot of direction, basically for myself. They may not use it, but I need to know what the characters are, or what they're doing, what they're holding. Props are extremely helpful. I take a lot of directions out before handing in a script, but not in ambiguous situations . . . Certain lines can be read in one of two ways. Whether a line is read compassionately or sarcastically can make all the difference in the world, so the attitude should be established. When I started I used to indicate things like "Party scene," "Director stages a football game," "Director stages a chase," and I used to believe in my soul that they'd work it out on the set and I'd come out looking really good. But it just doesn't work. You must be with your characters at all times. Who knows, maybe he wets his pants in the chase.

W. D. RICHTER: The freeway chase sequence in *Fat Chance* is five pages long, and I've described the action in it cut by cut. No doubt, a director's going to change it; I may change it before it even gets to the director. But I had to put it down on paper in a very specific way in order to convince myself that it would work.

I try to write a screenplay that is very readable, and in that sense, it's directed, because it's a story, it's not just a blueprint for somebody to step into and provide the imagination. I direct the movie in my own mind when I write it because I see it, but I don't specify everything I see. I try to go for a feeling. You should be able to see the story without specifying that a speech should be covered in a close-up. I use that when I really need it, when it's terribly important to me that it's not a medium shot. But that turns directors off, because they want to make that kind of decision themselves. Also, if you write "close-up" it's likely to be covered three ways anyway, so why write "close-up"?

LEIGH BRACKETT: On the B lots, at Republic, where I worked briefly before *The Big Sleep*, and at Columbia, where I worked later, they wanted a shooting script done scene by scene by scene — two-shot, medium two-shot, medium close-up — because it made it easier to break it down in order to draw up the production schedule and figure out a budget. When I went to work for Howard Hawks on *The Big Sleep*, I asked him, or I may have asked somebody else — anyway, I was given the instructions, "Just master scenes, do it all in master scenes." [That is, do not indicate or suggest camera angles for all or any part of the action and dialogue encompassed in a scene.] With a piece of action you do just enough to make the action clear — somebody enters or somebody exits, there's an insert of something. But, basically, you put in as little description as you can possibly get by with. I've always worked that way, except when I was forced to do the other, which I hate doing. No director worth his salt wants some writer telling him where to put his camera; even on the B's I wrote for Columbia, where I indicated all the shots, the director usually did what he pleased.

NUNNALLY JOHNSON: When I write a script and send it over to somebody else, it's not going to [end up as] exactly what I had in mind. It may be better. It often is.

this character, and in this test, he was screeching and raging. I said, "Look, are you going to play this fellow that way?" Ford said, "Who's being tested here, the director or the actor?" I said, "For God's sake, I can make a comment, can't I?" I could, but a lot of good it did. Ford was much too powerful for me, and it was just as if I were talking to him in Greek. He had a feeling for wild comedy — Ward Bond would hit John Wayne, and they'd all hit each other with flour bags, that kind of stuff. But anything softer than that, he just didn't understand. To him, a low, illiterate cracker and a low, illiterate Irishman were identical. They reacted the same way. Since he didn't know anything about crackers . . . and he did know about Irish, he simply changed them all into Irishmen. . . . I insisted that the script was better than the picture simply because of the way Ford directed these people. You send the thing in red and it comes out green.

"As a screenwriter," Alvin Sargent says, "you work with other people." There are screenwriters who would fault Sargent on his choice of preposition, and suggest that "for," "around," and "on" be substituted for "with."

Historically, the screenwriter, like the director, has been an employee responsible to a studio, a studio-affiliated production executive or producer, or an independent producer. When the writer works with a director in developing a piece of material prior to the involvement of a studio or producer, as is increasingly the case now, his accountability to the money people is likely to come at a later stage than previously, and it may be shared with the director, but it is inevitable nonetheless. A sensitive or imaginative, or at least receptive "boss" is as important to the screenwriter as to any "employee."

DONALD OGDEN STEWART: Irving Thalberg was . . . awfully close to being creative. He didn't actually create scenes, but he had such a clear recollection of every scene that had worked — it was like going to a computer. You put your script into Irving and the wheels went around and out came yes or no. But he was right in so many cases. He taught me a lot over the years about dramatic construction. And from his criticisms of my scenes I really learned an awful lot about writing for the stage and for the screen.

Hunt Stromberg I liked and respected, but he was entirely different from Irving. I'd write love scenes for *The White Sister* that I thought were very good love scenes, and Hunt would read [them] and then start walking up and down the room. He'd say, "Don, goddammit, I like this, yeah, this is — I think this is all right, but what's that dumb Scranton miner going to think about it?" He had this idea of what a dumb Scranton miner would go for, and you were writing love scenes not for Helen Hayes, but you were writing them for that dumb Scranton miner.

NUNNALLY JOHNSON (With reference to Samuel Goldwyn, for whom Johnson wrote parts of *Kid Millions* and *Roman Scandals*): He kept very close to it and his comments were all pretty good. He's an instinctive man about pictures, as if he had some kind of Geiger counter in his head, and thinks — well, in a way, like Zanuck. Darryl was a great editor. He'd read a script, and the minute it got dull, or didn't move, or went off the track, he said, "It stopped. Now where did this dullness start?" And he'd go back two, three pages, and then he'd figure out where the movement stopped, or where the movement went wrong. He couldn't pass that mark until he got it straightened out. Well, Goldwyn had some of that, but Goldwyn left a good deal of it to directors. Darryl's idea was to get a script and call in the director. The director was not only permitted, but expected to make suggestions, make his contribution, but it all had to be on paper before he went out on the set. And Darryl had to okay it.

Zanuck was the master of the story conference. When the first draft of a script was finished he sent copies to, I don't know, half a dozen, maybe eight, of the people who advised him, and Casting, and so on. Then he'd call me, and the director, if there was a director assigned to it, and we'd discuss the parts he wasn't satisfied with, or his dissatisfaction with the whole, and we'd also take up each point that was made in these notes from his advisors. He'd say, "Well, I don't believe what this fellow says. I had no confusion about it, so forget it." Or he'd say, "He's got a good point here. Now that I look back at it, it seemed that way to me too. Now what can we do to reconcile these differences?" Eventually, after I'd done a number of scripts for him and he had some trust in me, he would get to a point where he would begin to improvise. As often as not his improvisation was not to my liking. (He was inclined to the cornball stuff.) I wasn't going to say that to him, but I'd say, "Will you let me work on that a little longer?" He'd say, "Okay." When I came back in with the revised version, and I'd altered that, rewritten that particular part of the picture that Zanuck had "improvised" on, it didn't matter to him whether I'd followed anything he suggested or not. Not as long as it made dramatic sense. He never made another mention of it. I don't even know if he remembered. But if it fit and felt right, it went.

When I'd bring him back the first revised script, he'd say, "Well, this looks pretty good. I like the way you straightened out so-and-so, and could we get a little stronger ending?" Now it was just between him and me, and we'd discuss two or three endings until we found something that looked like it might fade out properly and satisfactorily. Then, after the second revised script was done, we would discuss it, and he would say, "I haven't got but two notes here. One, I don't think that the fellow ought to wear a beard," or something. He would mention some tiny thing like that. "And two, the guy's a little too harsh with the woman. I don't think he would be that harsh with her." I would say, "All right, that's easily fixed." He would say, "All right. Do those. Send it to Mimeograph and we'll go to work."

Now that happened script after script, the same routine. He was far and away the most valuable man I've ever been associated with in the business, one of the very few who really made contributions and was a collaborator. And I suppose for every one of those corny kinds of suggestions, he had three or four very good suggestions. As you can see, I have the greatest admiration possible for him.

LONNE ELDER III: Even though the producer had consented to the approach I was taking in writing *Sounder*, he was in many instances fighting for preserving to a certain degree the novel's focus on the dog. Also, the woman in the story — it seems like every time there was a problem, every time she was on edge about something, she'd start humming the same spiritual. She was always reaching for the Lord, starving to death but reaching for the Lord. The producer really wanted this type of thing. And I said, "No, if anything, this woman is going to become bitter. She may not indulge herself in bitterness, but it would certainly be apparent in her responses to things and responses to people. She certainly wouldn't be breaking out in a spiritual." Well, he wanted it badly, and I fought it all the way. We had quite a few battles, in a sense, but they were honorable battles. There's this thing with producers; they hear you out, but when they go to make the movie they do what they wanted to do in the first place. But they didn't do that with *Sounder*. They hung in there with a basic attitude. They actually heeded my warnings in terms of what not to do.

w. d. richter: I functioned almost autonomously on my first draft of *Fat Chance,* because the producer, Irwin Winkler, was busy with other productions at the time I was writing it. I was really interpreting *Deadfall* for myself, with Irwin's suggestions considered. The book is a stylized piece of writing, and a lot of its charm is in its description. Though the dialogue is very good, the way the book describes a person crossing a room suddenly makes you smile. It has a third-person wisecrack narrator with an incredible flippancy. In doing the first draft, I hit upon the idea of using a tongue-in-cheek voice-over to get the effects achieved by the novel's narrator. I thought it could work. It wasn't right. It might, as a result of extremely deft direction, work, but in the script itself it seemed ponderous. The flippancy was amusing in the novel if you read it for twenty pages and picked it up a day later for another twenty pages. But if you had to endure a movie of it unendingly, it kind of drove you through the floor. Irwin was the first to say this. He has a good story mind — not necessarily in terms of proposing solutions, but he can put his fingers on problems. He took the first draft apart where it deserved to be taken apart (the voice-over), and

I hadn't been as successful in simplifying the story as I had hoped. So I went back and did it again without a voice-over.

Because of ignorance of actual working conditions or an inability to find an alternative and equally concise label, critics and commentators often refer to film scripts by more than one writer as collaborations. In a footnote to his discussion of the postwar Italian neo-realist film in Volume II of *What is Cinema?*, André Bazin writes:

> Nearly all the credits of an Italian film list under the heading "scenario" a good dozen names. This imposing evidence of collaboration need not be taken too seriously. It is intended to provide the producers with a naïvely political assurance. It usually consists of one Christian Democrat and one Communist (just as in the film there is a Marxist and a priest); the third screenwriter has a reputation for story construction; the fourth is a gag man; the fifth because he is a good dialogue writer; the sixth because he has a fine feeling for life. The result is no better or no worse than if there had been only one screenwriter, but the Italian notion of a scenario fits in with their concept of a collective paternity according to which everyone contributes an idea without any obligation on the part of the director to use it. Rather than the assembly line of American screenwriters, this interdependence of improvisation is like that of *commedia dell'arte* or jazz.

Bazin's blanket assumption about the assembly-line nature of American screenwriting "collaborations," though not fully correct, is understandable. The most widely publicized of these concern the contract writers who, working in relays, fashioned the scripts of the MGM movies of the thirties, though the procedure was common at other studios as well. The following pages document the workings of the "assembly line" and note variations on it, some of them approximating the "Italian" model described by Bazin.

NUNNALLY JOHNSON (With reference to 1933's *Mama Loves Papa*): Arthur Kober was assigned to me. They had all kinds of odd categories then; Arthur was called a continuity man, and I was the dialogue man. Which I found out only meant that every now and then Arthur wrote "Cut" or "Fade in" or "Fade out," or something like that, and was getting more money for that than me. Often writers coming in from New York felt rather above the mechanical form of a script. They just wouldn't bother with it, and it was a simple thing, cutting, wiping, iris in and iris out. They could run you crazy with those things.

There was a producer at Paramount in the early 1930s named Harold Hurley . . . and one day the story editor told me to report to Hurley's office. There were about five of us, five writers, and Hurley assigned each of the characters in a film to one of us writers. I had a sailor, a sailor with a parrot, and I was to think up funny things for this sailor and this parrot to do. . . . Joe Mankiewicz had some other kind of character, and we were all to put them together. There were all sorts of demented ideas in those days.

[With reference to *The Gunfighter,* for which story credit goes to William Bowers and Andre deToth, screenplay credit to Bowers and William Sellers, and producer credit to Johnson]: As I remember it, Bill Bowers brought *The Gunfighter* to me; I think he had been writing it with Andre deToth. I guess they separated, and what Bill brought me was about sixty pages, about half the length of a script. Bill wanted to sell it right away. . . . I asked Fox to buy it, and they bought it and I expanded it, really not altering the structure or the story Bowers had written, but injecting scenes here and there that I thought would make it a little stronger and also make it long enough to shoot. . . . Instead of doing it in one step, you make it three steps. If he's being chased, they overtake him and he holds them off again and gets away. Maybe some of it was with the scenes with his wife. I may have done something like that. None of it was concocted outside of the line of the story as Bowers and deToth had done it. . . . William Sellers is an unknown to me now. I don't know, I never heard of him and . . . can't remember anything about him at all, because he certainly didn't write anything after Bill Bowers handed it to me.

DONALD OGDEN STEWART: Irving Thalberg was in a little bit of trouble with a picture called *Smilin' Through.* They started shooting with Norma Shearer and Leslie Howard and Freddy

March . . . and they were in trouble with dialogue and scenes, and Irving wasn't at all pleased. There were two or three others, old silent writers, on it. But I was the new sound person. And I was the guy they needed; he needed what I had to give. . . . David O. Selznick needed an ending for *Dinner at Eight.* They needed a laugh at the end and I gave them a laugh. And David was so grateful for that that he gave me screen credit for having only done two or three scenes on the picture. . . . I can't remember — I was called in and I added some dialogue to *No More Ladies,* and possibly a little reconstruction. . . . I gave them an ending to *Red Dust* that Hunt Stromberg liked very much. The general feeling was that it saved the picture. . . . I just wrote some scenes for *The Prisoner of Zenda,* and I think David O. Selznick gave me screen credit. John Balderston was a very good writer, and they had a good script. David just wanted some more dialogue, I imagine.

HOWARD ESTABROOK (With reference to *David Copperfield,* on which he is credited with the screenplay, and Hugh Walpole for the "adaptation"): I wrote the screenplay and Hugh went over it. And where it needed more Englishing than I had given it, he was able to do so. For instance, the expression used by Miss Trotwood, "But pray, but why should he do this?" "But pray," see. Now that was valuable; we wouldn't have thought of that. The treatment I wrote from the novel before actually writing the screenplay — that was really the "adaptation." We had no other credit to give Hugh, so we gave him the adaptation credit. But what he was really adapting was the dialogue. Walpole gave us valuable information all the way through. He immediately agreed to our cutting out all the incidents in the novel that did not directly affect the character David Copperfield, but advised us to include some ostensibly extraneous incidents on the grounds that they, or the characters in them, like Little Emily, were beloved by the British public.

MILOŠ FORMAN: The development of *Taking Off* [which Forman directed] had three periods. I worked with Jean-Claude Carrière about six to eight weeks, and the result was some kind of treatment. When Paramount became interested, we sat down with John Klein and worked, I guess, about two months. Then Paramount dropped the project and Universal stepped in, and I spent another five weeks working with John Guare. . . . I always work with three people, which is very good because if any two are in disagreement, the third one can bring the judgment. If one falls asleep, two can still work.

ALVIN SARGENT (With reference to *Gambit,* on which he shares writing credit with Sidney Carrol and Jack Davies): The story was there, the caper was established. But the characters apparently weren't working. I was called in about ten days before they started to shoot and I never saw another writer. I seem to remember that that piece has some long history. I think it was originally written for a man; it was around for years, and then Shirley MacLaine saw it and said she wanted to do it, so someone rewrote it for her. Basically, I worked on that character (though I also did some things with the character Michael Caine played), which needed shaking up a little. It needed to be tilted, the girl did. Not a polish — really, they should get rid of that word. When people call and say, "Polish, hurry we need a polish," they've got the wrong word. What they usually need is for the piece to be shaken up, have the gloss removed, get down to the heart of the matter. It's already "polished"; that's the problem.

LEIGH BRACKETT (With reference to *The Big Sleep*): William Faulkner was the senior writer; this was my first screenwriting job of any consequence. He simply greeted me very politely the first day of work, and opened a copy of the Raymond Chandler novel, and said, "We will do alternate sections. I will do Chapters X and Y and so on, and you will do those." I never had a meeting with Mr. Faulkner or a conference with him. He did his and I did mine and we handed them in to Howard Hawks. I never saw his material; he never saw mine.

Mr. Hawks would come in once in a while and talk to me (and, I suppose, to Mr. Faulkner) and I would carry on along the lines he set down. The stylistic consistency between the material I wrote and the material Mr. Faulkner wrote was, I think, achieved partly as a result of Mr. Hawks's guidance and partly because we both tried to stick as close to Chandler as we could.

When Jules Furthman came on I was off on something else and Faulkner was off on something else. Mr. Hawks, who does a great deal of shooting off the cuff — if he gets a good scene going he'll let it run and to hell with the story — had, at one point, an awful lot of film shot and X amount of script to go — far too great an amount. So he called in Furthman to rewrite the ending and shorten it. I never met Mr. Furthman; I didn't meet him until *Rio Bravo*, approximately twelve years later.

Jules Furthman and I got on famously. At the time, I still had not learned to think on my feet out loud. I was used to writing by myself, alone with my typewriter in a little room. Jules Furthman, on the other hand, just hated to put anything down on paper. So, in story conferences with Howard Hawks, Jules did most of the ball-carrying. He and Mr. Hawks would talk the scenes out, and I'd contribute as much as I could. If I thought something was absolutely awful I would politely say so. And very often Jules would back me up. It was a give-and-take business. Basically, though, I would put down on paper the scenes that Mr. Hawks and Mr. Furthman had talked out, shape them, reshape them if necessary, and put them together, adding a few things of my own in the process.

W. D. RICHTER (With reference to *Melinda*): Metro had a short story in rough treatment form, which I can only assume, because it had nobody's name on it, was written by the executives. They said, "We'll pay you five thousand dollars if you think you can write a screenplay from this." I went all the way through a second draft, and then they moved in all the black personnel to make the movie. I was suddenly a very conspicuous outsider. I was replaced by Lonne Elder, who wrote the screenplay that was shot. His first draft was just spun off, literally, a feature script written in two weeks, ostensibly as a dialogue polish, but really a black power play, an effort to prove I was unnecessary and to get a black writer on the project officially.

LONNE ELDER III: I had been called in on that particular picture. They had already had a screenplay on it that was totally unsuitable, and what happened was that I had to throw it all out and start from scratch and write a new screenplay altogether. I knew what kind of picture it was and what kind of picture it was going to be — I knew what kind of picture Metro-Goldwyn-Mayer wanted to release. Basically, an exploitation picture, which we might call a black exploitation picture. On the other hand, I had the notion that what I would try to do was to lend it a certain degree of substance — you know, a certain degree of quality within the context of a crime-adventure story. I knew that I wasn't going to get everything. I knew that there was going to be a constant battle to retain any — even an ounce of substance. I mean, from MGM's standpoint, Melinda is a tramp. To them, it was a waste of footage to have people intimately talking to each other or trying to reveal themselves to each other or trying to come to grips with each other. That was one fight. The character Terry, they said they could have done without her altogether. And the bank scene, they were really upset. They didn't want that scene in it at all.

DONALD OGDEN STEWART: You should never be the man that writes the first draft. That is what my agent Leland Hayward was awfully good at. Leland would wait until he knew what the shooting date was going to be before he got you the job. So that they couldn't get anybody in between you and the shooting date.

The screenwriter's dialogue is eventually spoken, often by star-actors who bring their own set of prerequisites to a piece of writing. Though scores of postmortems have been written on the star system and the star vehicle, both are alive and well under different names and in subtler, more aesthetically defensible forms: Films now are rarely officially described as showcases for actors, but roles are "reconceived" for them. The writer might engineer the reconception prior to the start of filming, or the actor might, with the director's indulgence, alter his role himself by means of on-the-set improvisation. Though actors' improvisation

in films is probably as old as the medium, its highly touted re-
surgence in recent years has resulted in a kind of writers' back-
lash. There was hardly a screenwriter in Hollywood in 1973 who
had anything complimentary to say about *Last Tango in Paris*.
Just about all the objections to the film arose from the widely
reported fact that Marlon Brando had "written" or rewritten, by
means of improvisation, a substantial portion of his character's
dialogue. "It's not scripted," was the most frequently heard "criticism." One wonders if the writers' opinion of the film would be
upgraded if it had been reported, or assumed, that Franco Arcalli
and Bernardo Bertolucci had written every word spoken in the film.

MILOŠ FORMAN: I like, before the final draft is written, to know
   approximately who will be in the film because it helps you to
   develop the characters.

LEIGH BRACKETT: Every film I've done for Hawks I knew who we
   were going to get before I started; in the first one, Bogart, and
   after that, Wayne. If you know who you're writing for it helps.
   You learn to utilize what an actor has that is peculiarly his own.
   Every one of them can do something that nobody else can do
   quite that well. Also, you learn what type of scene isn't particularly becoming to an actor or actress and tend to stay away
   from that.

ALVIN SARGENT: Writing for Michael Caine in *Gambit*, he's terrific. While they were shooting I was writing "on the set," and
   there is something so specific about Caine that, once you hear
   him and watch him, you can go back and write for him. Of
   course that was a fast rewrite and Caine, fortunately, offered
   his own style which made the work easier, though it wasn't
   what I'd call very good writing — all surface.
      I don't necessarily sit down and write for a personality, for a
   star. I'd rather not do that. But, with *The Sterile Cuckoo*, I
   couldn't help it. Just meeting Liza Minnelli once before I
   started writing — we had dinner at Alan Pakula's house, it
   was very easy, Liza was herself, she went home and that was
   that — I could never get her out of my head. From then on,
   I could see her move, I could hear her voice, I could overhear

that kind of manic thinking that goes on in her head, and
applied all that to the character. I can't imagine anyone else
playing that role.

LEIGH BRACKETT: On *The Big Sleep*, Howard Hawks would very
often sit down with the actors, and they would go over a
scene. And somebody would come up with an idea — "Why
don't I do this and why don't I say that?" — they'd get something going. Where Bacall visits Bogart in his office and does
the bit scratching the knee and they go on with all this dialogue
— that wasn't in the script as I recall it. It's somewhat difficult
to cite specifics in terms of that particular film, because we
never had a final script; we went into production with a temporary. Mr. Hawks didn't use me as much on *The Big Sleep* as
he did in later years, when I would sit in on these conferences
on the set.

RAY BRADBURY: In *Moby Dick* Orson Welles wrote most of
Father Mapple's speech himself, for himself. I learned that
Orson Welles came on and was not satisfied with my writing of
Mapple's scene. I agreed. I never got that the way I wanted it.
Mr. Welles got it exactly right. He did a brilliant job. This is
one thing we have to acknowledge when it occurs. If somebody
can do something better, then bravo.

HOWARD ESTABROOK: W. C. Fields was improvising on the set of
*David Copperfield*. He would be inclined to go overboard if you
let him, and I think, as I see the picture again now, it should
have been toned down a bit. He wanted to put a juggling act
in. Everybody hollered murder — they said, "Oh, no!" — and
he gave up.

BUDD SCHULBERG: I remember with Marlon Brando in *On the
Waterfront*, that he was kind of screwing up some of the lines.
But he is awfully creative and often he can improve the lines.
But, at the same time, he can also fuck up a favorite line. And
sometimes he would do that, and sometimes he would make it
better than what I had done. I still believe in a script, I will
always believe in that. Despite all the talk about the "impro-

vised" taxi scene, that scene was played exactly as written. Kazan balances cinematic inventiveness with loyalty to the script. At the same time, I do feel that improvisation can co-exist [with a script], but the writer, unless he is involved in the making of the improvisation, is being tampered with too much.

ALVIN SARGENT: With *The Sterile Cuckoo*, the actors would take the essence of a scene and start talking about it and then improvise the scene, as you would in an acting class. It was very helpful to them. Pakula is fantastic with actors, and improvisation allowed them to be freer with one another. They learned to understand the relationship better. Out of that, the actors and the director, and even I sometimes — we'd get a sense of something more. But then they'd go back to the script and they'd do the script. When a scene is written honestly, then you can go back — you must go back — and do that scene without having to change it. If a scene is not working — there were problems with *Love and Pain*. We got a lot out of the improvisations in the rehearsals preceding *Love and Pain* that I took and incorporated in the script. Maggie Smith and Timothy Bottoms are very inventive people. I would go back to my hotel room and work with what they contributed during rehearsals. This was done on a few scenes. It wasn't generally the case.

In the best of all possible filmmaking situations, the writer is closely involved with the director in the shaping or reshaping of the screenplay, is either physically present or consulted during the filming, and permitted to contribute ideas or suggestions to the editing process.

BUDD SCHULBERG (In regard to working with Elia Kazan on *A Face in the Crowd* and *On the Waterfront*): We talked it over first, so that we were in agreement on what we were trying to say. Then I wrote it, and then we would go over it again. Of course, there were situations that arose in which he would say, "I think it is too long," or, "It's in the wrong place." And I would say, "I'll think about it." I don't remember any rough situations. We weren't always completely together, but we were pretty close.

LEIGH BRACKETT: Howard Hawks gives you the material; he sits down with you for one long conference and gives you his thoughts on what he would like, and then you go away and write it. You're not likely to see him again for weeks or months. He doesn't stay with a writer, he tends to let a writer very much alone, which in one way is awfully good, but can drive those writers who are used to daily story conferences or having their stuff gone over right off the deep end. "I don't know what he wants," they say, "what does he want?" As time went on I found that the one thing he wants is a lot of stuff — a lot of pages, a lot of scenes, a lot of ideas — and then he can take what he wants. Oftentimes something that you will suggest will trigger off a new idea in him, and vice versa of course. In that sense, it's a very close collaboration.

I learned a great deal about my craft in the period between *The Big Sleep* and *Rio Bravo* — he hired me originally because I was good at writing dialogue, but structurally, in those days, I was not exactly brilliant — and so, on the later pictures, I was able to contribute more. He began to gain a measure of confidence in me, and I began to understand how his mind worked. Very often I knew what he meant even though he didn't say it. Still, I think I did about four scripts on *Rio Bravo*. Mr. Hawks would sometimes start out thinking he wanted one thing, and after you'd broken your neck trying to do it he'd decide it wasn't a very good idea. You had to wait for him to find out what he wanted.

ALVIN SARGENT: When you meet a director you search him out and try to get in touch with him. You look for that part of him that you can understand and relate to and hope you can have some kind of dialogue with him about . . . life — everything. Alan Pakula and I understand each other very well, we really are very much in touch with one another. We have similar views on a lot of things — humor, pathos — and we really are kind of in sync. He likes bold strokes, as I do, and he encouraged me to try for them in *Love and Pain*. I had a lot of problems with *Love and Pain.* There was real collaboration there with Alan. While the writer and the director have to understand each other and be in some kind of harmony about what they're doing, you still want to bring directors things they don't expect. I have to write surprises. Whatever the director expects after a story conference . . . it should be less than he gets.

I never really got to know Peter Bogdanovich. We addressed ourselves immediately to the work; we went right to the script. Paramount had asked me to do *Paper Moon* before he became involved with it; they sent him my second draft, and he committed himself to direct it. Peter and I had about six sessions together, and he asked for certain things. He knew what he wanted, he knew what he wanted fixed, he knew what he wanted added. He wanted to add some things from the book which I had chosen not to use. We worked well together, I think.

He was very good in regard to the relationship of Addie and Mose [Ryan O'Neal]. He kept it tough, he saw where they were tough with one another, and he wanted to keep that conflict always going throughout the film. Always at each other, never giving in. I didn't have that at first. I tended to be a bit more sentimental, more painful, in the sense that I wanted to show her looking for something a little more obviously, more openly, more needfully. I had a scene in the film which I wish he had kept in, a scene where Addie talks Mose into settling down. She convinces him to buy a house, and she's so happy. she goes to school with these grubby little kids, and this schoolteacher is lecturing about life and the Depression and . . . reality, somehow. Addie's overjoyed to be a part of something. Then she goes home and finds out that they don't own the house. They've been swindled; they bought a house from somebody who never even owned it. So they get a taste of their own medicine. She sees what they've been doing to everybody else is happening to them. That's the point; it's the thirties, everybody's desperate, and who do you trust? I would have liked to see more of the pain of the thirties — it was a painful time. This scene — it's a nice scene, I'm really proud of it — pointed that up to a certain extent, but Peter didn't want to use it, it just didn't work for him. I wish it had.

LEIGH BRACKETT: Elliott Kastner, my old friend and former agent, approached me about adapting Raymond Chandler's *The Long Goodbye,* on which he was executive producer. I worked first with Jerry Bick, the producer, and Brian Hutton, who was going to direct the film. Prior to meeting with them in London, I did virtually no work on it. You read the novel and make notes on what you think is good and what you think is bad and what you personally would like to see done with it — what ideas you have — but nothing beyond that.

When I was working with Jerry Bick and Brian Hutton, they were still playing with the idea of doing an early-fifties period piece, and I don't know exactly what made them change their minds. I don't know where that final decision to update it came from or the eventual reason for it — I imagine it was partially budgetary — but not knowing initially when the story was going to take place made it a bit of a problem. And we ran into some plot problems too. The book starts out telling one story and then breaks off in the middle and tells another one. The whole thing is pinned together on a series of coincidences that to me were very difficult to swallow. So we haggled and haggled and haggled and had a great many heart-burnings and finally decided to throw out a tremendous lot of the book which, for its genre, was an unusually long book. We took a lot of liberties and did a thing at the end . . . I had made one suggestion for an ending, which Brian Hutton didn't like, and he said, "I'd rather see Marlowe kill the guy." I thought, That sounds pretty good, let's do it that way. The original ending, the one in the novel, was inconclusive in a way, and didn't please any of us, so we thought we'd go for broke and see what happened. . . . There was a plot gimmick that was Mr. Hutton's idea. I wasn't very happy with it and said so, but he was very happy with it, and I thought, Well, I'll try anything, because I can be wrong. But it just wouldn't work — it stopped you dead, it wasn't logical, people were sort of coming out of their boxes and doing things and then going back into them. I'm sure that that would have been changed, but by the time I had executed it Mr. Hutton had terminated his involvement with the project and we never had a chance to discuss it.

Robert Altman came in as director. He and Jerry Bick and I

would sit in an office and kick it around, and I would go back
to my hotel room and write up everything that had been discussed that day — do an outline, in other words. I would take
that segment of the outline back the next morning and we'd
go over it and then go on to the next part. We got it done in
about a week, and it worked out very nicely. I went off on my
own and wrote the script and didn't see Altman again until I
did two or three days of revisions — minor things — at the
time he was testing Nina Van Pallandt. The chief difference
between the version of the script I worked on with Brian
Hutton and the one I worked on with Bob Altman was the
elimination of the troublesome plot gimmick. It was simply a
matter of dropping that and doing a straighter line. Also, the
heroine, Nina Van Pallandt's sister, whom Marlowe, in the
novel, became briefly but emotionally involved with, was
dropped.

DONALD OGDEN STEWART: Some directors, like George Cukor,
really would want to work with me. I'd go down to the set and
see how it was going. Some directors just got the script and
then set up the cameras, like Woody [W. S.] Van Dyke: "All
right, that'll be the take," and so forth and so on. Which made
you lose interest. A lot of the pictures I wrote I've not yet seen
because I didn't know what the hell they were doing and nobody seemed to care very much about what I had written.

BUDD SCHULBERG: In *On the Waterfront*, for example, Kazan and
Sam Spiegel and I consulted, and we would all express our
ideas. Finally, we decided that we would cast the film together.

LONNE ELDER III: Yes, they consulted me. I agreed with the casting of *Sounder*.

NUNNALLY JOHNSON: Jean Negulesco directed two or three pictures for me, and I was very fond of him. But actors came to
me and said, "He doesn't tell us. He doesn't say anything. We
keep doing it the same way." He'd leave it to a dialogue
director to go over the lines, and that's not good enough. So,
on *How to Marry a Millionaire*, I made a deal with him. I never

heard of anybody making a deal like this and I don't know if
anybody else would have permitted it. I said, "Jean, would
you let me rehearse the actors and their lines before each
scene?" He said, "I'd be delighted." He'd break on one set, and
he'd call me and say, "Look, we're moving into the apartment.
You want to come over and rehearse these people?" So I'd go
over. There was Lauren Bacall, Betty Grable, Marilyn Monroe,
Bill Powell and David Wayne. I'd go over the scene with them,
let them read it first, and then I would read it. Although I'm
not an actor, at least I knew where the emphasis went, and I
could give them something of the tempo. The actors were
pleased as hell, Jean was pleased, and the picture turned out
about five times as good as anything Jean had done before,
simply because somebody had taken the trouble.

BUDD SCHULBERG: I think that Kazan spoiled me. One time, I kind
of talked up, and I think it was in the middle of a take. He said,
"If you see anything that you don't like, just come up and tap
me on the shoulder, and, then, when it is finished, we'll just
walk off and I'll hear what you have to say. . . ." On the screenplay, he could protest but I was the Supreme Court. Then it
was just the opposite on the set; I could protest, but he had the
final say.

The first or second day of shooting on *Wind Across the Everglades* I went up to Nicholas Ray, put my hand on his shoulder,
and I think he jumped eight feet. He said, "For God's sake, nobody is going to tell me what to do. I am the director here." And
I sort of went back and . . . I do like much about that picture,
yes. I think the idea was good. I think that had we been closer
to the script it would have been a good deal better than it is.

ALVIN SARGENT: Peter Bogdanovich was very true to the script of
*Paper Moon*. He was very fair, he wasn't rewriting, and when
he wanted to change something he'd call me on the phone. He
had invited me to come to the location in Kansas, but I couldn't
because I was working on another film. He'd say, "What do
you think of this?," "I'd like to add this line, I'd like to change
that line," "I have an idea . . ." Things happened on the set, of
course, but, for the most part, it was amazing: there was almost

nothing changed in that last draft. He works fast. No waste, no deadwood. I tend to overwrite. I learned a lot from him about getting to the point. I have a tendency to put people to sleep, myself included.

LEIGH BRACKETT (With reference to *Hatari!*): Howard Hawks went to Africa with a company, spent about six months there, and came back with the most marvelous footage, but very little in the way of "people." Not much more than "There-goes-a-giraffe-let's-get-it" scenes. All of the scenes in which the characters and the relationships developed remained to be done. I'd already written four or five scripts, but they more or less went out the window one by one. That was one year I was trying to sell Mr. Hawks a plot, and he wasn't buying any plot that year. And, there again, he'd keep changing his mind and throwing in new characters. He'd see an actor or an actress he'd like and say, "Write in so-and-so." I was on the set every day, working till ten o'clock at night writing the scene they were going to shoot at nine o'clock the next morning. What I'd write might be based on what had gone on during the preceding day's shooting, and also I was constantly going ahead trying to shape it toward something. We'd come to an agreement and have another little segment of the thing done, and then you'd see where you had to go from there.

We had a gigantic storyboard, with the different color cards — red for chase scenes, and so on. You'd look at the board and see there were too many red cards all lumped together, so let's spread them out. The trick was to devise the people scenes and then work them into the chase scenes. There were certain pivotal people scenes that, once they were shot, had to be used because they tied in with something else that had been done in Africa. So I spent a fair amount of time in the editing room, looking for places in the previously assembled footage where a scene might be fitted in. John Wayne's wearing a red shirt in this exterior, so he mustn't be wearing a blue one in this interior that precedes or follows it — not exactly "creative" writing.

ALVIN SARGENT: I think the writer does have a place in the editing of the film, can be very helpful at that stage, because it returns to the area of writing again — editing is just an extension of writing. In the middle, it's the director and the actor, but then you're back to the script transcribed into visual form; it's been written on the screen. In *The Sterile Cuckoo* there was a moment up front . . . I remember saying, "You should cut to the father's face here. If you were left with the image of [his] face and then went to the bus, it would be much more effective." This isn't really much, though. But it's writing. It's the same process. If somebody said, "Hey, come on, let's spend three months editing this," I'd love that. I think the writer should have his own cut.

W. D. Richter's account of the genesis of *Slither*, his first original screenplay to be filmed, indicates he was an important participant at every stage of the realization of his work. Though he suffered various frustrations, particularly in dealing with MGM, his experience on the film was close to ideal. As Richter notes, he would not, could not, have been as deeply involved in the making of *Slither* had he not also been its associate producer. In recent years, a broadly-based effort by writers to control, or at least be consulted about the translation of their material has resulted in a marked increase in so-called hyphenates — writer-directors and writer-producers. It goes without saying that the author of an original screenplay is more likely to be able to negotiate himself into a situation where he is able to retain some authority over his work than the adapter is. The author of an original screenplay brings the product of his own imagination, complete, or substantially so, to the marketplace, while the adapter comes there to sell his services to a producer or studio who owns or has optioned the screen rights to the work of another writer. Whether the long-term results of writers of originals becoming, either by choice or out of expediency, writer-producers are salutary is a subject for debate. Those who view the producer negatively claim that the role of the producer and that of the writer of original screenplays, who is possibly the only truly "creative" person in filmmaking, are intrinsically inimical.

W. D. RICHTER: I wanted to write a story — I don't remember why — about a guy of thirty-three or so now [Dick Kinipsia, played in the film by James Caan], who was the greatest thing going when he was in high school. I thought it would be amusing to figure out, if it had been all downhill since then, where he'd be today. By that time I had started to connive when I sat down to write, because I'd done about four originals and was told everyone liked my writing but nobody wanted to do the specific project in question because it wasn't commercial enough. I was determined to write something so strangely unique and castable — that is, the leading character wasn't twelve years old, or fifty-five, but of an age that any one of several leading actors could play — that it would have to be taken seriously. I was programming a lot of things into it, besides telling the story I wanted to tell. Trying to find some handle for the thing — somehow that led me into the hook of the campers, which I was interested in just as a phenomenon of the California road. I bought a camper magazine, and with the idea of the character I had in mind, sat down one day during a slow period — I wrote *Slither* while I was a story analyst at Warner Brothers — and started roughly banging out the ideas. That's the hardest part for me; once I actually start writing it's easy, but it's figuring out the story that stymies me. My friends always ridicule my endings, but I usually like them fine.

I forget the exact chronology, but *Slither* was optioned by Daniel Melnick, while he was at Talent Associates and not yet a Metro executive. It got to Melnick because of a fellow named Jack Sher, producer of the film itself, who shares agents with me and had known Melnick for quite a while. He had brought *Slither* to Melnick at Talent Associates and convinced him to option it, and because Jack is a writer and a great champion of writers, he insisted that early on I be included as associate producer. [Then MGM president James] Aubrey hired Melnick, Melnick took *Slither* with him to Metro. When Metro acquired *Slither* — which they never really "wanted"; Melnick wanted it, Aubrey never wanted it — Melnick brought with him from Talent Associates a contract that said I had to be associate producer. I would never have gotten that from Metro. It's just impossible. With a first original screenplay sale they would have backed me out the door. But that clause really guaranteed me nothing other than a salary and my name on the

screen as associate producer; my actual involvement depended
on how I got along with . . . for instance, the director. When I
did get along with him, that guaranteed my intimate involvement with the whole production.

MGM was eager to get Howard Zieff to direct *Slither* very
early — not all that long after they bought the script. Howard
flew down to Florida, where I was doing a rewrite on a film
called *The Master* [released as *Lady Ice*], to talk about *Slither*,
to make sure that we weren't thinking about a different
movie from the same script. Once we agreed that we were trying to make the same movie from the script, it just fell into
place so effortlessly that I don't ever want to hold this experience up as something you can expect. When I came back
from Florida the *Slither* company had offices at MGM, and I
just moved right in and began working on it with Howard Zieff.

It would consist of our having two- or three-hour meetings
during a seven-week preproduction period and talking things
through, just completely discussing it. I'd agree for the most
part with what he had to say, because his instincts were right
on the button, emerge with a couple of pages of notes, go and
execute them. I'd come back, Howard would look at the revised
pages, we'd tinker with them a little bit. But, essentially, we'd
keep moving forward. We had problems with the script because, in trying to satirize the type of plot the film follows, you
can also trap yourself into making it a lame caricature. The biggest criticism leveled at the film has been that it has a shaggy-
dog story quality, and we were always trying to minimize that
*while* preserving it. It was critical to us that what happened at
the end did happen — there was no payoff — but a lot of time
was spent finessing that around, dealing with Barry Fenaka
[Peter Boyle], whether he was going to reappear or not. . . .
Things weren't being changed drastically in a structural sense,
just within each scene. It was always minor adjustments back
and forth.

Howard brought a lot of ideas to the project. Howard
wanted to work forties music into it. The scene in the Polish-
American club came out of our talks about how to justify that.
We made Barry Fenaka a musician — previous to that I hadn't
thought of what he might do for a living. We had him play that

period music at the club. The bingo game wasn't in the original script either; it came about as a result of the studio asking for things and the director asking for things. Originally, there was to be an accident involving a propane gas leak in the camper that caused Dick to do away with an unspecified number of the villains. The studio insisted this be changed; the hero of the film couldn't be a murderer, even an inadvertent one. The bingo game came about as a mutual decision by Howard and me, but for the most part I worked out what would happen in it on paper.

The studio had agreed that Howard was preparing his draft of the script, so they stepped back for a while — a month or so — and didn't demand to see what I was doing every day. They stepped in heavily when "Zieff's draft" was finished and made a lot of irresponsible suggestions and, in a few cases, helpful ones.

Their objection to our reducing the number of vans from two, for instance, to one caused us to recoil, to fight with them, to argue, but finally produced the structure in which a second van appears in the middle of the movie, which I'm delighted with and never would have come up with if they hadn't objected to our having only one. But they made a lot of asinine suggestions, primarily because they operated under a strange kind of committee system where several production executives all had their opinions solicited and all responded in a detailed way. It was Melnick's project, so he had the greatest say, but we were forced into meetings where four Metro people would be telling us what they thought would improve the script. I think that the greatest threat the project ever faced was losing its own identity by having a favorite fillip embellished to appease this executive or that executive every ten pages.

The day before we began shooting we were summoned to Melnick's office and given a list of twenty or thirty deletions or changes in the script that Aubrey had sent down to Melnick. And they were the most inconsequential things: "On page thirteen, change this word." It's not that we could get annoyed; it's just that we wondered why, when we were about to spend two million dollars of their money, they were bothering us with silly little things. The only one that comes to mind is in the

small scene in the truck where the farmer picks up Caan hitch-
hiking and says, "I got a kid like you, I broke his arm last
week." [Executive] Saul David said, "Nobody would say that."
Well, what do you mean, "Nobody would say that"? You can
tell me it's not funny, it's dumb, it's something else, but you
can't tell me nobody would say it. And we struggled for the
longest time and ended up having to put through a page in
which the line read, "I *about* broke his arm last week." Well,
we did one take of that and did all the rest, "I broke his arm
last week." They saw it in the dailies and loved it our way, so
that's the way it's in the film. They play little games like that,
and if they ask you to do something you have to at least make
the effort to do it. But then you have to figure out a way to do
it the way you want to do it and cover it so that if they're right
you have it their way, but if they're wrong you can at least
demonstrate to them how they're wrong. I must say, we got
through things in the script that I thought they were never
going to let get through.

I knew all along that I was writing a very outrageous story
with a realistic side to it, and if you didn't approach the filming
of the movie very realistically — try to get as much realism into
the look of the movie as you could — you would amplify the
outrageous aspects of it so that you'd make a joke out of it.
I communicated my feelings about the look of the film to Zieff.
Howard and I talked about the look of the film and inspected
photographs, books of photographic essays. We looked at the
*Time-Life* series on *This Fabulous Century*, we looked at
any number of books on California, we looked for photographs
of overcast skies; we wanted to find examples of the kind of
light that might achieve the look we thought the picture should
have. We really got into the details, and I didn't have to be as
forceful or as vocal as I might have had to be with another
director; Howard really thought the way I did about it. And I
think I helped him in that respect. He needed someone around
who thought the way he did so that he wouldn't think that he
was the crazy one. Because no matter how successful you are
in one field, as Zieff was in commercials, when you make your
first feature film you're thrust into a new world, with all these
people telling you, "We do it this way here, we don't do it that

way." I was present at Howard's discussions with [director of photography] Laszlo Kovacs, but I couldn't say I contributed anything. I might be able to contribute something in conceptual terms, but nothing when their discussions centered on lenses and so forth.

I went on location-scouting trips, both because I was an associate producer and because I was following Howard around writing revisions at the time the locations were being scouted. I had prescouted this film in a way. The previous year, I had taken a trip up the California coast with my wife Susan and then another with Susan and my parents, exactly the route of *Slither*. The film was plotted very specifically; I set it in the only area of California I knew. Howard had a terrible fear of making a "California movie"; he didn't want palm trees, he didn't want another television movie with a we-had-to-make-it-here-because-it-was-the-only-place-we-could look. So, some of my suggestions were dismissed only because he brought other prerequisites to it — I wasn't concerned about palm trees. Yet, I had a lot of effect; he listened to me, he asked for my opinions, and I think that was just because we got along very well.

I was involved in the casting. Howard has an interesting technique; he videotaped the actors' readings for all the roles except the leading ones, which were filled by stars. I sat in on all the readings, and I even read with actors a few times myself. Howard had very strong opinions, and I deferred to him because I want to direct someday myself; and though I'd welcome an opinion from someone I respected, I wouldn't want somebody jumping up and down if I made a decision he didn't like. When there was doubt — you get three or four good actors reading, and each shades it differently — there was an open round-table discussion. Howard would ultimately go away and make the decision, but he heard us out. I got to say what I thought.

I wrote into the production stage a bit, but not all that much. I changed scenes here and there, but the bulk of the revisions were done in the seven-week rewrite before we began. I was around if something didn't play, if we got into trouble, if we needed a little more here and there. Howard asked me all the time; he never altered the script without asking me. There are snippets and phrases that were contributed by the actors, or by Howard in rehearsals and run-throughs, but almost everything found its way onto paper before it was said. We never turned a scene loose to improvisation. Allen Garfield embellished some of his stuff as he went along, and it got us into trouble in places; it gave us scenes that were out of whack in length. By saying two lines where one was written, or three where there were two, he made a scene that was supposed to be three minutes long, five minutes. You could sit there and watch it while it was being filmed, and it was a wonderful comedy routine, but when you inserted it in the context of the film it was blatantly too long. We were all rather shell-shocked with the results of this improvisation. And if you're on a thirty-seven-day schedule, as we were, you'd better stay pretty close to the script.

After filming was completed, I went away for about a month while Howard put together his rough cut. Then he asked me to come back. From then on, it was probably two or three days a week, and toward the end, five days a week, sitting in the editing room while Howard and [film editor] Dave Bretherton cut the film. Howard would call me over and say, "Take a look at this, take a look at that." I approved deletions; I didn't have final approval, but I was aware of every change being made.

I made suggestions that were incorporated into the final cut. Once, Barry Fenaka's line in the car about not jostling Mary [Louise Lasser] because she goes batshit over stuff like this was played over the view of the van coming over the hill. When I saw that, I can recall saying, "That's wrong, the line should be *on* Barry, you should see [him as he speaks it, and then] the van right after that." And Howard said, "You're right." It's not something that Howard wasn't concluding simultaneously as he was watching it on the screen, because he and Dave Bretherton had previously seen it only on the moviola themselves, not on a big screen. If I hadn't been there I think Howard would have sensed that, but maybe not. But I said that right away, he agreed, and that change was effected.

At the very end of the film, when the van goes into the water, we had an awkward, dull moment. Kitty [Sally Kellerman] and Dick jump out of the car, run to the precipice, look down, and there's some dialogue about "it's dead now." Then you hear the second van whining in reverse toward them, and they run back into the car and try to start it up. The whole movie just fell into the toilet at that point because there was no momentum, the dialogue was delivered lifelessly — it had been a bad day on location, and you could see on their faces that they didn't care. We were going crazy trying to figure out what to do. It occurred to me that they never had to get out of the car because of the way we had it covered. Howard ran back to Dave Bretherton, and Dave said we could do it. We did it, and that's the way it is now. So I cut out half a page of my own script.

MGM did things with the cutting of the film that affected it enormously. There's a thirty- or forty-second sequence missing from the film and is a prime example of MGM's editorial intervention. After the scene at the Polish-American club, there's a jarring cut to black and the doors open on the Airstream [camper trailer] and Dick and Barry standing in a backlighted area that, if you look quickly enough, you realize is somebody's home workshop. Originally, there was an elaborate pullback on the Polish-American club scene, with Barry and Mary on the dance floor — pure schmaltz and intended to be just that — and then a flat cut to a giant padlock, which Barry opens to disclose a room which is his workshop. And sitting in the center of it is a two-man submarine made from the wing tank of an airplane, a bomber, ten feet long, all aluminum. They circle it, and Dick's a little concerned that Barry has some plans for this submarine. Barry tells him he doesn't, but it was a red herring that was supposed to make you think that nobody's going to build this thing and not use it later in the film. It's not something that's intended to make you bellylaugh. It should perplex you and, perhaps, make you smile. But Aubrey's sense of humor doesn't run along those lines, and for no reason other than it didn't strike *him* as funny, he said, "It comes out and that's all there is to it." And it came out. Silence on the part of the preview audiences bore this out; they don't understand a smile at MGM, you have to hear a laugh or it's not funny. It didn't destroy the film, but it disoriented me. Now, it would have been one thing if we were told we had to cut it out of the script. In retrospect it makes me a little bitter, because we had very little time to shoot the film, and we certainly could have used the time and money it took to build the sub and shoot the scene somewhere else in the film. But it made me realize how lucky we were, because a million things could have struck Aubrey as being as unnecessary as that submarine, each in and of itself unnecessary, but contributing to the texture of the thing.

I can't defend the bingo-game scene on the grounds that the studio tampered with it in the editing. [The locale of the scene is geographically unrelated to a supposedly proximate trailer camp. — D.C.] Ideally, that bingo tent would have been visible in some other view of the trailer park. But we did everything piecemeal. The bingo tent was on a sound stage, and a corner of the MGM backlot served as the rest of the trailer park. They wouldn't let us spend the money to take over a real trailer park at night or build an area large enough to do some kind of establishing shot, so you have to make an enormous assumption that somewhere in that trailer park there's a bingo tent.

In general, I guess I took this position: once I decided I respected Howard and his judgment, then I decided, "He's going to make a movie out of my script that will probably not resemble in every particular what I would do if I were making it, but I will defer to his judgment because I respect it." There is a certain kind of director who has enough of his own vision so that it's intriguing to see what he's going to do with my script. It may not be my movie he makes, but it'll be an exciting one. Yet, if I hadn't been so involved with the making of *Slither*, and the movie that's on the screen were still the same movie, I probably would have thought terrible things had been done to my script and felt disassociated from it. Because I was there throughout, and gave at least tacit approval to editing decisions, it came out being something that I was responsible for, or at least *felt* responsible for.

*

NUNNALLY JOHNSON: I was purely a storyteller, sometimes all right, sometimes not. I was never aiming at anything beyond what I put down on paper, the characters and what they did. . . . There

are people who have a view of what's possible. I can read
Pauline Kael, or I can read some stuff of Judith Crist's, just as I
can read Kenneth Tynan, and it will make me a little ashamed
of myself for not having the high aspirations that they have for
pictures.

# THREE
## The Actor

Puppet? Pawn? Or, center of the cinematic universe? Lazy, undisciplined bargain-basement version of his "legitimate" theatrical counterpart? Or, dedicated professional who must have an almost superhuman ability to concentrate, synthesize and carry through? Machine-tooled projection of the studio moguls' and the public's fantasies? Mere personality? Or, bona fide artist, more capable, because of the film's intrinsic closeness to nature, of conveying "truth" than the interpretive artists of other media?

As a species, the film actor — particularly in America — is probably all of these things. In the course of a career of any length, a single actor may be any or all of them. It is even likely that an actor has fitted three or four categories while making a single movie.

What the actor is, and when, depends on the director and the nature of the material actor and director are addressing themselves to. But also — perhaps to a more marked extent than is the case with the director's other associates — the actor's function both during the filmmaking process and at the end of it — on the screen — is determined by the actor himself. The uniqueness of the actor's contribution — he is the only component of the movie-making mix who is personally visible, and the substance and appeal of his work is emotional rather than intellectual — makes him at once extremely powerful and extremely vulnerable. According to his personal and technical resources, he can work miracles, or have miracles worked on him, on both the set and the screen or he can be defeated in the former situation and embarrassed in the latter. His essential human-beingness somehow figures more importantly than that of any of the director's collaborators.

The notion of the centrality of the actor in the filmmaking process is the rock upon which the star system is founded. Under the star system, which reached its fullest development at MGM in the thirties, writers would conceive or tailor scenarios expressly to serve as vehicles for one or more contract players. Since the star-actor was thought to be a guarantor of box-office in those days, his showcases were designed to display his particular abilities, camouflage his shortcomings, and accommodate the personal whatever-it-is that made him a star in the first place.

CHARLTON HESTON: You need a persona. Many very effective — not only successful, but effective — film actors are not actors in the professional sense at all. Conversely, many very fine stage actors lack the persona . . . the absolutely unidentifiable quotient that a film performer needs to make him interesting on the screen.

Because the actor with a persona brings basically the *same* "unidentifiable quotient" to every role he plays, even his best efforts are likely to be written off as "personality acting."

LESLIE CARON: In the Hollywood of the past you became a great star, like Cary Grant, if you could develop a very good style of unrealistic acting. [Ironically, Grant's performance opposite

Caron in 1964's *Father Goose* was praised for its "realism" and its independence of the actor's familiar screen persona. — D.C.]

LYNN CARLIN: Before *Faces,* I was a secretary, and being wanted to be in a film is enough so that you come in and you're sort of open and you're willing to do anything they tell you to do. But as soon as you do one film that "actor" thing comes in and you're so terribly afraid of making a fool of yourself that you put that wall up and you want to establish that — continue to establish the image that — if you were successful with the first one you don't want to mess up on the second.

A persona, however, can be liberating as easily as it can be limiting. By providing the actor with a foundation for any character he plays, his persona can allow him to go beyond conventional "characterization." By decreasing the audience's perceived distance between actor and role, a persona can help foster an impression of life duplicated, not merely imitated.

JEAN-LOUIS TRINTIGNANT: Even during the great Hollywood era — the thirties — there were some actors who played in a strikingly truthful style, not merely "realistically." For example — I don't know if Garfield belonged to that period, but there was a Bogart already.

Regardless of whether a screen actor has a persona, or whether he is a star, the range of his opportunities is ordinarily defined by strong aesthetic and practical considerations peculiar to the film medium.

JON VOIGHT: Some people are just movie personalities. I'm a character actor. . . . Character acting is difficult. It's much harder. . . . I have a great deal of respect for Mike Nichols. But . . . well, you see, I look a certain way, and he hired me [for *Catch-22*] for the way I look.

HENRY FONDA: [After being engaged to appear in Sergio Leone's *Once Upon a Time in the West*] I went to an optometrist and had myself fitted for contact lenses that would make my eyes dark and grew a moustache which was a little bit like John Wilkes Booth's. I was trying every way that I knew to look like a period heavy. And I arrived in Rome and went on the set and [Leone] took one look at me and said, "Off!" He wanted the baby blues, he wanted the Fonda face.

Like Ford and others, Hitchcock knows, he knows when he is casting, what he can expect from an actor, what kind of a performance. . . . He is not mute. I just don't remember very much talk as to how to play a scene, or what kind of man I was [in *The Wrong Man*].

LESLIE CARON: When you are hired they know pretty well what you are capable of doing. They expect you to come with a prepared idea of your character. Unfortunately, because of economic circumstances, the director usually doesn't have time to come to the leading actors and prepare them. You would be surprised how many directors have a very vague conception of your character. They have the sets and they have all of the equipment to think about. They are wondering which cameras and which lenses they are going to use.

The film actor's self-preparation for performing in front of the camera, that time when, in the words of Nina Foch, "you are standing there stark naked in front of everybody," may involve interior or exterior research, or a combination.

NINA FOCH: You build the character in your mind by asking such questions as: How does the person approach a stranger? Does this person walk in straight lines or in curving ones? What does this person eat? Is this person constipated? What is this person like in bed? . . . You are going to be stark naked, so you must be totally clothed within this human being.

JEAN-LOUIS TRINTIGNANT: . . . I raced in several automobile competitions before beginning *A Man and a Woman*. I wasn't satisfied just to talk with racers, I really had to race myself.

INGRID THULIN (With specific reference to *Winter Light*): I have it all in my sight before we start. I don't learn it day by day. I have read it and thought of it and decided on it. But I haven't decided on it in an exterior way. I have completed it psychologically, inside. So, however Ingmar Bergman changes it, I have a basic person there. You can find a pillar, and whatever you hang on that pillar, the pillar cannot go away. It has to stand. . . . And then I forget it and start the film.

LIV ULLMANN: Bergman hates to discuss and analyze. . . . He feels that you can discuss away your fantasy. I feel that he is right. I would hate to work with actors where you have to sit down and talk about the background of the character. Maybe I do that subconsciously, but I try to act out what is in the script. I try to capture what sort of a person it is. . . . [For *The Emigrants*] I had to learn that dialect. We had to learn to wash clothes the way they do it with the horses. [We] went for days in the fields. It's fun for a day, but after three days it gets a little tiring. But it was an experience, and for me I think that it was the best experience ever.

CHARLTON HESTON: [To prepare for *Khartoum*] I used a British vocal coach for about two months.

LESLIE CARON: I usually put aside one month and work a minimum of four hours a day. I read the script until I feel as though I have lived through it. Then I start out acting moments that I feel. The main thing is to study the script as if you were the director. The climaxes and the "unimportant" parenthesis moments and learning the structure of the script are the most important things to study.

It is often assumed that if actors (and directors) had their way, the shooting of a motion picture would be preceded by a rehearsal period similar to that preceding the first public performance of a stage production.

Advance rehearsals have not only relieved actors of some of the uncertainties of self-preparation in isolation and the pressures of on-the-spot creation on the sound stage, but have also aided them in arriving at and refining their conceptions of character. Irvin Kershner says that under his guidance George Segal and Eva

Liv Ullmann in *The Emigrants,* directed by Jan Troell: "I had to learn that dialect. We had to learn to wash clothes the way they do it with the horses. [We] went for days in the fields."

Marie Saint extensively revamped their roles in *Loving* during the one-week rehearsal period that preceded the shooting of the film.

The standard excuse for not having advance rehearsals is that they take time and cost money, an excuse invalidated by the numerous instances in which time and money were saved because various difficulties were resolved in the course of preproduction rehearsals. A classic example involves the first day's filming on Orson Welles's *Touch of Evil*. According to Charlton Heston, advance rehearsal away from the studio resulted in the shooting of a sequence covering thirteen script pages, and scheduled for two and one-half working days, in exactly one day.

Yet Heston, who is a theater-trained actor, is doubtful about rehearsal as a rule of thumb. He says that Orson Welles (co-star as well as director of *Touch of Evil*) and Laurence Olivier (co-star of *Khartoum*), "both of whom are primarily theater people," are alone among his professional associates in their ability to use rehearsal time "constructively. Both Wyler and Peckinpah, enormously talented directors, didn't really get much out of the rehearsal time away from the sound stage."

Liv Ullmann explains the approach of Ingmar Bergman which has served them both so successfully: "He allows technical rehearsals. But then he likes to take on the first emotional reading, because sometimes that is the best take."

Once on the sound stage, the film actor performs his role in piecemeal fashion over a period of weeks or months, usually out of continuity and often in takes lasting no more than a few seconds. Long between-take and between-scene delays and the necessity of repeating his performance of a scene, or parts of it, so that it may be recorded from various camera angles are additional obstacles to concentration and consistency. The camera itself can be a formidable deterrent to unselfconsciousness, the *sine qua non* of film acting.

CHARLTON HESTON: Since I have a lucky retentive faculty I don't study the lines, because a day's work is never more than six or seven pages. You can, if you trust your retention, absorb the lines in six or seven pages in the course of blocking out the scene, so I never read the scene the night before. I read the whole script maybe once a week, and this seems to help me keep an idea of the structure of the whole piece more clearly in mind than if I examined each day's work the night before I did it, out of the context of the story. . . . I found that quite often an incidental by-product of such a method is that the lines you forget, the fragments you forget, are often ones that don't belong. You remember the line of the scene, the spine of the scene, what it's about. There may be something that really is incidental and not contributive that you may or may not want. But at least it allows you to make a judgment about it.

LIV ULLMANN (With specific reference to *The Emigrants,* the action of which spans many years): I would read the script many times, to try to block it into sections. I would think, This is the section where this is happening to her, and now she goes a little further with this section. . . . Between scenes I may try to read something. I try to get away from it if [on an outdoor location] the sun is apparently to be away [and shooting delayed] for one hour. It will ruin everything if you sit and concentrate. The best thing is to really relax with something that doesn't demand anything.

JON VOIGHT: Stage acting just requires the understanding of the distance between you and the people. In film acting it's the distance between you and the camera. . . . You have to know how much, what's being focused on.

ROBERT STEPHENS: You cannot be too quick on film because the camera can't move that quickly. . . . Billy Wilder would constantly say, "Don't go so fast because, technically, the camera can't travel as fast as you can in nature."

LESLIE CARON: I used to go through a great many exercises to learn to concentrate. But, after so many films . . . the camera becomes a friend, a listener, and not an intruder.

CHARLTON HESTON: While it is certainly annoying to have to deal with so many moves — you know, hit the mark, be careful the crab dolly doesn't run over your toes — each medium has its technical limitations, and the centrality of the camera is part of

Robert Stephens about to plant a courtly kiss on the hand of Geneviève Page in *The Private Life of Sherlock Holmes*, directed by Billy Wilder: "You cannot be too quick on film . . ."

the prime definition of what film is. The camera is the most important thing. The camera is what tells the story; the actor in a sense is merely the most important prop.

INGRID THULIN: Bergman is very close to the camera, and while he is sitting so close to the camera, you have no feeling that they are parted. The feeling that you have towards the director is also the feeling that you have towards the audience, which would be where the camera is. He is a very good audience . . .

LIV ULLMANN: . . . You feel that there is somebody who is really there.

INGRID THULIN: [Because of the short takes prompted by the temporal scheme of Alain Resnais' *La Guerre est Finie*], you don't let yourself go. . . . He has long sequences where [you don't feel so constrained]. And from these sequences you pick up feelings . . . of the person you are trying to express, of the human being you are trying to be. With a film like Resnais', it can be [more constructive than it ordinarily is for me] to look at rushes. After you have seen much more of the film you understand that flashback later on. . . . For the actors, *The Ritual* was quite good because . . . it was ten minutes a day. Ordinarily you take two minutes a day of film, and you don't feel that you are doing so much. You don't feel that you are working.

CHARLTON HESTON: Acting for the camera, you rapidly become aware that the director quite properly is often not really interested in your best performance of a whole scene unless . . . that's what he's determined to use. One of the reasons I welcome a long scene is at least it's a chance to play the scene. You can then begin to deal with the scene in acting terms and begin to structure it as you would if you were playing it on the stage. You begin to feel you have a little control over it.

LESLIE CARON (With reference to *Head of the Family*, directed by Nanni Loy): The Italians always shoot with several cameras. We had incredibly long takes. I remember one scene where we went through thirteen rooms and we must have had fifteen people, including three babies. It was all in one take. There must have been eight cameras, because the main dolly always had three cameras. One was taking the main shot, and two were taking close-ups with zoom lenses. It was very interesting, and wonderful for actors. You don't have to worry about hitting marks and about your face being in camera because there were always so many cameras there.

Decades earlier, Jean Renoir had already taken the methods used by Loy to their logical conclusion by postponing his decision about the placement of the camera until the actors had finished rehearsing. The "angle depends on the acting of the actor and not on the imagination of the director. It's why I so often use tracking shots, pans, et cetera. It is for no other reason than that I hate to cut the acting of an actor during his inspiration."

In addition to being advantaged by long takes, camera setups that accommodate his performance, and a director who "humanizes" the camera, the actor is also aided by the physical and emotional environment in which a film is made.

CHARLTON HESTON (With reference to *Khartoum,* in which he impersonated General Charles Gordon): We really shot in the Sudan. The Nile is the Nile. There you are, the same goddam river that Gordon sailed up to get his head chopped off. . . . *Will Penny* is a "winter" Western. We shot it in the High Sierras and, again, if you're really chasing a stray cow, one lousy stray cow up among the jack pine above the snowline in January, you know what it felt like to chase a lone cow in the jack pine in 1885.

I had as close a relationship with Sam Peckinpah on *Major Dundee* as I've ever had with a director. A location picture promotes that kind of situation to a certain extent in that there's no place else to go, nobody else to talk to but the people you're working with. I got very close to him, and we'd go out and drink bad Mexican brandy at night. I guess Sam directed me as much in those times as he did on the set, maybe unconsciously. . . . To an extent, Sam made me into Major Dundee, drinking beer and brandy in those bars at night. . . . The

Charlton Heston in *Major Dundee*, directed by Sam Peckinpah. "Something about the Mexican experience and the living all day in a Union cavalryman's pants and sitting on a horse . . ."

Ingrid Thulin with Dirk Bogarde in *The Damned,* directed by Luchino Visconti: "Visconti suddenly said, 'I want you to look like that. It's more . . . like Hitler.'"

Mexico of 1966, or whenever we made the film, is very like the Mexico of 1866. The villages are the same. We rode through one village that was over four hundred years old, and you can sit on a horse in uniform with a saber in your hand and figure how many soldiers have ridden down that street. The reality is more total, that's what I'm suggesting. We were living a lot of the experience. . . . Something about the Mexican experience and the living all day in a Union cavalryman's pants and sitting on a horse most of the day and drinking all night in filthy Mexican cantinas, made — I guess it was more . . . I don't like to say some mystical act of creation occurred. It was an involuntary creation.

INGRID THULIN: *The Damned* was a very heavy production, and living with these people and going through their problems — you talk to Dirk Bogarde and he is that, and you talk to Helmut Berger and he is that. You can almost carry over all the human feelings that you had to use to move the production. Dirk Bogarde — we were very good friends. At the end of the film we were going to die together. I don't know how he took it, but for me it was significant of building up through three or four months of life together. Suddenly something happens that adds exactly what you couldn't think of . . . because other people come towards you and react. . . . There are actors who are so aware of clothes and surroundings — I don't say that I am — but . . . when I got that violet wedding thing on I began acting right away because the whole style was carrying you. And then I was a little angry because I was white in the face [because of the pasty pallor of the makeup designed for the scene]. . . . I thought it was too much of a jump, and then Visconti suddenly said, "I want you to look like that. It's more . . . like Hitler." And I said, "It's Hitler. He's dead. He was a clown. He was stupid." So I decided to be Hitler and acted that way. Dirk Bogarde wanted to hold me under the arm, and I said, "I don't want," [and moved away from him]. "I want to die all by myself." And he got so angry at that moment and the whole thing came off. . . . The whole thing was just an accident of the moment.

The failure to get a fully audible and noise-free recording of the actor's voice at the time of actual shooting necessitates the postdubbing, or looping, of either individual lines or whole scenes of dialogue. While looping is considered part and parcel of the actor's job in Europe — especially in Italy, where direct sound recording is relatively rare — actors in American films usually regard it as an onerous chore. Even the most distraction-ridden filming site has more "reality" than the vacuum of the dubbing room, where the actor essentially gives only half of his performance — the nonvisual part — and often gives it alone, without the benefit of the presence and interaction of his fellow performers in a scene. Still, both the actor's performance and the film it is part of can benefit from looping.

CHARLTON HESTON: Up to *Touch of Evil* I had always regarded looping as a necessary evil. They were just scenes where you hadn't gotten a clean track and you replaced it with a clean track, but I had always felt that, as an actor, I never could do as well and at best could just match what I had done. Orson persuaded me that it was possible to do more and, I think, taught me how to do more, and since then I have always regarded the looping process as another chance. It is often surprising how much you can change. . . .

LESLIE CARON: The Italians dub everything. They have no respect for sound. Many times the script is completely rewritten at the time of the dubbing. Why not? It makes sense. You should be more elastic and flexible. There is a real advantage in putting new sentences in the actor's mouth. What if you cut a scene out? Or what if the sudden juxtaposition of images creates a situation which was unforeseen? Often, different words might be infinitely better.

When film actors talk about their work on specific projects, what they are apt to remember most vividly is the way the director communicated with them, the extent to which the director allowed them to participate in the shaping of their characterizations. In the next several pages, actors — including an actor-director and an actress who worked as a director's "associate" —

Jack Benny, right, in *To Be or Not To Be*, directed by Ernst Lubitsch. "He would play the scene first, ahead of me."

Nina Foch (seated), with Dyan Cannon, Jennifer O'Neill and Ken Howard, in *Such Good Friends*, directed by Otto Preminger: "He knows when he comes in exactly how he will shoot; where you are going to stand; where you are going to go and how you are going to get there."

describe their responses to (and/or the rationale behind) working situations in which, to one degree or another, the actor did not participate as fully as he might have.

LESLIE CARON (With reference to her work in the episode of *Three Fables of Love* based on La Fontaine's "The Two Pigeons"): René Clair treated you like you were a moron. René does the part for you with a stopwatch. It is to the last detail that he portrays what he wants you to do. He has the precise turn of the head just when he wants it. Somehow you imitate what he does, and it is absolutely stupendous. You can't present anything better than what he asked you to do. This frustrates me as an actress. Finally, I told him that he made me feel like a grand duchess visiting his set. I didn't feel as though I were working. From that moment on, he let me bring suggestions to the part. After a while he accepted my participation.

JACK BENNY: (With reference to working with Ernst Lubitsch on *To Be or Not To Be*): He would play the scene first, ahead of me. I'll tell you how badly he played it. . . . Before he was ever a director, he was a corny comedian in Germany, a real corny comic. But you knew by what he was doing exactly what he wanted. He knew that if I watched him play a scene . . . that I would do exactly the same thing, except in my way.

NINA FOCH (With reference to working with Otto Preminger on *Such Good Friends*): Basically, he's a fine craftsman. He's so good at his own work. But the way he goes about getting his results! He knows when he comes in exactly how he will shoot; where you are going to stand; where you are going to go and how you are going to get there. But he doesn't give you a chance to probe, to define, to explore. . . . I don't think Preminger casts well. He traps himself. Then he is forced to tell everybody what he expects of them to the smallest detail. Of course, for the actor it is much more productive to be allowed to feel out the part . . . to have options open.

Ingmar Bergman speaks of working in an atmosphere of love. Otto Preminger, yelling and screaming, sets up an atmosphere under which most people don't work well at all. To hear him scream at this eight-year-old kid was almost too much. . . . I would do my part of the scene, and then he would make Dyan Cannon cry so hard that she would play her part of the scene in a way that completely surprised me. If I'd known she was going to play it that way, I wouldn't have played my part the way I did. His behavior is definitely counter productive.

I don't think it's the way things should be done. Of course, there are always exceptions. . . . In *The Diary of Anne Frank* I worked as an associate for George Stevens. I worked with the young actors. Basically, he doesn't like to talk to actors in detail. . . . One young actress couldn't get angry, couldn't burst into tears and get really resentful and angry. I had Stevens's permission to do some drastic things, so I said to the assistant [director], "I'm going to get her angry — but you had better tell me ten minutes before she's due to be out there." I went into her room. She had one of those model's bags, a big one. I kicked the bag and said, "What the hell is this?" I started throwing her things around. I was careful not to touch something that might be irreplaceable. I threw them. I broke them. I smashed them. By the time she came out of there, she was a mess. But she was right in the scene.

JOHN CASSAVETES: (Speaking of directing the middle-aged woman who appeared with Peter Falk in the London casino scene in *Husbands*): She was a ballet dancer who . . . it's so crazy. You see somebody sitting there and you've got to have her in the scene. . . . The woman was tight. She didn't know what was expected of her, and it was too late for her to find out in the course of filming. I would say terrible things to her, just awful things. She would fight them off like a lady. She reached a point where she could do everything by herself. She was grateful for that attitude of not giving a shit about what anybody else thought, because everything bad had already happened. From there on in, she just started to play.

Cassavetes, an actor himself, is obviously sincere when he says that, as a director, he loves and respects actors. He is upset by charges that his method in the instance discussed above was harsh, explaining, "We're all there to get something good."

Though Leslie Caron remembers her experience working on *Head of the Family* as one of her most satisfying ("the only time that I have had the privilege of discussing a part"), some of Nanni Loy's means could be said to manipulate or use the actor.

LESLIE CARON: I found myself in a position where I was clay in the hands of the director. I knew he could direct, and I followed what he said without question. . . . He will prepare you for a scene by telling you that at a particular moment the character is very depressed and worried because one of her children is in love and the other has troubles in school and the third one has some physical illness. . . . I would rehearse like that, and then just before we were ready to shoot he would tell me, "Now you are very happy because . . ." I would say to him, "Nanni, you have just told me the contrary thing." I don't know why he did that. I think it must have been to get a fresh emotion. . . .

HENRY FONDA: Ford . . . won't talk about it. If you start to ask Ford questions about your part he will turn you off. If you get too insistent he will just take the page and tear it out of your script, and there is nothing you can do. . . . But he's got a great instinct for things. The "good-bye" scene in *The Grapes of Wrath,* when Tom Joad says good-bye to his mother, was a very emotional scene. It was fairly difficult technically, because the camera had to come out of the tent and then take Ma and Tom down the side of the tent until they finally sit down on a bench beside the outdoor dance floor. There was a pan and a dolly, I believe. It took an hour or more for the cameraman to set it up and be sure that he knew and could anticipate our movements. We rehearsed the movements a lot. We never once rehearsed the dialogue of the scene. Now, Ford didn't make a point of that, saying, "Look, I don't want you to use it up." He never talked about it, as if he had something else on his mind. So, Jane Darwell and I were like a couple of frustrated race horses champing at the bit. When everybody was finally ready, Darwell and I were *so ready* that when we took our places both of us broke down with emotion . . . we had to hold it back. . . . We shot the scene and Ford just got up and walked away and we never did it again.

Henry Fonda and Jane Darwell in *The Grapes of Wrath*, directed by John Ford.
". . . Jane Darwell and I were like a couple of frustrated race horses champing at the bit."

In one of those Okie camps — or Hooverville camps — Ma Joad starts to prepare a stew. When it is ready there is a semicircle of children about thirty feet away, just standing. . . . The Joad family are aware of the hungry children watching them eat, and they are embarrassed by it. We came in and we rehearsed the scene, and I think we even shot it one time. Then Ford stopped, and he picked on the actor playing "Unk," one of the family. I wasn't looking at "Unk," so I don't know what he did. But evidently he started to "act" — seeing these hungry children — and he must have done something with his face, because Ford chewed him out in front of the whole company to such an extent that it just destroyed him. And when we shot it again he was numb — which is what you are supposed to be. You are without emotion, you are drained of emotion. . . . That is Ford's kind of communication. He will chew you out to stop you from acting.

LESLIE CARON: Vincente Minnelli never gives you one goddam piece of direction. I cannot remember one full sentence of direction that Vincente gave me. He puckers his lips and starts stuttering, and then you have to guess what he wants to say. Then he moves on. He watches the swans or the lilies or the horse in the background. You have to work with antennae to guess if he wants it stronger or more comical or more satirical. You keep trying until something seems to please him. And you know when you have done it right. He never tells you, but you do sort of sense it. He usually tells you the swans were great. . . . He is inarticulate, but he has monumental talent. And all his films bear his inimitable style.

CHARLTON HESTON: William Wyler prepares extensively . . . but I am convinced he doesn't really do the creative work that makes him William Wyler until he gets on the set. I made a grievous, grievous error with Willie quite early in the extensive preparation of *Ben-Hur* when I wrote a thirty-page essay on the life of Judah Ben-Hur prior to the story.

It's no fun at all doing a picture for Wyler. Now, as it happens, Wyler is a friend of mine. But on the set . . . he is so locked in his concentration on what he's doing and has, I have come to feel, really quite a limited interest in or trust of actors. He just knows that he has to use them and he knows how to get them to do what he wants, and it's a nerve-racking process for him, and God knows it is for the actor too. . . . He does not communicate his ideas to the actor as resourcefully as some directors — Orson, for example — but when it's right, it's right.

When you shoot he sits down under the lens and . . . watches, and you finish the scene and . . . he'll say, "Okay, let's do one more. And this time when you talk to the girl, don't make it so obvious that you decided not to take her with you. That has to come out in the course of the scene. You're beginning with that, that's no good."

So you do that, and he'll say, "You know, let's do one more. In fact, you should be warmer in the beginning because the scene the night before. . . . Be warmer, Chuck, for God's sake."

And you say, "Okay," and be warmer, and he'll say, "Yeah, that's better, that thing you did with the glass is good, but do less with it, not so much. . . ." And you do two or three more takes, and he'll say, "What happened to that thing with the glass? That was good." You say, "Well, you said do less." And he'll say, "Yeah, but that's too much less." And so you go on, and then he'll say, "Don't do the thing with the glass at all. That's a terrible thing. I'm sorry, I shouldn't have told you to do it."

And then he'll say, "What are you so nice to her for? This isn't a love scene, you know. You're leaving her." You say, "Well, you said . . ." "Yeah, but it's not good. Don't do it that way. I'll tell you what, we'll do one where you stay over here and . . . Chuck, look, if I don't say anything it's good, huh?"

Finally, you would do — I would say that it takes an average of about nine takes. And you'll finish, and he'll say, "Yeah, okay, let's do the close-up where the girl comes in."

Wyler covers extensively [i.e., he films scenes or portions of scenes from many angles]. But he often does not, I realized after two long pictures with him, print the best take — your best take of the whole scene. Your best take overall may have been five, but he may print two and six because there was a thing at the beginning that you never got better. Wyler puts a scene together like a man repairing a watch. . . . It's very hard

A Belle Époque décor and Leslie Caron in *Gigi*, directed by Vincente Minnelli. "You keep trying until something seems to please him. And you know when you have done it right."

to sustain any kind of an acting concentration working for
Wyler, because the effect of his direction comes from an ac-
cumulation of details, each of which you recognize to be correct
or you'd say, "Goddammit, Willy, I can't remember all that stuff.
There's nothing left to the scene; it's just pieces. . . ." I've often
observed that doing a picture for Wyler is like getting the works
in a Turkish bath — you damn near drown, but you come out
smelling like a bloody rose.

JON VOIGHT (With reference to working with Mike Nichols on
   *Catch-22*): I could never really get cooking with the kind of
   character he wanted me to go with. He wanted me to do a
   Mike Nichols [routine] all the time, and I did it. I tried to get
   my own thing. But I couldn't find any way into it, really. I just
   didn't find it. I wanted to play the role as a kind of fuckup. I
   wanted to play him like the kind of guy you want to help all
   the time . . . his hat is on crooked and his moustache was — like
   the book. And he always had stuff in his pockets, but he could
   never find the thing he wanted; like he'd have to play a whole
   scene looking for something and he'd never find it. And mean-
   while he'd be selling you some kind of insurance, and by the
   time you'd helped him find . . . whatever, he had sold you a
   policy for three million dollars. Well, Mike didn't want that
   because then, at the end, you see the paperhanger become
   Adolf Hitler. And that's what I wanted to do — have this kind
   of inept guy who had absolutely no values win . . . all of a
   sudden he was the winner. And then he didn't understand why
   people were picking on him because he was killing people.
   . . . Mike Nichols rejected it. He wanted it played as the all-
   American boy, and I didn't want to play him as the all-American
   boy because I don't know what the all-American boy is.

   For any or all of a number of reasons — the economic exigen-
cies of moviemaking, the inaccessibility of the director, an implicit
trust in the rightness of the director's choices, a low self-opinion,
habituation to nonparticipatory acting — it seems to be an un-
written rule among actors that the director's wishes must be
carried out.

Jon Voight with Anthony Perkins in *Catch-22*, directed by Mike Nichols: "He wanted it played as the all-American boy . . ."

CHARLTON HESTON: As an actor, it seems to me part of what I'm paid for is to adjust to the way they want to work.

LESLIE CARON: If the director doesn't like what you have prepared, then he would tell me and I would change it. I would try to satisfy the director.

LYNN CARLIN: I put total faith in the director and I will always do what he says. I might discuss, but . . . I will never disagree.

HENRY FONDA: I have been known not to agree with a lot of things, and I've even had disagreements with Ford a couple of times. But . . . "insist on something." Not with Ford, I don't. Not with Otto [Preminger], either.

The conflict between remaining true to one's instincts, when they are contrary to the director's, and maintaining a reasonably harmonious relationship with the director can dictate a self-protective deviousness.

NINA FOCH: I protect the part of me that is pure, that doesn't believe in stealing, that doesn't believe in cheating a person that you love. That is the thing that you protect when you say to the director, "Why, yes, sure, right." You don't go against him. You do what he wants . . . but you can bring your truth within the framework of the director's desire.

JOHN CASSAVETES: [As an actor] you can't divorce yourself from what the director wants. The director could be an absolute imbecile, but if he says it, we are so trained and oriented that we've got to do that. . . . In directing I try to break that down in actors. It was my attempt to have an actor do something better.

It is not surprising, of course, that an actor-director, or actor-turned-director, should be cognizant of and sympathetic to an actor's problems.

CHARLTON HESTON: All of us work better . . . if we are constantly stimulated and alert, and this is difficult in film. A great many scenes you do in films are not very interesting. Orson was more successful than any director I've ever worked for in persuading everybody that each shot we did was in fact the most important in the film. He communicates his own enthusiasm and creative energy to everyone involved. . . . In the course of solving any kind of a problem — talking to the cameraman about the kind of angle he wants — he will say something terribly funny about something that happened with another cameraman. . . . I don't mean just jokes, but some inventive thing to excite your effort to solve whatever the problem is. It keeps it bright and sharp; it isn't the way you've heard it before. . . . He is himself an actor of considerable ability, and he can tell you things about the scene or tell you routes to solve it that you never thought of. . . . He knows about acting, his specifics about it are quite pragmatic things. I remember that he said something that impressed me enormously. He said very few leading men understand the importance of the tenor range. The more I thought about that, the more I realized it's true, and I have since attempted to explore this truth to my profit. I was able to raise my voice largely into a tenor range to play Chinese Gordon in *Khartoum*. I probably would not have thought of that . . . if, ten years before, Orson had not made that singularly unusual observation.

HENRY FONDA: Some directors . . . have an ability to talk to an actor and put words together in a certain sequence that makes sense to an actor. . . . Sidney Lumet is an actor's director who knows how — because he was an actor once himself — to communicate with an actor. I chose Sidney to direct *Twelve Angry Men* because of his known ability to get more out of you by word, which Ford doesn't do.

Unfortunately, there is no correlation coefficient between the degree to which the actor is permitted to make or contribute to creative choices and the quality — or effectiveness — of his performance. Whether Fonda's work in *Twelve Angry Men* measures up to his work in *The Grapes of Wrath* or in Fritz Lang's *You Only Live Once* ("a too-tortured nightmare to make") is, quite apart from any consideration of these films *as films,* open to ques-

tion. Jon Voight suggests that his working relationship with John
Boorman, who directed *Deliverance,* was basically a complementary one and that had it been more collaborative — or had Voight
written or directed the movie or been less tired physically — his
character would have been markedly fuller and richer. One doesn't
know for sure whether Voight's additions and refinements would
have benefited the film as a whole or upset its already precarious
balance between metaphysics and high adventure. Yet it sometimes happens that the actor's participation in the "authorship" of
his role causes him to modify and expand both his characterization and the movie that encompasses it. Irvin Kershner says that
only during the rehearsals for *Loving,* undertaken so that George
Segal, Eva Marie Saint, and he as director might "find the fullness
of the people," did he begin "to see the picture taking form for
the first time." Segal, who confided in a member of the shooting
company that "this was the one movie where he really had a
sense of participation," extended his boundaries as an actor in it,
and Eva Marie Saint did her best work since her award-winning
film début in *On the Waterfront* fifteen years earlier.

The following extracts record actors' impressions of working
situations in which they felt a sense of participation, without
attempting to evaluate the performances that resulted or the films
they were part of.

JON VOIGHT: When we first met, John Boorman said to me, "You
    know, I'm very good at making film. I can make a scene work.
    I mean, we get together and I can figure out how to make it
    work. Where I'm not so good is depth of character; at depth
    I'm not very good." I said, "That's what you're really not good
    at — huh! I'll tell you what I'm good at: I'm good at the archi-
    tecture, I can make the story work for the character. That's
    what I'm good at. That's what I can give you." And he said,
    "That seems to be a very good combination." And it was.
    Exactly that. He can make it work. He can photograph it. . . .
    We didn't get to completion in a sense. It wasn't complete work
    but it was good work. I didn't feel I completed it, but I did what
    I had to do under the circumstances well, and he did what he
    had to do well. . . . How I would have changed it, if it was my

movie . . . I would have made it much more from the point of
view of [my character] Ed. I would have gone into his getting
up in the morning and leaving on the trip, showing a little of
his life before. When he climbed the cliff I would have shown
it almost from the point of view of what he saw. I would have
shot moments of decision, making a certain move and not being
able to make another move, and have all the stuff of the shooting of the guy on top of the cliff from Ed's point of view. I
mean, I would have . . . turned him right into an animal with
the camera. . . . I kept trying. I'd say, "You know, well, you
could do a little of this." But I was so tired I really couldn't
pursue that very far. By the time I got to the major scenes in
the picture — the decision scenes — I was wiped out.

What I am trying to do is nurture the things in me which I
think are really me. So how do I find the directors to get some
of this stuff out of me? . . . I am always looking for someone to
save me, because all actors need help. All directors need help
from good actors. With John Schlesinger, it was absolutely the
best collaboration with anybody . . . because he gave me lots of
room. And he also gave me lots of help. I like to be criticized
when I work. But I don't like to be told what to do. . . . I made
a terrific scene in *Midnight Cowboy*, the crux of the film really.
I've just had a good night with that girl I picked up. I made
some money as a stud. I come back with all this stuff — pills
and soup and clothes. I come back and Dusty Hoffman's sitting
on the bed. He's sick. Now I — the way the scene was written,
"See, I've got some stuff for you. Ratso, goddam, we're gonna
make it . . ." Then Dusty says, "I ain't feeling so good, Joe," and
I say, "Oh yeah, what's happening?" We played the scene. It was
so sentimental. We were acting it well, but something was
wrong. John couldn't figure it out. He called up Waldo Salt, the
screenwriter. [Waldo] comes down to the studio. We go through
the scene, and he says, "Well, you've got to remember that
Joe is very selfish. He wants to leave Ratso." Bing! Here we
go. So I changed a few lines. I said, "I've got some stuff in there
for you *too*." I pulled out this stuff. "I've got some socks. Looks
like socks, see? I've got some stuff in there for you *too*." I'm
thinking I'm going to be out of there in a couple of days be-

cause, man, I'm tough stuff. I find him sick and it makes me angry. And then I don't know what to do because the responsibility is on me. . . . And that's the beginning of a dramatic section that finally winds up with his decision to go to Florida with Ratso.

LIV ULLMANN: Working with Bergman, you feel that you are a part of something. . . . I know that he will help me and he will know what I am trying to express. If I don't do it, then I know that he will help me. . . . After a take in which the actor felt uncomfortable he would change the blocking of the scene. He feels that if you the actor can't express it or don't know how to, if it is an actor who knows his job, then it might be something wrong with the blocking. Maybe you should be standing instead of sitting. Very often he is right. Often a change of position helps you to get the feeling that you didn't have. He listens to the actors and he watches them. He tries to get out of them what they have to give, not what he would want to do in a particular situation. He sees what you are trying to express and he builds on that. He helps get it out of you.

I have a say as an actress. Bergman is . . . open for suggestions. He hates it if you start to analyze, but he is very open to your own kind of interpretation of the kind of woman he has written.

In my experience, improvisation started in *Shame*. We are sitting by a table and drinking wine and eating. Then we fall down on the grass. We knew what Bergman wanted to say. But the way that we did it was more or less left up to us. . . . There was the dinner party in *The Passion of Anna* where the four [principal characters] each tell their own story. That was our own complete freedom. But we had to stick to the character. First it may have been Max von Sydow's turn. He drank red wine, and all of us could ask him questions. He had to answer as the character while the camera was on him all the time. Bergman did the same thing with all four of us. Then he cut it together. He didn't really feel that [the film] was good. He took it away, and after the picture was finished he asked us to come to the studio and to speak as the actor [in what became the "interview" scenes].

LYNN CARLIN: *Taking Off* was a love venture. Everybody felt terribly involved and cared. They took great pride in their own work and they cared very much about you and your work and went out of their way to make it special. . . . When I first was crying on the couch telling my husband to go out and look for our runaway daughter Miloš Forman told us the scene and what we were to say. He said, "I don't care what happens; if you laugh or if you cry or if you scream. Whatever feeling is there, whatever happens happens." And that's kind of the way it was through the whole thing. That was early in the shooting, and I realized then that he wanted me to behave, I think, wanted me to behave in each situation, given the guidelines of the character, more or less as I would behave.

JOHN CASSAVETES: We started working on *Husbands* as a natural extension of people wanting to continue their lives in work; use what you think you've learned and try to find the subject and deepen it. . . . Falk, Gazzara and myself started with ourselves and a kind of a simple idea of a guy dying; what would it mean to us if one of our close friends died?

We in the film were always putting ourselves up, discovering things about us that we wouldn't ordinarily know.

Actors are your arms. . . . I'm going to tell you how to behave, how you should sit? It is better if the actor has an overall understanding of what he's doing or what you are trying to do. You can talk to him as you talk to a writer about a character. . . . As director, I went under the assumption that sooner or later Peter [Falk] would know what he was doing and sooner or later Ben [Gazzara] would know what he was doing, and we'd wait it out until we did know what we were doing. . . . I was shocked by Peter's choices. I mean, it really surprised me that he would go off in a certain direction.

PETER FALK: I dislike very, very much when I walk onto a set and I know the director has an idea ahead of time where he wants that camera to go and where he wants the scene to go. As soon as you sense that, then everybody's dead. As a director, you can't come to conclusions too soon. You can't work it out ahead of time. You've got to see first; you've got to see what's going to

Lynn Carlin in a scene with Buck Henry in *Taking Off*, directed by Miloš Forman. "He wanted me to behave . . . in each situation, given the guidelines of the character, more or less as I would behave."

Peter Falk, Ben Gazzara, and John Cassavetes in *Husbands,* directed by John Cassavetes. Falk: "It's very hard to just start a scene and see what will happen, what will come out of it . . ."

happen. . . . Yet we all have instincts about beginnings, middles and ends. We know what a climax is and what a dramatic moment is. It's very hard to get rid of that thinking. It's very hard to . . . rely on and trust something that is smaller, subtler, but more genuine. It's very hard to just start a scene and see what will happen, what will come out of it . . . without imposing on it some idea that you have. That is hard to do, and [in *Husbands*] I didn't do it. I did it sometimes. I think as the film went on I did it more, but in the beginning I was hanging on to an old way. . . . I was just confused . . . angry and confused because I was working without a part. There was no character. There was me. . . . I wasn't willing to settle on anything, to settle on whatever happened, whatever I was feeling at the moment.

I would like to do a film like *Husbands* again. I would be curious to know whether or not, if I did it again, I could be better. . . . I don't think I gave enough, because I couldn't zero in on exactly what was going on and how to do it. Maybe the next time I wouldn't, either, but I think I would have a better chance.

Improvisation has become so closely identified with participatory film acting that many actors measure their contentment with an assignment — their participation in a film — by the amount of improvisation a director allows them. And many critics and commentators now hunt for "improvised" scenes with the same fervor they once applied to tracking down "symbols" or directorial touches. John Cassavetes, who has *probably* used improvisation as extensively as any narrative filmmaker, rankles at the freehanded use of the word ("Nobody knows what improvisation is. I don't know what's improvised. Tell me!"), but points to one of the pitfalls of improvisational methods:

We could improvise the rehearsal and come out great. Then all of a sudden there would be cameras, cables, guys around, people saying, "We can't move this thing over there," and the actors would be of very little importance. And you start to preserve what you have and you start pushing, and all of a sudden, it's gone. What had been terribly concentrated in rehearsals would dissipate.

As Cassavetes's remarks suggest, improvisation in rehearsal, particularly rehearsal away from the sound stage, can result in a "script" that is to some degree written by the actor. Keeping this script fresh (or adding freshness to a writer- or director-written one, for that matter) can be accomplished by using it as the basis for additional improvisation on the set. If the improvised rehearsals for *Loving* were intended to get at "the fullness of the people," the improvisations on the set of the film, Irvin Kershner says, "were to find the fullness and truth of the moment."

Eric Rohmer employed what could be called a variation on improvisation in the preparation of his script for *Chloe in the Afternoon*. The dialogue that Zouzou was to speak was written after a series of tape-recorded conversations with the actress. Though Zouzou was disappointed that none of her ideas on child-raising and the institution of the family became part of the character of Chloe, Rohmer says his conversations with her were valuable because they resulted in lines she could read well. A somewhat similar approach is used by Ingmar Bergman who, according to Liv Ullmann, "knows which actor is going to play which part when he writes the script. There might be parts of you which he puts into the character that he wants you to play."

In a way, the methods of "personal" filmmakers Rohmer and Bergman, whose characters are developed with an eye to the comfort and capabilities of the actors who will perform them, seem perplexingly similar to those employed by the fabricators of big-studio American star vehicles. But while the star vehicles serve the actor-as-icon, the films of Rohmer and Bergman (and Kershner and Cassavetes, among others), by fostering a closer and deeper correspondence between performer and role, serve the actor-as-person, as vessel of truth.

*

JEAN-LOUIS TRINTIGNANT: Actors now plunge into life, shoot in the street without any makeup at all — this last point is very im-

Jean-Louis Trintignant, apparently wearing little or no makeup, with Anouk Aimée in *A Man and a Woman,* directed by Claude Lelouch. "Previously we were heavily made up. To be adorned like this was very irritating, it distorts everything."

portant. Previously we were heavily made up. To be adorned like this was very irritating, it distorts everything. It is not the fact that you have makeup on your face. The truth is that it entails a whole behavior which is projected through it.

LIV ULLMANN: . . . You want people to recognize what you are doing, if not in themselves, in somebody on the street. . . . The cinema is also life.

# FOUR

## The Director of Photography

In America the director of photography — the man most instrumental in transferring onto film and making accessible to other eyes the director's mind's-eye vision of what a movie will look like — is also called the cinematographer, the cameraman, and, in reference to silent movies, the first cameraman. His British counterpart is known as the lighting cameraman, which is perhaps the most precisely descriptive of all these labels. The director of photography's primary function is to light the scene; someone else — the camera operator — actually "films" it.

The director of photography is a painter of motion pictures who uses light in much the same way that the painter of still pictures does and can be said to employ lenses to accomplish what the still painter achieves with brush strokes. His use of various combinations of light and lenses in photographing a given scene can result in pictures as different in texture and emotional weight as the renderings of the same subject matter by, say, a Flemish master and an Impressionist master.

The Flemish or Impressionist master decides not only the over-all "look" of his painting (and then chooses his light and brushes accordingly), but determines also its composition (what is to be included in it) and its perspective or vantage point (the relative distance between the work of art as a whole and the individual figures or objects in it and the spectator). The director of photography, a member of a team captained by the director, may or may not be involved in arriving at the photographic concept of a film. He may or may not be involved in composing individual scenes. And he may or may not be involved in determining the point of view from which these individual scenes will be shot. What he contributes in the way of ideas or suggestions about look, composition and point of view, and the extent to which his contributions are used by a director, vary according to his relationship with the director and, probably, according to the director's and the cinematographer's individual and shared closeness to the material they are working on. The one constant in all filmmaking situations is the amount of sheer work, in terms of man hours of concentrated activity, that the director of photography does. Required first off to decide how to carry out his own or a director's conception of the lighting of a scene, he then supervises the placement of the lights and remains a vigilant observer of their functioning during the rehearsal and shooting stages. He is, by some accounts, the busiest man on a film set.

In silent movie days, according to veteran cameraman Joseph Ruttenberg, "the cameraman was God." A combination of factors having to do with both the nature of the silent film and the conditions under which many silent films were made suggests that Ruttenberg's statement is not nostalgically hyperbolic. The film medium in those days was essentially a visual one; the cinematographer's pictures were the prime storytelling device. The duties of the cameraman were also more extensive than they were to be later. He operated his own camera for the most part, and was also responsible for the execution of the optical effects — fades, dissolves, double and triple exposures, etc. — in the camera at the time of shooting. The comparative primitiveness of the technology at his disposal made constant demands upon his ingenuity and inventiveness. And already there was the star system. Performers, especially, but by no means exclusively, women performers, took their favorite cameramen with them from picture to picture, sometimes investing them with the status of royal consorts. So, the authority and influence of the first cameraman were great. (The second cameraman placed his camera as close to the first cameraman's as possible in an attempt to get a "duplicate" negative that would be sent to the European market.) And the achievements of a host of gifted first cameramen, particularly after the development of panchromatic film in 1924, matched their authority and influence.

The advent of sound signaled a temporary and endemic decrease in the cinematographer's power and a "decline" in the quality of his work. The mobility of the camera was substantially reduced by the necessity of accommodating the microphone, and even the use of multiple cameras did not prevent the majority of early sound films from looking like photographed stage plays. By the mid-30s, with the improvement of sound-recording techniques (and, no doubt, a rapprochement between the sometimes truculent sound engineers and the bedeviled cameramen), cinematography had largely rallied as an art. Though the tremendous power amassed by the studios and studio-affiliated stars by the 1930s involved many cameramen in glorified beautification projects — the rotogravure studies of MGM stars and *Town & Country* treatments of MGM sets are the obvious but by no means only examples — as many imaginatively, organically photographed films probably came out of that decade as the 20s.

The introduction of various color and wide-screen processes demanded additional adjustments be made, but the general feeling is that neither type of innovation occasioned a setback as pervasive as that resulting from the coming of sound. Though the first all-color film was made in 1935, black-and-white was used for all but musicals, Westerns and other types of spectacles until the mid-50s, and only one studio — Twentieth Century-Fox, which patented CinemaScope in 1953 — began using wide screen for all of its releases almost immediately after the process was available. (In the early days of color — and at some studios, until the 1950s — Technicolor Laboratories provided special color consultants to advise as to the photographability of the individual and combined colors of the sets, costumes, etc., and to assist the cameraman in lighting them. While the consultants, in all likelihood, provided a necessary service, many cameramen looked upon them as intruders. "The Technicolor people . . . had a technician with you, so it wasn't altogether my picture," Ruttenberg says.)

Gradual refinements in color and wide-screen processes, increasing sophistication in their use, the comparatively recent introduction of faster film and lighter, more mobile camera equipment — all have helped extend the range of the cameraman's possibilities and contributed to the dawning, in the mid-60s, of what many commentators have called a new "great age of cinematography."

Yet, to suggest that the history of American cinematography since, say, the mid-30s is a relatively continuous one and infer from this that the "renaissance" which began in the mid-60s is a natural outgrowth of the achievements of the preceding years would not be fully correct. Restrictive and strictly enforced union regulations laid down in the 1930s prohibited all but a handful of cameramen from beginning careers in feature films in the 40s and 50s. (The regulations, designed to protect the cameramen who entered the field, quite often in the most casual manner, in the late silent or early sound days and continued to work for four or five decades, were relaxed in the 60s only after death or old age greatly reduced the number of functioning union members. A cameraman who has been denied entrance into the union and thus the opportunity to work, or gained it only after a long, embittering struggle, is apt to blame the regulations on union members, especially the older ones. The older union membership is apt to blame the regulations on the Producers Association which, it is claimed, substantially dictated their form. Everyone now agrees that the regulations should be revised, but there are differences of opinion as to how much and how fast.) As a result, there is today a missing generation gap of Hollywood cameramen. There are older cameramen (from age 60, roughly, on up) and young cameramen (age 45, roughly, on down). It is the young cameramen who are credited with the cinematographic renaissance — some say, "revolution" — of the 60s. Their combination of new technology with a rediscovery of techniques that have lain in disuse since silent screen days, and an increase in location filming, have lent film photography a new freshness and spontaneity. But the "inspiration" apparent in their work is too often self-conscious and lacks the steadying influence of the careful, unobtrusive craftsmanship that distinguishes the work of the older generation of cameramen. An open dialogue between the older and younger generations of cameramen could set things in balance and help make future developments in cinematography evolutionary ones.

"You can follow my style like a thread through many directors' films," Lee Garmes says in Charles Higham's *Hollywood Cameramen*. Though a great number — perhaps the majority — of cinematographers will deny that they have a discernible style, and maintain instead that their style is always determined by the requirements of the story and the director, logic and, often, empirical evidence refute this modest stance.

JAMES WONG HOWE: There are no two photographers who photograph the same, as there are no two artists who paint the same, and it doesn't matter, really, how you do it as long as you accomplish what you want to do and you do it well.

GORDON WILLIS: Yes, I do have a style. If you took all the movies I've shot and ran them side by side, at first they'd tend to look different, but if you looked at them carefully you'd see the attack on the movies, mechanically speaking, or even from the standpoint of "look" — a lot of it's the same. The mechanical philosophy — I mean, how I achieve something — is the same. It's like putting suits of two different colors together using the same sewing machine; the stitching would be the same. [My style] generally has to do with equipment or the use of equipment in executing things. . . . At an interpretive level [the notion of an individual photographic style] is very thin.

If [another cameraman] does a movie with a director and I do a movie with a director, you're going to get two different things. And it's not only "photographic style." It just boils down to two people working together. You end up with something different; the influence on each other — it's something different.

LASZLO KOVACS (With reference to Robert Altman's *M\*A\*S\*H*, which he was set to photograph until an ultimatum from the union — of which Kovacs was not then a member — forced his removal from the project): Not to take anything away from the cameraman who eventually shot the film, but if I had done *M\*A\*S\*H* with Robert Altman it would have been quite different, especially the look of the interiors. Not in terms of lighting, but in terms of composition. They would . . . suggest more insanity. We had designed — the director, the art director, and I — the scenes on different planes; the foreground, the background, and so forth. [Altman] wanted to be freer with the camera [than he ended up being]. Because of various difficulties during production, he lost patience with the camera and went with the relatively more conventional photographic approach the cinematographer was more comfortable with.

The photography — and everything else — should serve the story and the director's concept of it in an organic way. Still, I can see, maybe, a certain "look" in all my work, and this could be why I'm not called by certain directors. The experience of seeing this country that lies between the two coasts, different life styles, a different reality during the filming of *Easy Rider* changed my outlook a lot, especially my feelings about nature, and has influenced my compositions, I think. I like to use nature — the landscape — with compassion. I try to incorporate nature into a dramatic context whenever I can. If it's well placed and well balanced in a film it can be very effective. [In *Slither,* a film which treats the landscape — even its trash-blighted portions — with admirable understatement and generosity,] I tried to juxtapose the landscape and various facets of American life, used in a very realistic way, with Jimmy Caan being lost and confused.

The light which the director of photography uses to paint his motion pictures is focused on sets and locations whose design or selection is largely the responsibility of the art director (also called the production designer), and on the inhabitants of these environments — the actors.

JAMES WONG HOWE: In the set designing and the camera setups *Kings Row* was preplanned down to the last detail. [Art director] William Cameron Menzies would make sketches of the entire picture and he would, on the sketch, mark what lens you use. He'd say, "A forty at that point; a forty fits perfectly." It was wonderful. You just take the drawings. He sketched all the highlights in, and you'd say, "That's it." How many art directors do that? But how many directors would let an art director lay out the shots for him?

HAL MOHR: Whenever Warners would get in trouble they'd call on old Hal to come and dig them out. I dug them out on *A Midsummer Night's Dream*. There was a man photographing the picture who had a very good reputation as a cameraman. [But] he didn't have enough strength to say what he would do and what he wouldn't do. And he was being pushed around by the art director and the others, [being] made to do what he knew he couldn't do. . . . I went out and looked at some of the rushes. The thing that was wrong was that they had taken two stages, two of the biggest stages [at Warners], and had built a forest. They literally built a forest to the point where there was no sky. Where there is no sky there is no place to get lights in. So the poor guy couldn't get any light on the set. I finally agreed to take the picture over, but I said I would do it under one condition. I said, "I'll take it over but I don't want anybody to tell me a damn thing. I'm going to do it exactly the way I want to do it. And the art director has nothing to say about his sets if I want to change them; not arbitrarily, but to meet my requirements."

I accepted the assignment on a Friday afternoon. I planned in my own mind what the hell I wanted to do. . . . We cut the tops off all the trees and thinned out branches. I had them light all the lights down one side of the stage. Then, with these lights burning, I called the paint crew in. I said, "Take aluminum paint and wherever you see light hitting put aluminum paint on that from the side the light is coming from. And then, on the other side of the set, where no light is hitting, spray everything with orange shellac. The trees, the ground, everything, with the orange shellac." So I painted in a source of light onto the set.

A scene from *A Midsummer Night's Dream*, directed by Max Reinhardt and William Dieterle. Hal Mohr: "They literally built a forest to the point where there was no sky. . . . We cut the tops off all the trees and thinned out branches."

I had a gang of special effects men come in with cobweb machines . . . and spray everything on the set. Every tree, every blade of grass; everything was just covered with cobwebs. I went down to a casket company and got a few hundred pounds of this stuff — caskets used to have these little golden flickers on them, golden reflections of light, like little particles of glass — and they sprayed it on. The whole set became like a huge gossamer veil covered with millions of fireflies. Then I had wooden frames made to put in front of the camera with invisible piano wires strung across about two or three inches apart. I sprayed cobwebs on that thing and flickers on that thing. . . .

And the topper of this thing is that when everybody walked onto the set the next Monday morning to start shooting they all wanted to blow their brains out. Because I had completely destroyed the set. But, you know, strangely enough the old guy, [the director Max] Reinhardt, [just] said: [lip noise]. That's all he said.

GORDON WILLIS: I talked with Dean [Tavoularis, production designer on *The Godfather*] both before and during production about lighting [though not about construction], or we'd discuss color. I knew what he was doing and he knew what I was doing. There were no opposing forces in that area, [and the result] holds together. Actually, his work is so good, and always looked so nice, that it was never necessary to discuss things at great length.

LASZLO KOVACS: [Production designer] Polly Platt played a very important role [in the making of Peter Bogdanovich's *Paper Moon*]. Her selections of particular locations and interiors and the way she handled them — dressed and prepared them for the camera — it was really a heavy contribution. Polly actually had many choices for each particular scene; she didn't put the director in a situation where she would say, "This is what you've got, this is where you have to shoot it." That could limit a sequence as to how you could cover it or photograph it or block it.

I took a trip with Peter and Polly — after looking at photographs [she took on an earlier location-scouting trip] — and we were able to make specific selections. The three of us discussed each of our problems. Many times Peter would say, "You make the choice, because I don't want to limit the kind of coverage I had in mind. So you tell me if it's possible to do this kind of coverage. What do you think?"

Stories about actors' ego, so amusing to recount, are probably pretty hellish to play a part in. At a remove of decades, James Wong Howe, laughing, recalls that, early in the filming of *The Prisoner of Zenda,* leads Ronald Colman and Madeleine Carroll both told him that they preferred to be photographed from the same best (left) side. Joseph Ruttenberg says, levelly, that he won favor with that consummate professional Katharine Hepburn after he devised a flattering method of photographing her neck in a test for *The Philadelphia Story.* Howe also relates that he was employed as Mary Miles Minter's cameraman on a series of films in the 20s because, during their first picture together, he accidentally hit upon a way of lighting the star so that her pale-blue eyes weren't washed out. But perhaps it is William Daniels's long association with Greta Garbo and Ruttenberg's with Greer Garson that best substantiate Hal Mohr's remark: "If you photographed a star like nobody else could do it, you were there as long as she was." Though present-day film actors are said to be generally less self-involved than those of the past, the fact is they *are* concerned with how they look.

GORDON WILLIS: I don't pay any attention to actors' ego — no, that's an oversimplification. The picture always comes first in my mind, which doesn't mean I don't deal with what's best for them. I won't put the picture under because somebody feels they look better this way than they look that way. But I'll do everything I can to make sure an actor is comfortable — without stepping over that line where you say, "There's a close-up of a terrific-looking actor." I'm not going to turn out an eight-by-ten glossy in the middle of two unrelated things in a movie. What's good about Barbra [Streisand, whom Willis photographed in *Up the Sandbox*] is that she'll work with you. Barbra's honest, she'll say, "I don't look well this way, I have a problem with this or a problem with that." She won't lay it all on you. She'll bend a lot to make it work. Brando had [artistic, nonegoistic] opinions at the beginning of *The Godfather*, which I did a lot of nodding about, but the truth of the matter is that his opinions were quite correct!

Though the separation of function between the director of photography, who lights the scene, and the camera operator, who executes the shot, is a heatedly debated subject, it is, due to present-day union conditions, a given in most filmmaking situations. To insure as close a correspondence as possible between the cinematographer's (or, as is more likely, the director's *and* cinematographer's) concept of a shot and its execution, a good working relationship with the camera operator is obviously necessary.

CONRAD HALL: The cameraman should have the prerogative to operate if he wants to. . . . Let all the first cameramen be operators and let all the operators be first cameramen, and let them work interchangeably whenever they want. I love operating. You get to see the movie before anyone else does. It gives me the greatest emotional satisfaction of anything I do, except seeing a terrific shot in the dailies. . . . [Yet] there are a lot of times when I don't want to operate, when I'm too busy thinking of other things to want to operate.

HASKELL WEXLER: I operate when I feel like it, which is often.

GORDON WILLIS: Good operators . . . take a lot off your shoulders. Same thing with good first assistant cameramen. [Operating] is very tiring, and I don't have physical and emotional time to deal with it. I'm too busy at a mechanical level in lighting and at an interpretive level with the director. And if you use energy [in operating], you don't have as much to deal with at the other levels. I can stand behind a camera and I know exactly what's been done. If he's made a mistake, I'll see he's made a mistake.
    I only operated once. It was on *End of the Road*, and it was purely an interpretive thing. It was the material; it had to do with the horseback riding and a lot of thousand-millimeter work and it was just hard for me to say, "Do this, do that." There was

nothing I could say to my operator that would make him execute this shot, because I didn't know myself how to execute the shot. I had an idea about the scene, so I did the execution myself. And then he was brooding for a day or two, and I said, "Well, when you do your first movie [as director of photography] you'll want to operate." And he did. On his first film he did all his operating.

JOSEPH RUTTENBERG: At MGM, I always rode the camera with the director on the camera movements, and the operator would watch these movements, but the operator actually did the taking of the picture. . . . On many pictures I'd ask the operator if I could sit with him [during the execution of a shot].

LASZLO KOVACS: The camera is your tool, and it's difficult to do it through another person, however talented. It's not *you*. . . . [*Getting Straight*] was very carefully designed for the rack focus. It was a very exciting idea that started somewhere else, a little earlier in my career working with Dick Rush, when we had been associated on more limited productions. Maybe we were too enthusiastic; in a way, I suppose it was like discovering the zoom lens for the first time. But anyway, it was my first IA [short for IATSE, International Alliance of Stage and Theatrical Employees] picture, and I tried to get permission from the union to operate the camera myself where we were going to be racking. It was a long battle, a senseless battle, and needless to say, we lost it. It's not fair to blame the operator, but my execution of it would have been very different; not calling as much attention to itself. I still think it's an interesting and justifiable technique, dramatically, if used properly.

GORDON WILLIS: That's a hard relationship to build.

HASKELL WEXLER: My assistant on many films, little ones we did in Chicago and others better known, like *America, America*, *The Loved One*, and *The Hoodlum Priest*, became my operator on *In the Heat of the Night* and *The Thomas Crown Affair*. He began on *Medium Cool* but didn't finish. He was and is my very good friend and an excellent operator. He is more conservative

A demonstration of rack focus technique in *Getting Straight,* directed by Richard Rush and photographed by Laszlo Kovacs. The plane of vision which Elliott Gould occupies is not as sharply focused as that which Candice Bergen inhabits.

politically [than I], and we had to undergo pressures in Chicago in 1968 not usual to the protected, privileged position a film company enjoys on location. He didn't like certain things. I respect him for it, but we couldn't work together at that time, so he went home.

LASZLO KOVACS: I have a great rapport with my operator and I've used him on every film since *Alex in Wonderland*, with the exceptions of *The Last Movie* and *Freebie and the Bean*. We [are] similar [in] the way we see things. My whole camera crew — key grip, gaffer, et cetera — is the same whenever possible, kind of my own repertory company. Yet, if I feel it needs me, I just do it [operate].

The cameraman's relationships with his contemporaries in the field can occasionally be as influential as those with members of the creative team he is working with on a specific project.

JOSEPH RUTTENBERG: I would never go out and see other pictures when I was working . . . because I might have an urge when I saw an interesting lighting effect or something to imitate it. . . . When you're working on a set all day long, you get into a sort of groove. It's difficult to judge lighting. My trick was, when I found myself in that position, I walked off the stage, took a walk or got a cup of coffee and came back. I used to walk on to George Folsey's set and comment . . . and he would come on my set and look around and make a suggestion. It wouldn't make either of us mad if we didn't adopt an idea. Many cameramen don't like other cameramen to come on their set.

Today, the younger generation of cinematographers are particularly enthusiastic supporters of the idea of a continuing dialogue among professional colleagues.

GORDON WILLIS: [The older generation of cameramen] were never willing to teach. They were dying with their secrets. It's really only in the last five years or so that there's been any air in this town. I'll tell anybody anything. If they can learn something from it . . . fine. . . . I admire Gregg Toland as a thinking cameraman, an interpretive cameraman, but I have no desire to imitate his style or his techniques. I would love to work in black-and-white and use deep focus if it served the story, but not arbitrarily. When you [indulge] in photographic or directorial imitation, you get a Woolworth's reproduction of somebody's idea. It's self-conscious and unhealthy. Imitation can be a kind of refining process — early in my career I punched out a lot of [imitative] crap — but then *you* have to come to the surface.

LASZLO KOVACS (Whose black-and-white, deep-focus photography on *Paper Moon* is among his best work): Tradition should be respected and studied — and used, made richer. There is this silly tradition that cameramen shouldn't trade their "secrets." There should be more contact among cameramen, some kind of forum where we can get together informally and discuss our work. The A.S.C. [American Society of Cinematographers] used to be something like this, but I think we need . . . something new.

The cameraman's relationship with the director is the key factor in his work. It is the prime determinant of what and how the cameraman will contribute to a film.

JOSEPH RUTTENBERG: When I was first introduced to a director I'd always say, "I have a habit of making suggestions as I see them. Now you don't have to use them, but I warn you ahead of time. It's sort of a habit."

CONRAD HALL: Everybody should bring ideas. The director is the one who orchestrates the ideas. He uses them — his own, everybody's.

LASZLO KOVACS: The director surrounds himself with the best collaborators he can get to help him realize his end. . . . There is the director's concept, and that must be supported by everyone. But to it we may add our own [concept]. The reason a director hires me is because he expects my opinion, perhaps *demands* it; he doesn't want a yes-man. Visuals are so difficult to verbalize; in making those two visions [i.e. the cameraman's and the director's] into one, you have to get inside the director's head, you must really get to know him so that you are sure you mean the same thing. For *Alex in Wonderland,* a film that is very dear to me, I spent five or six days — days and nights — a week in discussion with Paul Mazursky [for a six-to-seven-week period prior to production]. He wanted to bring me close to it. He conveyed his ideas to me for visual translation, and we story-boarded for a certain coverage. [The "storyboard" is of the type mentioned by Gene Allen in Chapter 5 rather than the kind mentioned earlier by Leigh Brackett. — D. C.]

GORDON WILLIS: There's always a rendezvous period . . . where people get to know each other. Generally speaking, you might be thinking of the same thing, but by the time you realize you're both talking about the same thing — it may take eight weeks of working together.

HASKELL WEXLER: Talking with a director about the "look" of a film should be preceded by frames of reference. There are too many bullshit words about photography, and definitions gen-erally discount the subjective. If the cameraman and director can see films, photographs and paintings together, then there can be an immediate shorthand reference recall.

A director's familiarity with the technological aspects of movie-making influences the way he communicates with his cameraman. Communication is obviously facilitated when the director is knowledgeable about the camera, but there is always the con-tingent danger that a technically oriented director will diminish his cameraman's sense of participation to a demoralizing degree by oversupervising his work. A director who is not particularly well versed in terms of the camera is of necessity dependent on his cameraman and thus increases his cameraman's authority, but the director's difficulties in communicating with him in specific terms may result in an altered translation of his vision.

GORDON WILLIS: I like making movies [with débuting directors]. I just have a stronger grip on the technology than the first-

time-around director. It's an advantage for them. It does and it
doesn't [increase my responsibility]. Knowing how to cut put
[former editors Aram Avakian and Hal Ashby, whose first
films, *End of the Road* and *The Landlord*, respectively, were
shot by Willis] about ten times ahead.

   Alan [Pakula] hasn't been directing very long . . . and he has
problems at a mechanical level, which he's the first to admit. He's
very happy to say, "Look, I want to achieve this and I want this
to happen." And then he'll go away for twenty minutes and try
to deal with script problems and all of the actors. He'll come
back and he'll look at it, and he'll say, "Fine . . ." And if he's
unsure about something, then you'll talk that out so that he
feels better about it or he realizes it's right or wrong. You
relieve him of that. That's not unusual, there's nothing wrong
with that.

JOSEPH RUTTENBERG: Cukor is a great director. Spends a lot of time
rehearsing. On *Gaslight*, when he was ready for a take, he would
give me a rehearsal, then discuss the setups, and left the technical details to me. . . . Vince Minnelli was a great guy for setting all his action with the camera. Oh, yes, Minnelli in particular [when asked for advice]. He would say, "I would like this
kind of a shot," and I'd say, "Well, you'd have to use a certain
lens." He wouldn't know the lenses, you know. . . . George
Stevens was a technician. He had been a cameraman. He was
very particular and he used to spend loads of time on finding
setups. I remember we had a scene in *Woman of the Year* where
Spencer Tracy and Katharine Hepburn were coming out of the
marriage license bureau. Stevens spent the whole morning, with
nobody around, trying to pick out a setup. He was very helpful
to me, to any cameraman, I think.

HAL MOHR: Now, Sammy [Fuller, for whom Mohr shot *Underworld U.S.A.*], there's a case where the director had a hell of a
lot to do with the camera. Sammy was a man who wanted to
rehearse a scene looking through the camera. I'd line it up with
the operator and we'd get it all set, and then Sammy would
watch the rehearsal through it. If he wanted to change anything he would talk to me about it and we'd make the change.

But he was one of the most invasive directors — that's *in-vasive* — directors I have ever worked with because he had his eye . . . ninety percent of the time.

In the next several pages, seven cinematographers comment more specifically on their work with directors during the prepara-tory and shooting stages of filmmaking.

LASZLO KOVACS: *Paper Moon* is a good example of one way of arriving at the visual concept of a film. Peter [Bogdanovich] said, "It's going to be black-and-white" — which is a major decision. Once he decided it was going to be a black-and-white film, which was *his* decision, we really started to talk about it; what specific look and what specific feeling we should go for.

JOSEPH RUTTENBERG: *Gaslight* would have been a color picture if I hadn't suggested that I thought we could do much better with black-and-white dramatically.

LASZLO KOVACS: After reading the script of *Five Easy Pieces,* I thought, It feels like Chekhov. I never consciously thought of this while shooting the film, but it influenced my approach throughout. As an "inspiration," it helped me a lot. Within Bob Rafelson's concept, I always added that, I think.

HASKELL WEXLER: [The preparation of *America, America* con-sisted mainly of] talking to [Elia] Kazan. We looked at a lot of old photographs, looked at thousands of old photographs of the period, a lot of pictures of his family. We went to Greece and Turkey and looked for the locations. I shot some tests of the kid, Stathis Giallelis.

WINTON HOCH: [John Ford] wants you to make sure that you pre-serve what he's trying to do. He told me on *She Wore a Yellow Ribbon,* "I want the feeling of the Remington pictures." That means that you reach for those Remington colors. And he helped, we all helped in the costume selection and set [design to achieve this].

Patricia Neal and Paul Newman in *Hud*, directed by Martin Ritt. James Wong Howe: "I said, 'I'd make it as desolate as you could, and keep that [illusion of] space that shows you his next neighbor is about ten miles away.'"

JAMES WONG HOWE: [During the preparation of *Hud,* Martin Ritt] said, "Down in Texas, I don't know whether you'll be very happy. It's just blank skies and strips of land and nothing much to photograph. By the way, do you think we could double-print clouds in the sky?" I said, "Sure." So, for a whole week we looked at clouds, stock stuff. I said, "What kind of clouds? What kind do you want, Marty?" He said, "I can't tell until I look at them." When he got tired of looking at clouds, he said, "Let's go down and look at the location." I knew the script. So I said, "Look, Marty, you're crazy to try and put clouds in." He said, "Why?" I said, "I would shoot it with nothing but blank sky, and if there were clouds in there I would use, maybe, a light blue filter and make the blue go white so the clouds wouldn't show. Wash it out. Because it's a black-and-white film." He said, "Why would you?" I said, "I'd make it as desolate as you could, and keep that [illusion of] space that shows you his next neighbor is about ten miles away. That shows you how much land he's got to graze his cattle, but this hot, dusty sky — that's why Paul Newman wants to get the devil out of there. Sell out. He wants money. Turn it into oil or something." When we got down there we had some beautiful shots with clouds, but I used a filter to wash them out.

GORDON WILLIS: Before [*The Godfather*] started shooting, Francis Ford Coppola and I discussed what the film was going to look like. We agreed never to use zoom lenses, for instance; we agreed that it was a tableau form of moviemaking, that the film should be held in a framework, so to speak, and that contemporary mechanical items were not to be used. And that's basically how the film was executed. I would say that Francis forgot [our discussions] twenty minutes after we started the movie, and so, I spent five or six months executing it [as discussed] and reminding him that that's the way we had talked about it. He would veer between one thing and another; he'd want to do something *cinéma vérité* one day and want to use a thousand-millimeter lens the next day. It was a juxtaposition of ideas that were not related to what you were doing at the moment. As far as the photographic quality and the color structure of the movie, we rarely talked about that at all. I just did that.

We decided that's the way it was going to be, and that's the way it was.

[Irvin Kershner] loves to make movies, and he's trying to get ideas about everything into one particular piece — which is wrong. It's like, This is my one chance to do everything I ever wanted to do. It doesn't work; you can only do one painting at a time. So, if directors tend to work at five different levels at once [and] you generally work together to reinforce the one idea, they'll generally get back to [the] idea they had at the beginning of the movie and which they had forgotten about because they're into some other idea. Nobody can think of everything — I know I can't — so it's better to work . . . I'm not a believer in the singular filmmaker. I believe two or three people working together make the best movies. The ideas are stronger, they're reinforced. That doesn't mean that the director doesn't have the idea to begin with, but in sifting it, in executing it, that's where you end up making it better. You make a singular vision out of ten other visions. I did this with Kershner on [*Loving* and] . . . *Up the Sandbox*.

Much of the location scouting for *Bad Company* had been done before Willis became involved with the film, but his recommendations, based on narrative and thematic considerations, resulted in the use of certain "specific areas."

GORDON WILLIS: There were only about five minutes of it that took place on the prairies, and the rest of it in gulleys, on hills and near streams. I convinced them to shoot more on the prairies. The prairies are essentially very boring; some of the critics said they were "endless, boring." Well, yes, they are, that's one of the story points in the movie!

In the spring of 1973, Willis was observed at work photographing a scene in *The Parallax View* for director Alan J. Pakula. Seven judicial-looking men in late middle age sit at a podium whose proportions are roughly those of the Panavision screen. (One is reminded of the opening dinner-table scene and the modeling-job-interview scene in *Klute,* an earlier collaboration between Pakula, Willis and art director George Jenkins.) The podium is bounded at the bottom by a jet-black floor and on the sides and at the top by a jet-black cyclorama. The scene's abstraction from identifiable, everyday reality is heightened when the centrally placed man on the panel begins an emotionless, measured-tone recitation of the findings of an investigation into the assassination of a political figure. Willis's use of a wide-angle lens will further increase the viewer's sense of physical and psychic dislocation by "distorting the image so as to make it slightly bowed."

GORDON WILLIS: This is all something I worked out with Alan. He had some ideas, I had some ideas — these things usually go in three stages. Alan had an idea about a kind of semilimbo kind of thing. I took it one step further and said, "Let's make it totally limbo, no people at all except those on the podium, one panel at the beginning of the movie and another one at the end. Nothing really changes except the people." . . . You try to purify the idea — or to keep the idea pure, which takes a lot of discipline because you'll say, Well, maybe we should shift the people, or have no people. You can protect yourself out of existence.

LASZLO KOVACS (Speaking of the cinematographer's role in selecting camera setups): Always wait for the director to express his idea first — if he has any. "Look, this is the way I envision this scene, this is what's going to happen." You absorb his idea, and your mind is moving along or jumping ahead evaluating things and thinking about how it works for the story. Sometimes you have an idea yourself, and you arrive at a unified approach. . . . Sometimes while working on a setup — doing the lighting — something feels very false, something bothers you. I call his attention to it, see how he feels about it. I might not have an idea, I just feel that it's wrong. In many cases, he'll say, "You're right, that's a good point. Let's work it out." We go back and reconstruct the whole scene to see how it fits, and many times it happens that he changes it. . . . In many instances, you feel the scene isn't right, and he'll say, "No, that's perfectly all right, just don't worry about it. I think it's going to work."

WINTON HOCH (With reference to working with John Ford): Very often he'll tell me what the setup is — what he wants — and sometimes he doesn't. Sometimes, when [Ford has finished rehearsing with the actors], he comes back and says, "How does it look through the camera?" In other words, he keeps you on your toes all the time.

JOSEPH RUTTENBERG (With reference to *The Swan,* on which he was eventually replaced by Robert Surtees due to quarrels with the director, Charles Vidor): There was a shot where Grace Kelly comes in in a carriage. She drives around the estate, and then you see her through an arch. I said, "Why don't we go above the building on a boom and show [the carriage] driving through; and as it comes, go down and show it all in one piece." Well, Vidor couldn't see it. He decided to do it two ways. "No, do it *one* way because it'll take a lot of time. If you want it your way I'll do it. I'm just suggesting that we try it from the top." So I got him up on the boom. He said, "That's very nice, but I'd like to do it both ways." Well, we argued and argued, and finally he said, "All right, all right. If you want to do it go ahead and do it that way." It was a beautiful shot. It sold the whole scene.

JOHN SEITZ: I realized how particular [Rex] Ingram was about his films. So I would set things up before — give him two choices. I'd make the setups and then he'd say yes or no. But I found out that's what the other cameramen didn't do. [Seitz, who shot twelve films for Ingram, says he was the only cameraman who worked for the director twice. — D.C.] They didn't have the initiative, and he liked initiative.

GORDON WILLIS: If I said I'm responsible for one hundred percent of the setups in a movie I'd be right, but at the same time . . . the position [of the camera is] based on a discussion with the director who wants to achieve this or that. After he tells me what it is he wants to achieve, if he's smart he'll go over and work with his actors and twenty minutes later he'll come back and I'll show it to him. He'll say, "Yeah, I like that, fine," or "Do you think it's too much of this or too much of that?," and

2-49

Gordon Willis: "Because you think it's a nice angle doesn't mean it works well in the movie. . . ." This low-angle shot in *Klute*, directed by Alan J. Pakula, has an aesthetic appeal, a dramatic logic, and is economical as well: Donald Sutherland, Jane Fonda and the Fonda character's pillaged apartment are captured in a single frame.

we'll talk for five minutes and I'll eliminate something he doesn't like or add something he does like. . . . If he says, "Let's be high over there," I'll say, "It's an eye-level movie, who's up there, who's looking down seeing the action from the ceiling? Because you think it's a nice angle doesn't mean it works well in the movie. . . ."

JOSEPH RUTTENBERG: In *The Great Waltz,* the lighting was all mine. The action, the movement and so forth was all designed by the director, Julien Duvivier, and worked out by him in conjunction with me. . . . Duvivier had fantastic ideas which would have to be worked out sometimes just when you got on the set. He could never put his ideas down in writing. . . . All those opera scenes, those were my setups. Those were things that I suggested. . . . I was so excited throughout the whole picture. For example, you remember the rays in the park when they were driving through. I was driving to the studio very early one morning. We were going on location. As I was driving up towards the studio near Culver City — there were a lot of trees — I saw the rays. The sun was just rising and there was a little fog and there were rays. I thought, My God, when I go out to the location I'm going to see what I can do to get the same kind of effect. So, before I left the studio I told the prop man to take as many smoke pots as they had in the studio. When we got out there towards evening, I sent all these prop men to spray the whole woods with smoke pots as the sun was setting, and we got this beautiful scene.

HASKELL WEXLER: If you are bored with a shot, if you don't feel as though you are experimenting in some small way, then don't do the shot, because then you have done it before and it's going to be dull. I don't mean you have to do something outlandish each time just to feel you are functioning. Sometimes, just the addition of an eyelight, barely visible for an instant in the final cut, can give immense personal satisfaction.

When creative people feel strongly about what they are doing, differences can be sharp. I argued with Kazan about many things on *America, America,* a very presumptive posture considering I was just starting in the big time and he had

From *The Great Waltz,* directed by Julien Duvivier. Joseph Ruttenberg: "All those opera scenes, those were my setups. Those were things that I suggested."

proven himself as a great director. We had a pretty hot discussion about the lighting of a scene where he thought the expression on the boy's face when the father slapped him was important and I wanted to keep the two figures in foreground silhouette. How trivial it seems now! Arguments between director and cameraman can be part of a productive, live relationship. As a cameraman you have the protection of the limits of the profession and the advantage of second-guessing. When you direct you are on the line, you are responsible.

When differences, based on questions of taste or principle, become too sharp or occur too frequently they can undermine the cinematographer-director relationship so that it is not only non-collaborative, but untenable.

JOSEPH RUTTENBERG: The director is the captain of the ship, and you do what he likes or try to discuss it with him, and if he doesn't agree with you either you do the picture or you get off the picture. . . . If he wants you to stand on your head you stand on your head — or quit.

JAMES WONG HOWE: I may not be one hundred percent happy, but I don't always have to be happy to photograph a picture. But as a matter of fact, the [second to] last picture I worked on, I didn't finish. I had a disagreement with the director. He had ordered from a nineteen-millimeter lens up to a three thousand millimeter. He wanted to use them all because he was responsible for renting them. We were paying a tremendous rental on one lens alone, and he had to justify the rental. He asked me to use it. I just said, "No." And he said, "Look, you and I just have different ideas. We must come to a separation." I said, "You're correct, because I'm not going to use this lens. I think it's wrong." I told him the reason why I thought so. He disagreed. I packed up and left.

Most of the excited talk about improvisation by actors and directors fails to take into account the important part played by the cinematographer in getting the improvised material on film.

A scene from *America, America*, directed by Elia Kazan. Haskell Wexler: "We had a pretty hot discussion about the lighting . . ."

JOSEPH RUTTENBERG: On *A Day at the Races* we always had to
have three or four cameras set up at the same time because
. . . they never did the same thing twice, the Marx Brothers,
never, no matter how they rehearsed it. . . . When we rehearsed
it we knew we should have a separate camera [following the
movements of] each Marx Brother. The long shot would naturally be [done with still another] steady camera.

CONRAD HALL: The actors are told this is the quality we're after,
and therefore you're not to know any lines beforehand but
you're to talk about this subject, and these points have to be
involved. How you arrive at them we'll find out when we say,
"Roll 'em." [As a cameraman] you try to follow the story.
Knowing what the story is, but not having marks, not having
focus marks or anything like that. All of a sudden you're moving in because you feel something happening that causes you
to want to go in, to see, and then somebody turns to somebody
else and you have the option to pan over to them or not.
Organic, that's a very good word, I think. It just grows out of
what you feel when it's happening, and it's all left to the operator unless the director is right there to sort of tap you.

LASZLO KOVACS: [The improvised empty-house sequence with
Donald Sutherland near the end of *Alex in Wonderland*] demanded that the camera accommodate the actor's movement in
an interior. Paul Mazursky gave us a briefing. Everyone was
told to expect the unexpected. I didn't want to plant lights
because you didn't know exactly where he'd move; everything
was [lit] from the outside, through windows. Originally [for
the beach interlude centering on a discussion of masturbation]
there was dialogue written, and written well. This was thrown
out, and with just a basic concept, an idea for the scene, and
instructions to exercise some self-discipline and restraint and
remain within character, Paul turned the actors loose. [After]
some planning — not even a rehearsal, just judging distance —
I put two cameras on it, and said, "Whatever happens . . ." I
was on one camera, my operator was on the other. Before we
started I said to him, "You're running a camera, I'm running a
camera, let's not talk about it, let's improvise."

The feeling dictates what you do. The scene was shot in one take. . . . [Improvisation] gives a scene a freshness. I enjoy working that way, but the ideal thing would probably be to use both improvisation and conventional methods of staging and framing [in a single film].

GORDON WILLIS: I am a believer in improving all the time, in changing things to make it better. . . . [On *Loving*] there was a lot of improvisation the day before or [on the set prior to actual filming] to get an idea straight, but it was structured after that point. It was never a free-for-all. I hate the word improvisation because it's [basically] an undisciplined way of executing your work. It's very difficult to shoot that way, you really can't achieve anything. You become sloppy and incoherent. It's really chaos in the cutting room. You can shoot some scenes that way — in tableau form, a one-take exchange between actors [photographed] individually, close-ups — but really, it rarely works well. [In the psychiatric monologues of Jane Fonda in *Klute*] there was a lot of rambling, but that's fine, it worked. But that was one person sitting in a chair, just talking. There were twenty thousand feet, or whatever we used, and then finally it was cut up. A lot of people loved them, but I didn't particularly care for them. I just find . . . good things happen in movies by mistake a lot, but if you really boil down all of the mistakes and all of the *cinéma vérité* free-form shooting you'll find that little of it exists. Remnants of that form of shooting are around . . . but it doesn't hold up. Many films that are shot at that level, you say "exciting," and the first time around it is. You see it again and you begin to see these huge, gaping holes in it. It's a very flashy way of getting through it, but it has no structure, so it becomes boring. It may have been very exciting for [the actors], inside themselves, but when you look at it on the screen you want to rush up to the screen and tear it down because it's such a mess. So I'm not a great believer . . .

The younger generation of cinematographers are, or seem to be, more reflective, opinionated and self-critical than their older counterparts. Whether it is natural inclination or circumstance that makes them so is difficult to say. To a degree, their independence of major-studio contract obligations may afford them the luxury of volubility. Their free-lance status also provides them with the opportunity, once a certain professional standing has been attained, to be selective in choosing assignments.

LASZLO KOVACS (Responding to the critic who wrote that the Kovacs-shot *The Marriage of a Young Stockbroker* looked as if it had been photographed through a windshield): Perhaps my work reflected a mediocre attitude.

GORDON WILLIS: If I hate a scene my work'll be better than average, but it won't be *right,* and the reason it won't be right is that, probably, the scene is wrong for the movie. [Without commenting one way or the other about the quality of his execution of it, Willis discusses a scene in *Klute* which he feels is "wrong."] The first scene in which [Jane Fonda's] being stalked — I would have cut that shot of Charles Cioffi in the basement and that bit where [Donald Sutherland] opens the door on the kids having a pot party. I talked to Alan about [the pot party scene], and he said, "I know," but said something about it being "commercial." I never thought it would end up in the movie. I'm sure that if he were questioned about it today, Alan would think it was pretty bad too. All you needed was the noise and to show [Donald Sutherland] going up to the roof to look for whoever's terrorizing her.

HASKELL WEXLER: At different times in life you are willing or able to make a more conscious decision about the kind of picture you work on. I always try to be associated with films which reflect my views, or at least say something about things I am interested in. This is not always possible in features, and that is why, from time to time, I have gone off on my own to make a documentary.

GORDON WILLIS: First of all, do I like the idea or the subject matter? But the people involved may be wrong for you or wrong for it. If there was an imaginative director, or a good bunch of people, I'd go with them. If the material is doubtful in its present state, usually the people involved will bring it around to where it makes sense and it's a good movie. You can go with very good scripts and get killed by incompetent people. So it's more the people than the script.

LASZLO KOVACS: The script plus the director. But I think I would rather go with the lesser script and the more exciting director.

In addition to working with the director, the actors, the art director and the other "creative" personnel involved in filmmaking, the cameraman is called upon to deal with the producer and/ or the studio, either on a one-to-one basis or with the director as (it is hoped) a combination intermediary-ally. The cameraman's discussions — or, as is more likely, conflicts — with the production end can hinge on aesthetic questions both during and after principal photography as well as the sometimes related matters of time and money. The long, mysterious between-take and between-scene "delays" that are anathema to most screen actors are taken up largely with the director of photography's primary activity — lighting. Therefore, the speed with which the cameraman lights a scene concerns the producer as much as the director's speed in staging and shooting it. During the course of a career a cameraman gets a reputation for being either "fast" or "slow," adjectives for which some producers would just as soon substitute "good" or "bad."

JOSEPH RUTTENBERG: The production department at MGM, particularly during the 30s and 40s, had spies on the set. The moment you did something wrong — you would say you're ready, for example, and then the director would take a long time to rehearse a scene, and you'd say, "I'd better change that light over there to improve the shot." They'd go right to the telephone and report it, and the script girl would put it down that Joe Ruttenberg was all ready and then he changed the light.

HASKELL WEXLER: Knowing when to stop is the most important decision in lighting a set. Sometimes you get caught either because the director changes staging or the sun has moved and the beautiful backlight of the plan has become hard sidelight.

You need time to change. We used to work deals with actors so they'd have to go to the honeywagon, thus giving time to set a scrim or move in the silk. In Italy we had a signal with one of the electricians up high — when I touched my left eye he'd pull the plug on a big unit as if it was a bad connection, just enough to give us some time to fix the look of a scene. Many times we'd wait for the soundman or director to call for another take rather than have camera "take the blame."

GORDON WILLIS: There's a whole school of moviemaking — you go to Universal Studios. There might be ten, twelve cameramen punching out movies. You cut them all together, there's a sameness about it which is kind of a company sameness. . . . It's a mentality; it's a mechanical mentality. "Just give me a close-up there, this is a long shot here." If you allow yourself to photograph something in a manner which they like, that you don't like, then ultimately you're going to end up with something punched out of the cookie-press, because the closer you get [to what they want] the more they'll take advantage of it. They will boil everything down to kind of sixty-cycle tone, which is something that they understand. It's the same thing in cutting as it is in printing or processing: If they can do it mechanically, they'll do it. [But] it's impossible to do that if a movie is shot at a certain level. They can turn it upside down and it's not going to look any different.

A strong line producer can be an important positive force in moviemaking by, first of all, bringing the right people together, and then, once they arrive at a concept, seeing that they follow that concept through. Good producers do contribute an awful lot to holding a show together. If you get into trouble in a particular situation and you have someone who's dealing with a studio and dealing with you at the same time, it helps you maneuver the project so that you can achieve whatever it is you want to achieve and nobody gets hurt. If you have a good producer he'll make sure you can maneuver the material properly within the framework of what you have to spend without getting your brains kicked out. . . . I've had strong producers, but it was kind of like having a bull chained to the back door of your house. It was an unproductive kind of strength, based on lack of knowledge. Most producers today do not know anything about movies; they're dealmakers.

I'd like to shoot and coproduce. You take a good director, or writer-director, and I'll coproduce with him. That makes a lot of sense to me. You become a very solid unit. It would eliminate a lot of bullshit, it would increase your authority. So when you make a decision it's right there, bang, that minute. That's a lot better than calling the CIA every twenty minutes, or the producer at the pool or wherever he is. . . . I don't really want to direct. There's a point where [directors] leave off and I pick up. There are people who cast better, who deal with actors better than I can. What I do very well, I build, improve and execute very well. So if you put those two together [as coproducers], you're in a stronger situation.

CONRAD HALL: What happens normally is that if there is somebody like Sol Halperin [of Twentieth Century-Fox's camera department] in control of the photographic end of a studio and [in] the [postproduction] finishing of a picture, he [may] let the cameraman come in and mucky up how the print should look for drive-ins. . . . [Still], you arrive at a Sol Halperin kind of look, not a Conrad Hall look. That's one way [the timed — color-corrected — print of a film is arrived at]. Another way is the director gets used to what he is seeing, or finds out what he would really like to have [isn't what you've done] and then he doesn't want you there, so he does it himself. The other way is that nobody calls you and the director is not interested in it and there is no studio cameraman who is interested in it and it is left to the cutter. And the cutter does it the way he wants to do it. I don't know why everyone is so frightened of the cameraman coming in to do [the timed print]. I should think it would be the first thing they would want. They override you. It's their prerogative. That's why you have to get into directing if you want control. [Even then], you never get final cut unless you've established an enormous stature in this industry. The man who puts up the money has final cut. It's hardly ever the producer. And so, it's between you and the money man.

JAMES WONG HOWE: I take about two looks at [the answer print —
the first composite print]. Beyond that, they start crabbing.

GORDON WILLIS: [Working on a film in the postproduction phase
is] a courtesy the producer extends. I did it on *The Godfather*.
. . . I exchanged some ideas with [director Robert] Benton on
the cutting of *Bad Company* and I worked with the timed print
of the film until almost the end; there's a difference in the part
I didn't do. . . . I was one of the ones who pushed for the use
of continuous cutting techniques in the fantasy sequences of
*Up the Sandbox* instead of the usual Walter Mitty approach
[in which long fades or dissolves telegraph the spectator that
what follows is not "real"].

Conrad Hall's account of his work on *Fat City* resounds, in the
context of a single film, many of the themes explored earlier in
this chapter.

CONRAD HALL: The best way is to discuss it long beforehand. It's
best not so much because of what they'll get from you as far as
actual contributions to picking locations and that kind of thing,
but in the cameraman having the opportunity to be around the
director so that when the picture does start functioning and he
starts shooting, the cameraman will be an extension of the
director rather than his own personal artistic entity. . . . What
they're really interested in discussing is what you think about
how to direct the film. Any good director always asks people
what they think — how they would do it. And so you tell them.
That doesn't mean they have to use it.
   I talked over the concept of shooting [*Fat City*] with John
[Huston]; I didn't talk it over with [producer] Ray [Stark]
because I didn't see any need to. [John and I] agreed on the
style of the show by taking natural-light stills with a Polaroid
Land camera, and the lighting in these stills was just exactly
the way we wanted the show to look. We went up to Stockton
[California] and we talked about title material [i.e., scenes to
be played behind the credits]. He saw all of these great skid-
row bars and all the people wandering around the urban re-
newal project taking place in Stockton. So I went out with a

hidden camera in the back of a truck with black curtains and a zoom lens and shot a guy just sitting there having his hair cut . . . and a great sequence in the lobby of a rundown hotel, with people just sitting there watching the traffic. I was trying to capture the feeling of people's lives going down the drain while they're sitting there staring into space not doing anything about it. It's really devastating stuff — unbelievable! — and John looked at it and he just fell in love with it. I overexposed everything about three stops and then printed it down, and it has a nice pale quality. He said, "Oh, Conrad, I've never seen color like this in my life." I shot this material so that we saw it about the day before shooting. And everybody was really excited until we saw the first day's dailies [of scripted scenes involving professional performers]. It's a different thing entirely when you photograph actors and actresses *portraying* people's lives going down the drain. It looks like acting all of a sudden, and it doesn't look real; [the rushes from the first day of principal photography] didn't look good.

I could never understand why they took a lot of the material into sets, but we had an art director named Dick Sylbert, who is a very good art director, and he built a lot of sets. . . . For some reason or another, a decision John Huston made, a lot of the sets were built on a — not on a sound stage, but in an auditorium in the Stockton Fairgrounds. I think it's always tough to make sets look really real. That first hotel room — that's my favorite shot in the picture — where Stacy Keach is lying down and he gets up and he's looking for the cigarettes and matches. That was a real room that looked like a real room.

The style I was trying to use comes from the material, which takes place in dingy afternoon bars. It's dark, you can hardly see anything. And then, when you come outside, you can hardly see anything — it's pure white. So I went for really dark interiors and I worked right on the edge, using very little light, wide-open stop, and letting the windows go completely white, so then the exterior material, when it appeared white, would have a sense to it. When you looked from the inside out it was white, and then when you go outside it was white. . . .

There was a lot of hassling during the [shooting] about not having enough light on the actors. . . . Ray Stark wanted to see more light on Earl [played by Curtis Cokes, a black actor] in the bar. It would have looked phony. I chose not to do it. And I think you see him well enough. We had the front office looking at the dailies, and if they felt it was something that wouldn't project properly at the drive-ins they would send somebody on the set who would come over and say something like, "There's nothing on film." I got very angry finally, and we had it out. I said, "Ray, you got one option. That's to call Hollywood and get another cameraman, and I'll work until he gets here. Otherwise, I'm going to do it the way John and I have decided we're going to do it."

Later on, John turned on me and sided with Ray about a scene he felt I had made too obscure. It's the scene where they're taking the buses in early morning; we went out about four o'clock one morning [when], it's called the shape-up, takes place. It took place in an area where there's no light. You have a few little fires going, and you hear the bus drivers hawking the type of work the buses would take you to. There was a sense that I got from it, [it] was [one] of wandering through and not seeing anything and having the story told to you through an audio sense. The story is what has to be served; seeing everything is not necessarily the most important thing. I thought it was fascinating to hear all these people and to get the mystery of the thing, and then get on this hot field [later] in the morning and have it be an immense contrast. But when we saw the dailies, John said, "Conrad, I can't see anything," and I was sorry that he didn't like it. I don't try to do something that only I like and not try to do what the director wants to do. He wanted to reshoot it, but because there were so many extras and things, they didn't.

I couldn't get an operator I had worked with before, whose work I knew. So I hired somebody who was a very competent operator, but he wasn't getting what I wanted. I would discuss it with him, and he was trying, but for some reason or another, he was not understanding me . . . [about] what headroom should be in a close-up, what headroom should be in a medium shot, what headroom should be in a long shot. The way I like it, not how it "should" be. I let him go and decided to operate the rest of it myself. They [the studio] hired somebody on their own and sent him up, but I continued to operate. He could go off and make a promotional film, which he did, or do anything else he wanted to do. [I operated], I'd say probably a quarter — a little more, maybe a third [of the film].

John chose . . . to eliminate conventional cutting by shooting as many scenes as possible in one shot. Instead of making it for the cutting room, where you have a close-up, a master shot. To get a natural-light picture, and to get naturalism into the picture, we decided to play everything in one scene and to work out how to do it so that the camera followed the people around and told the story the best way it possibly could without any kind of coverage at all. Now, we started to do this, and we did it. And again, Ray got very nervous and uptight about this technique and [started] hammering at John.

All of the boxing in *Fat City* is improvisational. I just followed the action with a camera. Each fight was handled differently, but the last fight was handled in the following manner. John would talk things over with the actors . . . what story points were involved in that round. Then he'd say, "Gentlemen, let's have a round of boxing," and somebody would say, "Bong!," and I used three-camera coverage — everyone on the risers outside of the ring, back, very comfortable, no hand-held stuff — and these guys did a round of boxing, three minutes, and tried to incorporate the story points. And then we'd let them rest, and then John would say, "Another round of boxing." I really didn't do anything special, like getting really low angles or cutting holes through floors. I wanted it to look like TV fights, like Saturday night fights on TV. I tried to get that sort of mundane quality of Saturday night fights. Unfortunately, after we did that, then John would say, "Well, we better cover that point," and then he started setting things up and things looked staged.

[The scene at the end of the fight, where the Mexican fighter walks down a corridor in semidarkness] was planned to be very dramatic-looking. It's a little too on the nose, I think. It's not real life.

The scene at the bar, several angles of it were improvisational from a camera standpoint. . . . Susan [Tyrrell] in the center, Stacy [Keach] to the right and Curtis [Cokes] to the left in

Susan Tyrrell and Stacy Keach in *Fat City*, directed by John Huston. Conrad Hall: "The scene at the bar, several angles of it were improvisational from a camera standpoint."

the foreground. The camera was set on a long lens when she was talking to Stacy. It was supposed to be a two-shot. And when she turned to talk to Curtis, that would drive the camera frame to a two-shot of Curtis and her. And there was no way to tell when she was going to turn. So you just sort of hung in there and went with however you felt. But you could only go on a movement. And if you didn't get it right away, if she turned too quickly, then it would look funny to have the camera subsequently . . . [and] arbitrarily travel over there. We did the take two or three times and printed all of them. And then they used the pieces that they liked. [In the final film, the scene has] a screwed-up quality . . . it seems very convincing to me.

What happens is that you are involved in the planning and shaping of a film, but then your involvement ceases at the end of the shooting schedule and somebody else is involved. When you see the end result, and it is different from how you planned it and you're not part of the thought process that went into all the changes, it really bothers you.

John Huston had his cut, and then Ray Stark started messing around with it. [The film] was such a downer that he said, "Give me a couple of up scenes." So he got a writer. Not *the* writer of the screenplay; some other writer. And he wrote a couple of "up" scenes. Dick Moore shot [these] two scenes. Now both of these scenes I had previously shot; not the same dialogue, but really in effect the same scenes. There's just more dialogue in [the Moore-shot scenes].

The theme of the story is people's lives going down the drain before they have a chance to put the plug in and fullfill them. [A dream sequence showing Stacy Keach at an earlier, happier time in his life was cut from the film. — D.C.] That's what's missing, what life was like. It's the key to making his dilemma *felt*. In order to appreciate what happens when life goes down the drain, you have to know the good times.

The concept of that barroom scene was . . . we would follow him in until he stopped because his eyes had not adjusted to the dimness. I had purposely not lit the bar interior so we would see nothing past his back, lit from the open doorway. What I wanted to have happen was to see beyond him and not see anything, just the shape of his back before cutting around to the reverse [angle view of the scene]. Well, they never did that. He came in and they cut immediately to a reverse. I think it would have been much more effective to come in, hear some music and voices and not see anything before you cut around to the silhouette scene and sort of lighten the scene a bit as it progressed.

A lot of it was hotter, the exteriors were hotter in the work print, I would say. They printed it down; they got chicken with letting it go white. It's [basically] little individual things [that were changed].

*

JOSEPH RUTTENBERG: I've never done a hundred-percent picture. I don't know anybody who ever did do a hundred-percent picture. You have too many people handling it.

JAMES WONG HOWE: You've got the producer. And the director. And the star. And the art director. And you've got to please your laboratory. You've got so many people to please. You wonder, When am I going to please myself?

LASZLO KOVACS: The preparation — that's when you really make the film. It's when you can really let your imagination loose and fantasize away, always asking yourself and the others, What would happen if. . . . During the shooting you're involved in giving life to a film, but when it's over the film begins to have a life of its own. It leaves you — you feel left behind. Sometimes you pass by a theater where a film of yours is playing, and you look at the marquee and feel that part of yourself is in that theater.

# FIVE

## The Production Designer

A production designer," according to Gene Allen, "is an art director who has an in with the director in the sense of having some authority."

A few years back, the art director was described for the Academy Awards telecast's tens of millions of viewers as the individual responsible for the "look" of a film. Sketches of sets used in the five films nominated for the art direction Oscar were provided as a visual aid.

If the art director's function consists mainly in the design of studio sets, as the Oscar show job profile and the title — architect — attached to art directors in German films suggest, then Kevin Brownlow is correct in asserting, in *The Parade's Gone By* . . . that "in the silent days, art direction was a late developer." Brownlow notes:

The earliest pictures were shot against flats decorated by the property man. If a scene painter was needed, he was hired from a local theatre. . . . The improvement in art direction paralleled the improvement in lighting.

Brownlow goes on to say that the sets for D. W. Griffith's *Intolerance* (1916), "built without an art director by master craftsman Frank 'Huck' Wortman, were a great impetus to the field," and that in the years that immediately followed many celebrated stage designers, such as Joseph Urban, were engaged for film work. The design of the German Expressionist films of the twenties, which many still regard as the apotheosis of art direction, was another impetus to the field in Hollywood. The American desire to imitate or reproduce the striking work done in German films brought about the importation of numerous German artists and craftsmen.

If, however, one takes a wider view and regards art direction as concerning itself with the total physical environment of a film — both designed and constructed studio sets, and existing structures and landscapes used in though not specifically contrived for a film — art direction was as "developed" in the earliest days of the film medium as it is now. In some essential way, every film ever made is "art directed," even if no one is credited with that function. In his preface to Léon Barsacq's *Le Décor de Film*, René Clair discusses the contrasting modes of art direction in the films of the Lumières and Méliès and suggests that they are expressions of contrasting world views.

> The Lumière Brothers, who came to film by way of photography, focused their attention on aspects of the real. (Their emulators today speak of "cinéma-vérité.") On the other hand, Méliès, led to the cinema by way of illusionism and the theatre, concerned himself less with reproducing what he had seen than with transforming it into what he had imagined. . . . Between the two extremes is the idea of the real imitated.

Largely in substantiation, Barsacq, who designed *La Beauté du Diable* and other films for Clair, *La Marseillaise* for Renoir, and *Les Enfants du Paradis* for Carné, remarks that

Each "school" of filmmaking from the "primitives" at the beginning of the century to the "neo-realists," and in passing the "aesthetes" of 1920–26 has had its conception of the décor.

Without stretching Barsacq's point, it can be said that each *film* has its conception of the environment. The art director's primary function is to translate that conception into visual terms. But, as Barsacq observes, "His functions are many and vary according to the films and the directors."

POLLY PLATT: The average art director walks in and says, "What do you want, how do you see it?" and goes and does it and really, essentially, brings nothing of himself to it. He picks up on exactly what the director wants, he doesn't begin to impose his own opinions on it at all. . . .

HARRY HORNER: That, in my estimation, is not enough. In terms of design, on *The Heiress*, for instance, my contribution, I think, was in another direction. [William] Wyler engaged me before the writers were engaged to write the screenplay. They were the same writers [Ruth and Augustus Goetz] who wrote the stage version from the Henry James novel *Washington Square*. Wyler felt that it would be good to first let the visualizer — the designer — think of how this story could be translated. Wyler said, "Why don't you, you know, visualize it?" . . . I first wrote down general reactions and suggestions for scenes. . . . I feel that I should stimulate a director to see more than he has seen. By "seeing" I don't necessarily mean something visual. To understand more, to widen or be more curious about a character, about a landscape, about the relationship between an interior and a character. . . .

POLLY PLATT: . . . You begin to ask yourself, if, as a designer, you're not overstepping your boundaries: I say, What is my function and what is the director's, and what is the writer's function and how do we all fit in and whose picture is it anyhow? For instance, classically . . . this next film [*Nashville*] that Bob Altman is going to make with me and with [writer]

Joan Tewksbury. The minute you have Nashville and the Grand Ol' Opry [as the setting for the story] a certain visual style begins to impose itself beyond either Bob Altman or myself. I went to see the Grand Ol' Opry originally when Peter [Bogdanovich] was going to do *The Getaway*. He had a whole sequence in the Grand Ol' Opry, and then for a long period in *Paper Moon* we were going to take [the characters played by Ryan and Tatum O'Neal] all the way through Kansas and into the South and use the Grand Ol' Opry. I started telling Bob about Nashville and how dirty and chaotic it is, and he said, "Let's have automobile accidents in the background that are ignored; that are just part of the background action." In other words, when I was telling him my impressions of the city he got that idea. . . .

HARRY HORNER: I would still say respectfully that the director is *auteur*; except that the other contributors like the cameraman and the production designer are also an entity. One doesn't have to define too carefully where one contributes and where one steps back and says the other one had a better idea. The main thing is the end result.

GENE ALLEN: A production designer is . . . what? An "idea man." His training in filmmaking has been such that he takes the often "flat" written word and transforms it into a three-dimensional image. Working with the director, he is constantly asking, "What if we . . . ?," or, "Why don't you . . . ?," or, "If you combined . . . ?" Yes, I'd say the production designer is a visualizer whose task is to take the screenplay and come up with a "look" . . . a style appropriate for a particular story.

Before exploring the production designer's working relationships, it may be instructive as an orientation to consider the reflections of Polly Platt and Harry Horner on the subjects of studio versus location filming and contemporary versus period designing.

POLLY PLATT: In the old days the function of an art director was to design and build the sets in the studio and go out with the director and find the locations, if any. It's really an expanding world, the world of art direction, now that more pictures are made on location. . . .

HARRY HORNER: I hate scenery. It's a strange perversion. I really find it rather old-fashioned and heavy-handed. It's marvelous to have belonged to that [scenery-dominated] period. I must say that I was very lucky, because I met many marvelous people who fitted into the period. . . . I find the new art director — I find there's a new sense of taste, a new sense of search for truth. . . .

POLLY PLATT: You would think that the art director would function less [today], but it's not so. You're faced with the whole world to choose from, and you have to exercise selectivity. You've got a whole city, now what do you choose to show in that city? You form the city as you see it. If you see a city as modern — now, Houston [the setting of *The Thief Who Came to Dinner*] has plenty of old buildings — you *make* the city modern. Altman used Houston interestingly — as a circus. And I screened *Brewster McCloud* before I went to Houston, because I didn't want to follow in Altman's footsteps and accidentally pick up on his theme.

HARRY HORNER: Most of *The Heiress* was designed before shooting started, which I now do not believe in. I think directors should not be burdened by a preconceived, drawn-out concept. But in a historical film — and I call *The Heiress* a historical film — it is difficult because you have to recreate a period and it almost automatically becomes theatrical. You are not on your own, you cannot go on the street.

POLLY PLATT: A period picture is more difficult because you don't have the freedom of choice in terms of where you can shoot it if you're shooting on actual locations. You have to find . . . a town that doesn't have too much modernization so you're not spending a lot of money on sets to cover up buildings that don't look right. There are tremendous limitations in doing a period picture that result in it being a challenge economically and creatively — and I love that. You have all these incredible prob-

lems, which become fun. However, I always breathe a sigh of
relief when a picture is not period because I realize that I have
complete freedom. But with the freedom of choice of locations
[comes the question] of how you are going to control your
freedom.

The only question that I ask myself is, Why does this *have*
to be a period picture? And then, when I find the answer, then
I can design it. . . . At one time I developed a theory that
when you do a period picture you should ignore the period.
In *Paper Moon* I tried to avoid the Depression. It seemed to
me that it was implicit in the story.

Apart from the director, the person most closely involved with
the production designer's work is the director of photography.
Even the vocabulary used to describe the functions of the production designer and the cameraman overlap: both, rightly, have
been called "visualizers," and both, again rightly, are responsible for the "look" of a film. Though their work is executed with
different tools and, sometimes, at essentially different stages in
the filmmaking process (on occasion, the production designer's
job ends before or shortly after a film begins shooting), their functions are complementary and interdependent. Ideally, the production designer's work is also closely integrated with that of the
costume designer. Studio policy or union regulations may require
him to function with, or alongside of, an associate, co- or standby
art director. A musical brings him into the sphere of the choreographer, an extensively preplanned movie demands that he perform
an editorial function, and a George Cukor film is likely to find
him in the bailiwick of the screenwriter. As Polly Platt says, "It
depends on the personality of the person who's doing the job. It's
like, What does the assistant to the corporate president do, in
what areas does he assist? I think it really expands according
to your own personal scope as an artist and as a human being."

GENE ALLEN: The production designer must be on guard constantly, making sure that approved visual ideas are not diluted
or lost. He attends story conferences to remind the director and
screenwriter of visual possibilities. He reads all "blue pages"
to make sure the rewrite has not eliminated something that

would aid in the telling of the story or add to the visual style of the production. In *A Star Is Born*, my first film with George Cukor, the first-draft screenplay by Moss Hart had the head of publicity, Jack Carson, describing the fantastic . . . the huge . . . the glamorous wedding he would arrange for Judy Garland and James Mason. You then cut to two drunks in a small-town jail applauding the justice-of-the-peace pronouncing Judy and James, man and wife. The rewrite went from Carson to something unrelated to what he was saying. I called this to Cukor's attention and he and Moss Hart sent new blue pages that again cut from Carson to the two drunks. [The credits for *A Star Is Born* list Malcolm Bert as art director, Irene Sharaff as art director and costume designer for the "Born in a Trunk" number, and Allen as production designer. Allen, along with Grant Stuart, is credited with the "adaptation" of Cukor's *The Chapman Report*, on which Allen also served as production designer — D.C.]

Stanley Kramer, prior to shooting *Champion*, worked with his production designer, Rudy Sternad, to see if the film could be made for a price, without losing any production values. Every shot in every scene was illustrated and the final storyboard [comprising the illustrations laid end-to-end] was in fact the final film; the only difference being it was on paper instead of film. The results prove that this approach should be given more consideration by the [cost-conscious] young filmmaker.

The production designer, as a member of the director's creative team, works closely with the cameraman and his operator. Usually there is no conflict. . . . I worked for eighteen years as George Cukor's production designer and can't remember a director of photography who resented my suggestions as to possible camera angles or compositions. It is a matter of casting. A professional director, such as Cukor, assembles a creative team . . . who are willing to leave their inflated egos at home.

HARRY HORNER: [I worked with George Cuker (on *Born Yesterday*)], who insisted that I make every camera setup and stage the visual action. George Cukor does not know or like the camera — which is very interesting — so that the production

designer who works with him . . . [is asked] not only to look
through the camera and establish what is to be done, but to
tell the actors you see, "Try the scene. And now then, if you
sit here and you sit over there, this will be more or less the
way it will work, because from here you go to the window and
. . . [to the camera operator] pan." This was extraordinary. The
crew would say, "He's doing the whole thing," and Cukor didn't
mind it. Certainly I knew I wasn't directing the film. I
contributed.

GENE ALLEN: Early in the game, I learned that Cukor's apparent
lack of knowledge about cameras, compositions, color, et cetera,
was a great hoax. By pretending not to be knowledgeable about
such things he forced you to explain fully what it was you had
in mind. Cukor is the expert on all elements of filmmaking. At
times, Cukor was the auctioneer allowing the production designer and the director of photography to bid against each other
. . . to see who could come up with the best method of visualiz-
ing a particular segment of a film.

HARRY HORNER: Every camera setup in *The Heiress* had to be
made by the designer, which was difficult — we had three or
four cameramen on it. [Leo Tover is credited as director of
photography. — D.C.] Wyler . . . he's sort of a scoundrel. He'd
say, "You always draw these sketches, but you can never make
the setup. You will never get this angle." It was easy to prove
that it could be done.
    [With reference to *They Shoot Horses, Don't They?*]: I felt
that it would be very interesting to shoot the flashback/flash-
forward [so as] to give a sense of timelessness. I wanted it all
in white. That means totally overexposed. The sets, which were
minimal, were actually only pieces of sets put into a totally
white space with no edges on it, no corners. [It] was like an
egg, the inside of an egg. Into that was put a judge's table or
the inside of a piece of an automobile — the police thing —
and the police station and so forth. That was the concept of
it, and I thought this kind of a definite estrangement — it
would have been something without contrast — would give
it a feeling of anxiety.

By the time Sydney Pollack started to shoot there was a . . . nervousness. [Pollack's services were secured after a lengthy and budget-escalating preparation period involving at least one other director. — D.C.] They left the flashback for the end of the film[ing]. I was told, "Harry, make all your sketches and explain what you want, and then I think you will have done everything." By that time I was on the picture like an annuity. I said, "Fine. I would like, however, to be present [during the shooting]," because it was a visual concept which came out of my pen, so to say, the director liked it. . . . But what happened was that the cameraman [Philip Lathrop] didn't have the courage to light it out, and so it became just as realistic and just as hard-edged as the rest, except it wasn't quite as bright, as colorful [Horner may be a little hard on Lathrop. In an interview with Michael Dempsey (in *The Hollywood Screenwriters*, Richard Corliss, editor) James Poe, coauthor of the screenplay of *They Shoot Horses*, blames Pollack for the film's photographic deficiencies in general. — D.C.] It had no essential difference and I felt one couldn't really quite understand what it was and I thought it mattered. I felt that it wasn't — it didn't succeed. It didn't succeed because there was suddenly no time to do it correctly. It was an expensive film, so this little additional expense probably would not have mattered, because it was built, the cameraman was there, I said I would certainly not charge — but they didn't bother. There was a feeling of "Ah, Christ, we don't really need it." So that happened, and it was a detriment, I think, to the overall effect of the film.

GENE ALLEN: Sometimes the production designer receives credit as art director, and the designer of the wardrobe, wigs and hats gets credit as the production designer. This was the case on *My Fair Lady*. Prior to Cukor signing to direct, Cecil Beaton was hired and his credit established as "Costumes and Production Designed by . . ." To avoid stirring up old battles, I will say only that Cecil was never involved in the actual filming of the production. I functioned as I always had with Cukor, working from the start to the finish with the director of photography, Harry Stradling, a fantastic and creative man, whose passing leaves a void in the ranks. [In Gavin Lambert's *On Cukor*, the

director attributes "art director" Allen with "the lion's share
of the practical work, as well as a lot of the designing. I
think it would be fair to say that Gene executed the sets and
made very important contributions to the conception of them."
— D.C.]

Cukor and I missed having aboard *My Fair Lady* our friend,
the gifted George Hoyningen-Huene. Huene, credited [on
earlier Cukor films] as "color coordinator," threw out ideas as
easily as he spoke five or six languages. His great delight was
casting and clothing the extras. Working with the assistant
director and the wardrobe department, George would create
as backgrounds "living, moving vignettes," often [inspired by]
a Picasso or Braque or another modern master. I've heard
George Cukor say about a Hoyningen-Huene background, "The
damned background looks better than my foreground."

HARRY HORNER: I worked with Edith Head, who designed the
costumes for *The Heiress*. I made rough costume sketches. . . .

POLLY PLATT: If [the credit reads] "production design," the production *is* designed by Polly Platt . . . or whomever. And that
means the clothes. I feel the sets and costumes should be
designed by the same person. I can't imagine . . . I think I
would be so crippled if I had to work with a costume designer.
I'm extremely opinionated, right or wrong, [and] I think I
would be agonized trying to . . . work well with someone else.

GENE ALLEN: We made drawings [of the Covent Garden set for
*My Fair Lady*] in the drafting room and as soon as a model
of it could be prepared and approved we showed it to Hermes
Pan [the choreographer]. Then we taped out that set on the
back lot, so he could start thinking about blocking out his
action.

Incidentally, I directed the "Ascot Gavotte" dance number
and various "atmosphere shots" of the running of the race and
of the Covent Garden market scenes. This was at George
Cukor's suggestion and with the full approval of Jack Warner.
The costumes Cecil created for the men and women of Covent
Garden were magnificent.

The designer begins his work by reading the script. "When you design a film," Polly Platt says, "in a sense you become a director. You attack a script just as a director does." But a designer is not director, the realization of which gives rise to an odd admixture of feelings.

POLLY PLATT: There's a sense of depression upon taking a film, because you know you have begun to follow out the old syndrome, especially as a woman, of dedicating yourself again for a certain period of time to a man, to a creator. It gives you a sense of drive and direction, because it's exciting to work for a director, to try to find out what he wants to do, to bring all of your creative forces to bear in order to inspire and augment and complete his vision. Yet you have a sense of depression. . . . I've often thought of what it would be like to work for Elaine May. And I'm sure that it would be the same experience. It's a kind of submission that is required. . . .

HARRY HORNER: [There is a certain] lack of character that lies in being a designer. By lack of character, I mean that you change, you are with each film another person. And that, I think, you should be. . . .

POLLY PLATT: You begin to hunt for the director's theme, you begin to hunt for what he's doing. And that's exciting. That is your function.

Bob Altman sent me a book called *Thieves Like Us* and said, "I'm going to do this and I want you to design it." [Platt eventually worked on the film in an unofficial, advisory capacity. — D.C.] I read the book and I thought, There must be a good reason why he wants to do this story. Nick Ray's *They Live By Night* is based on the same book, but I knew Bob wasn't doing a "remake." When I called Bob, I said, "Why do you want to make it?" And he said he wanted to make a love story and that he wanted to show — and I misquote him slightly — "to show what happens to a love affair when it leaves its own sheltered world of the bedroom and goes out into the wider world." He used the word "fragile," how fragile a love affair is out in the world. He took this sort of wandering tale and defined it. That's

Cecil Beaton's and Gene Allen's Ascot Races set in *My Fair Lady*, directed by
George Cukor.

an example of how a director imposed his personality [on a film] even before the picture started to be made. . . . There was the original story, there's the script by Joan Tewksbury [and Calder Willingham and Altman himself], there are so many elements involved. But he's managed to impose his theme onto this big story.

HARRY HORNER: The script of *The Hustler* is handed to you and you don't know anything about billiards. I personally feel a film about pool will not work. Nobody will come to see it. I am a reasonably interested person, but I am not curious to see pool players. I said that to [Robert] Rossen. He said for me to make it interesting. . . .

POLLY PLATT: You bring your own expertise and your own philosophy and, of course, that's why he hires you. . . .

HARRY HORNER: You read the book [by Walter Tevis from which *The Hustler* is derived] to get yourself more familiar with the characters. . . . I thought the film was a film of texture, of people who are rotting away — it's a decadent story. This kind of texture in [the designer's] reality is a cracked wall, a rusty pipe, a dirty floor. The feeling is that nature and weather does with a room as it does with a human being. In New York [where the film was shot] there are craftsmen who can age a place. They say, "Well, how old should it be?" And you say, "fifteen years" or, "sixteen years," and tell them how the people who live there would treat it.

GENE ALLEN: As soon as a deal is set, the production designer begins to surround himself with research . . . with tons of research. He must approach each assignment as if he knows nothing about the times and conditions it calls for. He organizes his research material and furnishes the director with copies of it [in the hopes it will] stimulate and guide him towards a visual conception that is often [at this point] only a vague notion in the back of the designer's head. On a Cukor film we would end up with fifty or sixty folders of research photos, each con-

taining material that collectively added up to the look of the
final movie.

Having been to London, where I took research photos of
Covent Garden, I found it not difficult to design a set that included all of the elements required by the story; the church,
the street, the pubs, and the market.

HARRY HORNER: [Prior to the filming of *The Heiress*] I went to
New York . . . and found that Washington Square at that time
— you could shoot, with certain modifications. I would have
had to lay cobblestones, which would be plastic, would be
just a skin, and minor things, but I could get certain areas in
the city of New York in 1948 where you could shoot a picture
laid in the 1860s. But Wyler insisted on the convenience of the
studio.

I found that the park, Washington Square Park in New York,
was a parade ground [at the time of the early scenes in *The
Heiress*]. It gave me a marvelous thing to show the progression
in time, because there is a sequence where the father is dying
and another sequence later when the father is dead. To show
a progression in time, the parade ground in Washington Square
later had a wooden fence. At one time I thought it might be
interesting to have the digging of the first gas pipes, and then
they would have gaslights. [The actual digging was never
shown in the film.] Not so anybody would say, "A-ha, do you
see the gaslights?," because I don't think anybody did.

Part of the "researching" of films to be shot largely or entirely
on location consists of finding locations appropriate to the story.
Polly Platt's experience demonstrates that the locale specified by
a script when it reaches the designer is not necessarily the locale
the film is eventually set in.

POLLY PLATT: As a designer, what you try to find is a place where
the story *could* happen. . . . Peter [Bogdanovich] leaned on me
heavily for that aspect of it. . . . I went to Chicago to see if it
would be a good location for *What's Up, Doc?*, and Chicago
had no complete feeling as a city. It's half New York, it's half
a lakeside city; and I couldn't grasp it in terms of a . . . place

51-50

Paul Newman and George C. Scott (2nd and 3rd from left) in *The Hustler*, directed by Robert Rossen. Harry Horner: "I thought the film was a film of texture. . . . This kind of texture in [the designer's] reality is a cracked wall, a rusty pipe . . ."

for *What's Up, Doc?* I told Peter my feelings about Chicago. I certainly didn't think it ought to be shot in New York, and he agreed, although there was some discussion about shooting it there. [An abortive, substantially different version of the film was begun by another director on New York locations. — D.C.]. But I just didn't see Barbra [Streisand] in New York. In a sense, she's *too* New York, and I just didn't see that character there. She would become a "Village character . . . " I thought she should be outside of all worlds. The character she played was a cartoon character, I didn't feel she related to any world. That's why I tried to design clothes for her that were nonevocative of any life style. San Francisco, so white and shining, was the perfect city for this insane, nonreal, comic-strip cartoon movie to happen.

I influenced Bud [Yorkin] to shoot *The Thief Who Came to Dinner* in Houston. The script was set in Chicago. And when I read the script I said "impossible." *The Thief Who Came to Dinner* is the story of a computer analyst who decides to become a better thief than all the corporations he works for — industrial, commercial, artistic thieves, the government. It's essentially a highly cynical story approached from a comic point of view. Now, I have been robbed, [and] I don't like sneak thieves, people who break into my house and go through my jewelry and take my mother's watch and my father's ring. Chicago is filled with beautiful houses belonging to people of taste, families of many generations who have made some attempt at culture. I thought if we were to make a movie about a man who was going to capitalize on the incredible corporations and the corporate thievery, then we had to go to a city with corporate money; new homes that had no past, sparsely decorated by interior decorators; people who had no roots in culture — the *nouveau riche* who could easily restore what was taken. Because of insurance policies, people with no real emotional investment in their possessions. It was all money. The jewelry the women wore, bought brand-new at Van Cleef and Arpels or Cartier, is easily replaceable, and is only to show how much money their husbands make; it was all a primitive demonstration of wealth. The thievery was no longer a rape — no passion. . . . I went to Denver, I went to Seattle, I went to

Dallas, and I went to Houston. Houston was the best. Not only did [Bud Yorkin] back me up on it, he embraced it. There are cities that have a personality that will dictate the look of a film. And Houston had a very strong personality: super-modern, astringent, clean-lined.

When I read *Paper Moon* I could not imagine that picture taking place in the South [where the novel from which it derives is set]. I'm so sick of pictures in the South, anyway — damn Southern accents, and the South is hilly and leafy and fertile and I saw [the characters] in an arid, flat land. I can't tell you how the idea for Kansas came to me, but it came right away. And the thought of Ryan and Tatum [O'Neal] in little cars in that flat land — it all just fit in one day. Peter liked the idea of Kansas right away.

Film, like politics, is a largely practical art, and practical considerations seem to increase at a geometrical rate when a production designer moves outside of the confines of the studio.

HARRY HORNER: The novel [on which *The Hustler* is based] plays in Chicago. This big center of pool playing. I went to Chicago to look at poolrooms and, of course, the famous poolrooms didn't exist anymore. Rossen said, "Let's see what there is in New York." We went, and I saw some marvelous locations in New York, in Harlem poolrooms . . . some marvelous colors and textures in these old, rundown places.

[Rossen] insisted that he wanted to have the freedom of taking out a wall or getting behind something or taking up a ceiling and shooting down. All this you cannot do on a real location. So, very reluctantly . . . we agreed that we would build [almost] everything. . . . There were six or eight different poolrooms in the story. We had two basic poolrooms and they were remodeled and reshaped — they all have different characters. The main billiards place was a loft on Forty-fourth Street. It was two stories and had great depth. We brought thirty or forty pool tables in. I put paneling on the walls and installed the cash register and a coat rack. It had solid walls and certain columns that were very good. It worked [as a "sound" stage] because there were very thick walls.

POLLY PLATT: The first house that Ryan O'Neal investigated in *The Thief Who Came to Dinner* was the most important to me because it was going to set the style of the picture. It had to be right. I had decided on green [as a motif] all the way back with Jacqueline Bisset's clothes: it was a movie about money, and the color scheme was my own little joke. It had to be a green house and it had to have that kind of horrible modernity and it had to be unlived in. And I had such a paucity of choice in Houston. [Finding] it was a miracle. The owners were terribly cooperative and moved out so that we could shoot for an entire week. (A sizable sum was donated to their favorite charity in recompense.) Their décor was essentially the same. She had the green rugs, and all I had to do was remove stuff that made it look lived in. She didn't let me repaint. The house was essentially green; green was her favorite color. We were just terribly lucky. But I have discovered in movies that you make your own luck. You can't give in, you have to say, This is what I want, and I don't care how hard it is to find it. If you insist and insist and push and push to get it you will get it.

In designing sets in the studio or selecting from among existing rooms that will serve as "homes," Harry Horner observes that "you really design the characters that will inhabit them."

HARRY HORNER: How can the set [in *The Heiress*], mainly the house, contribute? . . . When the father, Ralph Richardson, looks at the house, and when we see the house in terms of this father, it was like a shrine: the memory of his late wife who had had this marvelous taste. He always compares his daughter, Olivia de Havilland, with his wife who was so sophisticated and pretty; he reproaches the daughter, that all she knows and all she does is sit and embroider. The house — to the girl I wanted it to be a cage. So whenever we photographed her, without spelling it out too much, there were walls. We invented a kind of Victorian greenhouse-winter garden in the back of the house. . . . She was caught behind the grillwork of this Victorian building, like a bird. In the eyes of the young lover, Montgomery Clift, this place was supposed to be the most marvelous castle — a crystal palace, the promise of wealth —

Tatum O'Neal, P. J. Johnson, Madeline Kahn and Ryan O'Neal in *Paper Moon,* directed by Peter Bogdanovich. Polly Platt: " . . . the thought of Ryan and Tatum in little cars in that flat land — it all just fit in one day."

Ralph Richardson and Olivia de Havilland in *The Heiress*, directed by William
Wyler. Harry Horner: "The house — to the girl I wanted it to be a cage." The
door that Richardson opens for de Havilland leads to an enclosed "kind of Victorian
greenhouse-winter garden." The sense of confinement is heightened by the small
size of the panes in the window at the left.

that he wanted to possess . . . with the girl. There was a sign, "Dr. A. Sloper," on the fence outside the house. It was a big brass plate that I thought would serve two purposes. It would indicate wealth, it would show that it was *Doctor* Sloper. It's a marvelous opportunity for the boy, who wants to go up to see whether he's all right in this brass-plated kind of place.

Piper Laurie's character [in *The Hustler*] was a very complicated one. Designing [her] little pad I found terribly difficult. She goes to a course at the university twice a week. She drinks. She has no moral strength. She drifts around at night. She takes men in. She is terribly lonely. Basically, she has a very good upbringing. I said, "Where would she live?" Probably in the Fifties or Sixties. On the West Side. Near Carnegie Hall I went to a place where they rent flats to students. We saw the place of a ballet dancer. I made rough sketches of this. They show the sloppiness, bricks on the floor with wood on top for a makeshift bookcase, the kind of books she reads. How people walk in corridors, doors with shiny locks that are replaced by each successive person that moves in. . . . To repeat it successfully is another problem. I now have the feeling that it was too large. Everything becomes so large on the screen. The problem was to design one room in such a way that you could see back into the bathroom. It's a Pullman flat kind of thing. The middle room, which was actually the entrance room, had a Japanese poster. It was never seen, never photographed. But I thought she had a longing for travel.

If well "designed," characters can be defined or expanded by the environments created for them. If inadequately or poorly designed, they can be obfuscated or diminished despite the screenwriter's skill in drafting them or the director's and the actors' ability to bring them to life, as Polly Platt suggests in her perceptive critique of Robert Altman's *The Long Goodbye.*

POLLY PLATT: *The Long Goodbye*, for instance, was not a movie that I thought was particularly well designed. I would have suggested we play those characters in vastly different kinds of environments. I would never have put the detective in that apartment. There was an incredible tension between giving

Montgomery Clift and Miriam Hopkins in *The Heiress*, directed by William Wyler.
Harry Horner: "In the eyes of the young lover, Montgomery Clift, this place was
supposed to be the most marvelous castle — a crystal palace, the promise of wealth
— that he wanted to possess . . . with the girl."

Elliott Gould a kind of pseudoromantic life style, with the old Lincoln and the apartment with its own private elevator, and his total noncommitment to that way of life as a human being. The character in the film was *not* the kind of man that would live in that kind of penthouse-apartment world. I felt the home of the woman in the film, Nina Van Pallandt, was wrong. It wasn't so much the beach, because the [Malibu Beach] Colony is the perfect place for her to live now [i.e., in 1973; Raymond Chandler's 1953 novel placed her in an Old Guard inland community. — D.C.], but the house she was living in — with all those plants. If there were going to be plants, they should have been strangling plants. . . . The interesting thing about Nina Van Pallandt's character was that she was not what she seemed to be. I would have made her home more impossible; plush, overstuffed. In other words, more of a denial of a beach life. I would have put her in clothes that were more of a disguise than the clothes she was wearing. . . . Just a slight refinement of what it was would have been better. I felt there could have been much more precision involved in the visualization of their lives and a much deeper, more subtle comment on what kind of human beings they were.

It is apt to be much more difficult to "design" characters according to preconceived scripted notions when existing structures are to serve as their homes than when studio sets are to be used. If the production designer and the director keep their options open, however, it can happen that an existing structure will redesign and, more important, amplify the character whose living quarters it is to represent.

POLLY PLATT: In *The Thief Who Came to Dinner* the girl [Jacqueline Bisset] was supposedly living in a very elegant home. I thought she was something of an eccentric — maybe she should have been more of an eccentric than she eventually came to be — and I couldn't imagine her living in a really "nice" home. When I went to Houston and found that big fifties-Modern house that was deserted and empty it just struck me as right.

The unfurnished house was never in the script; that whole

concept of a big empty house and the fact that her parents had left it to her. I saw the house and I kept saying, How can I use this monstrosity, this abortive Frank Lloyd Wright imitation? And I just had the idea, I was standing there and I thought, This is an absolutely classic example of what happens to bad money — this big, terribly expensive house in which, now, the three swimming pools are filled with leaves. . . . I . . . thought, My God, how great, if this is her house and she has no interest in it and she's let it go to pieces and just lived in one corner of it where she has an unpretentious warm little kind of home that she's made for herself. A good example of a kind of eccentric way of life of a girl who has taken as a lover a man who was a *thief* — she was attracted to him *because* he was a thief. . . . I didn't think Bud Yorkin would go for it. He really liked it. That really changed it, it had to be rewritten. All the dialogue was rewritten for the scene in which Ryan O'Neal first comes to her house, and all of the scenes that took place between Ryan and her in the house were changed because of the house.

The resourceful production designer equips his décors or looks for locations with structural elements that can enhance the drama of a film; the resourceful director makes use of them.

HARRY HORNER: You give the director possibilities which, in your estimation, are dramatic. [In *The Heiress*] I tried to find architectural elements that could be used dramatically. One of them, the staircase, became very useful. That was the invention of the designer. When [Olivia de Havilland] was happy and running down it she had a kind of joyousness and beauty, and when she was rejected and had to climb back up again it became a kind of obstacle. This staircase was very interesting because some of it you see in the mirror, you see the continuation of it so that it was really an endless staircase — which was very useful in the final scene of the film. The staircase was like à motif.

In *The Hustler* the door [of Piper Laurie's apartment] becomes a terribly important factor. The character played by Paul Newman is not reliable. There is the possibility that he would run away at any moment. She is never secure. How can I place this door? I still want . . . a kind of architectural reality. I start

Warren Oates, Ryan O'Neal and Jacqueline Bisset in the Bisset character's un-furnished house in *The Thief Who Came to Dinner*, directed by Bud Yorkin. Polly Platt: "The unfurnished house was never in the script . . ."

Piper Laurie and Paul Newman in *The Hustler*, directed by Robert Rossen. Harry Horner: "The door . . . becomes a terribly important factor. The character played by Paul Newman is not reliable. There is the possibility that he would run away at any moment."

with a ground plan, twisting it, remembering that it is a brown-stone. The kitchen might have an airshaft. I want . . . enough of a bathroom so that a dialogue can take place there between a man and a girl [standing fairly] far apart. The living room is a step higher than the entrance hall and the rest of the house. It worked realistically enough. It was one of those architectural monstrosities that happen. It gave me the possibility of being at a certain height with the camera . . . to have him stand lower than her and still have both faces together. Sometimes some-thing terribly superficial causes you to invent an architectural logic for it. When you have all this worked out, the lighting somehow works out.

[There were] things in *They Shoot Horses, Don't They?* I wanted very much and which I designed to be shot. There was a whole sequence with a restaurant on one side. Some of the scenes, I felt, would be very good at the bar, so that the dance — one would see the dance in the mirror in back of these people talking. Sydney Pollack did not like it. . . . He was rather difficult to communicate with — not in terms of general con-cepts, but in terms of detail.

POLLY PLATT: I think that directors love that, when you find something that enhances a dramatic situation. Like in *Paper Moon,* there is a sequence — the bootlegging sequence — where he gets the idea to steal the whiskey. [In the script] we open up on Ryan and Tatum in this moosehead lodge-type hotel, and she draws his attention to a bootlegging operation. The first town that I found in Kansas that was right for the picture had this wonderful hotel in it that we later used instead of the lodge. This is a case where a very good idea of mine — and Peter embraced it immediately — was used by the director to its fullest advantage.

In the script they sit in the lobby, and the whole scene is *described.* Tatum goes and looks out and sees [a suspicious-looking man] cross the field and comes back to Ryan and says, "He did this and he did that . . ." Well, this wonderful old hotel had this long outside porch, which I thought would be fasci-nating to use for hiding and long dolly shots up and down as she follows this man. The whole thing, instead of being played inside, would be played as an exterior outside the hotel using this long porch. It certainly did dictate changes [in the script] in terms of pure physical action — all of that was adjusted to the set.

Polly Platt's account of the evolution of a key set in *What's Up, Doc?* and how it functioned in the film documents the creative give-and-take between the production designer, the director, and the cinematographer. It also introduces the figure of the set decorator, who is charged with fleshing out and embellishing the production designer's vision, and indicates that under optimum conditions — a production designer who communicates effectively and delegates responsibility judiciously, and a director who is receptive as well as imaginative — the set decorator can make a material contribution to a film.

POLLY PLATT: The genesis of [the set which served as the home of the young millionaire played by Austin Pendleton in *What's Up, Doc?*] began when Peter and I first discussed this cartoon, this unreal world of the movie. And once that was decided. . . . Originally that millionaire was written as an old man. I couldn't design the set, I just couldn't make a set for him that wouldn't be clichéd. Peter and I know a guy who's young, who has a lot of money and is involved in giving money to worthy academic causes. He's very young and he's very pompous and he's very pretentious. And I did suggest to Peter that he change the character of the millionaire from an old man to a young man. That idea was eventually accepted. Once it had been decided that he would be young, his character became far more interesting; instead of the proverbial old-man philanthropist, he would be a pompous kook.

And then San Francisco, how do rich people live in San Francisco? My original choice for the young man, obviously, was a modern house, one of those houses perched on the Heights looking over the Bay, filled with absurd modern sculpture. And then I thought, Why not take the essence of San Francisco, which is these old Victorian houses on the hills, and have him in his total lack of taste destroy this beautiful house? Instead of going and building himself a modern house, he buys

The ballroom set designed by Harry Horner for *They Shoot Horses, Don't They?*, directed by Sydney Pollack. In the background, behind a railing, is the café that Horner had hoped would be utilized as the locus for dialogue scenes.

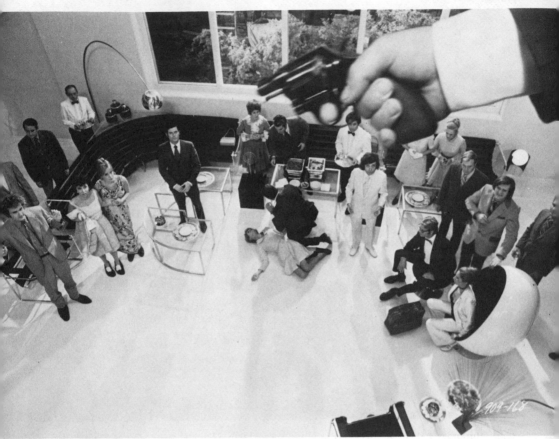

The "vulgar beautiful set" designed by Polly Platt for *What's Up, Doc?*, directed by Peter Bogdanovich. Barely visible on the far left is the steel-hoop sculpture found by set decorator John Austin. Another of Austin's contributions is the egg chair Barbra Streisand sits in on the right.

an old house and modernizes it. It seemed to me that was a classic demonstration of money without taste. I've seen so many people do this — take beautiful places and destroy them — and it enrages me while it is also amusing, it's funny. He took a beautiful old Victorian house and he ripped out the whole inside; the upstairs, everything. . . . Now it turned out to be a very beautiful set — I love that set — but it was meant to be vulgar also. It's a vulgar beautiful set that had everything wrong with it. It was wrong for the house that it was in; it was meant to make you ill at ease. . . . Most of those Victorian houses are long and narrow, so the set was going to be long and narrow and eventually very tall. The set formed itself within the structure of the house.

The wonderful thing about working with Peter is that he encouraged me in all these things, and without Peter it would never have come to what it did. You interest and you influence each other. For instance, I just wanted the set to be modern. It was his idea that the set be black and white. That was Peter's idea, and I loved it. It really set the form. Whenever I faltered in [executing] it he would encourage me. That's another [of the] director's functions: When a good idea happens, if he doesn't back you up on it or if the two of you don't force it through, it gets dissipated. Somebody will say, "Jesus, a whole black-and-white set?" Or the cameraman will say, "I can't photograph this, it's all white."

If you have any courtesy at all, or if you know anything about making pictures or the photographer's difficulties, the first thing you do when you have an idea for a set that's white and that has large windows in it is you go to the photographer immediately and you tell him what you're doing so that he can begin to think about how he's going to photograph it. You don't paint it a stark white, which will flare and glare and make it very difficult to balance the light. You tone it down; we call it tecking. Instead of a pure white, a bed-sheet white, it's a white that has brown in it. Laszlo Kovacs was consulted in the choice of the teck. I made a white floor, which really disturbed him, and he did a lot of things . . . he tried to experiment himself when he was photographing that set. He overexposed the film slightly, he opened up a few stops more than he would ordinarily. And he did what you call "pushing the film," to adjust for the over-exposure. It gives it a kind of soft quality. . . . You can have a concept of all-white walls, and if you're not working on a col-laborative basis with your photographer, if you don't explain to him what you're doing — and why — he can say, "I can't photograph this." Then, naturally, the walls are going to get painted a different color. If he understands what you're doing and if he agrees, then everybody gets what everybody wants.

I had this idea with this Plexiglas. . . . I designed the circular Plexiglas staircase. Peter came in, took one look at it, and said, "What can I do with this wonderful thing?" He staged that fight sequence on the staircase. He made it work in the most wonderful way.

The standby art director did a lot of work on *What's Up, Doc?* We really put him to work. He was a heavy organizer, and very helpful to me. And he made some suggestions too.

Working with the set decorator . . . [is] a wonderfully crea-tive experience when they're good. I hired John Austin on *What's Up, Doc?* You tell him what you're doing, that this is your concept of the set: [the young millionaire's house] is going to be totally modern, you only want modern sculpture, you show him a few things that you saw that you thought should fit in, you draw him some pictures of the type of things you want. I drew a picture of [the types] of sculpture, and when Peter saw the sculpture that John got for one corner of that room — a bunch of steel hoops welded together — he looked at it and said, "Wouldn't it be great in the fight sequence? The guy would fall against the sculpture and the sculpture would fall to pieces." And overnight the prop department made a balsa wood copy of that sculpture so that we could have that the next day for the fight sequence.

John had all the Plexiglas furniture made for me. I designed all the furniture that's in that set except for the big egg chair, which *he* found. . . . That was his idea. And all that wonderful staging that took place around the egg-shaped chair — where Barbra sat in the chair and Ryan O'Neal sat on a little stool next to her, the guy hiding behind the chair and the pie flying past the chair and hitting the wall — all of that came about as a

Madeline Kahn, Red Shaw and Austin Pendleton in *What's Up, Doc?*, directed by Peter Bogdanovich. Polly Platt: "I designed the circular Plexiglas staircase. Peter came in, took one look at it, and said, 'What can I do with this wonderful thing?'"

result of the work of three people: me, who designed the set;
the set decorator who found that wonderful chair; and Peter,
who looked at it and got this great idea.

In speaking of her work as production designer on an Orson
Welles film, Polly Platt paints that prodigious director as alternately vague and specific, intractable and infinitely flexible —
permissive, one is tempted to say — and as a master in at least two
senses of the word. The contradictions in Welles's methods suggest
the variations possible in the director-designer relationship within
the context of a single film, or, even more to the point, a single set.

POLLY PLATT: The film is called *The Other Side of the Wind* and
is not, I believe, complete. He needs more money to finish it. . . .
It's a movie about one day in the life of a movie director who is
. . . sort of a combination of Ernest Hemingway, John Ford
and John Huston. In conversation with Welles it came out that
the man was a self-conscious talent, like Huston — in other
words, one who had pretensions. But the main drive of the
character was that he was a Hemingway man. He was Hemingway, with all those macho Hemingway hangers-on; the only
difference was that he was a movie director instead of a
novelist. John Huston plays the character.
The film encompasses many different forms of storytelling.
There is a young man who is doing an oral history on him, who
is played by Peter Bogdanovich. There is a young team of
*cinéma-vérité* filmmakers who are doing a film on this director.
The director is making a film, the dailies of which he is showing
in the movie. So we are seeing a movie that is composed of the
real-life day of the director, the footage of the *cinéma-vérité*
team, the footage of the film the director is shooting.
I was involved with it for three months continuously on
location in Arizona, where the film that the director is shooting
was shot. We shot two different aspects of the film: we shot the
film that the director was making and we shot scenes at the
private home of the director where he was having a [press]
party at which he was showing dailies of his film. Orson would
read you a scene from [the movie] — I've heard whole scenes of
it and I've seen whole scenes from it — but you don't get to read

the script. He just tells you what he wants in the way of sets and then you go and get it for him.

A few of us literally, physically, built the sets ourselves for the film-within-the-film. Orson taught me how to use foreground miniatures. I learned more from Welles in three months than I think I will ever learn in an entire lifetime. This was my first experience with models, and particularly, his unique use of models. It's just extraordinary what he does . . . with real backgrounds and foreground miniatures. A great many of Orson's incredible shots — for instance, the whole opening sequence in *Othello*, the whole funeral procession — were done with foreground miniatures and real people in the background very far away, up on platforms. . . . You build, literally you build, a whole terrain in front of the camera, and then you put the moving, real actors up on twelve-foot parallels in the distance. . . . It just opens your mind, you have the most extraordinary realization of what you can do with miniatures.

He had me construct this big slanted, adjustable-height table about eight feet long and sixteen feet wide and raked like a draftsman's table. (It got to looking like an airplane because he was using these real wide-angle lenses — these eighteen millimeter lenses — which were so wide that I had to widen the table and the sides of the table began to look like the wings of an airplane.) He had me make these long tubes of Styrofoam, take a torch and burn them, and form these stalagmite shapes that he wanted coming up from the table to a point. They were very small, about twelve or thirteen inches high and two inches in diameter. I stuck them upside down in the table. This was in the foreground of the scene, and what happens when you shoot through the stalagmites with an eighteen-millimeter lens and put a character walking on a platform fifty feet behind with enough light for depth of field — well, it looks like a girl walking through a forest of twenty- and thirty- and forty-foot-high stalagmites. In other words, I created a set that was completely authored by Welles. . . . I was literally guided through the miniature scenes by Orson — not ever giving me any more information than just what he wanted and [then] he would look at what I was doing and tell me what else to do, and we would experiment.

And one day, after I built that board of stalagmites for him, he was going to shoot the sequence [using them] and he was very tired, and he said, "Go out and make a setup, line up the shot. Polly, you go do it, you have a good eye." You place the camera, which is essentially what we call the director's prerogative. Where the camera shall be is what many people feel is the essence of direction. . . . Line it up and look through the camera and decide how it should look: whether the stalagmites should cut off the left edge of the picture or whether I should raise up the camera to include the tops of certain stalagmites. You begin to understand the director's choices . . . what's to be in the frame. Orson did come out and he looked through the camera — Gary Graver was photographing the film — and he asked me to move some of the stalagmites over so that we could see the girl better. And we built something on the left-hand side of the frame because he didn't like the way it looked. It was his shot, it was absolutely his shot, but what other director would say . . . "You go do it, you have a good eye."

I'm talking about all the good parts; there are a lot of bad parts of working for a man like that. He does indeed eat you alive, it's true. We expect our geniuses to be gods in their personal lives — and they're not. And why should they be?

He'd give his instructions: "Polly, come up here, I want to talk to you." I'd come up to his big living room where he was writing the script. He'd have been typing the script all night and he was exhausted and irritable. "Now sit there and shut up. Don't speak. Don't even nod. I want a tower, I want you to use the great whale." (We had this big black sheet of plastic that the wind would get under and blow up; the dust made it all dirty and gray instead of shiny and black. We were using it to create pretentious shapes in this pretentious film [-within-a-film] that this director was making.) He said, "I want a tower, build me a tower, and it has to be this shape." He drew me this shape.

"How tall should it be, Orson, how big?"

"I don't know how tall it should be, I don't know."

"Ten . . . ?"

"I don't know. As big as this house."

I made a mental note of "forty feet."

"And don't nod like that. Just go and do it."

"Well, when do you want it?"

"I don't know. As soon as you can get it ready. Don't ask me any more questions. Just go and make it with the whale and use whatever else you can to make it."

So I left the room with the knowledge that I had to go make this very tall tower out in the desert and of this material that we had. And then, as I was going out of the door, he said, "Oh, yes. And it has to be able to fall over." This is really an apocryphal story.

*

GENE ALLEN: You take an idea and try to fight that through to get it on film. It is sometimes a tremendous battle. . . . A part of that battle, for me as a production designer, is the fight against the notion that "we're paying for color, so give us lots of it." On all of Cukor's films the creative team fought to keep out color. We felt that the unexposed film was itself too colorful. We set guards against color creeping in, against the prop man or decorator adding something at the last minute to "lend a little color." George Huene carried with him neutral-colored netting so that he could quickly eliminate an unwanted color in a dress worn by a background extra, a tablecloth . . . whatever. . . . What the big directors in the past have learned is to try and get somebody working with them in a certain area that will help them execute their ideas all the way along.

POLLY PLATT: In America the director was neglected for years, and then we learned in the 60s, we read *Cahiers* and we developed a certain theory about . . . how directors in America have managed to impose their personalities on their films in spite of the restrictions of the studio system. Now that greater freedom has been allowed the director, there are no longer any barriers, such as being assigned a certain script, being required to use certain actors and actresses under contract to the studio. And having been allowed this freedom, the director, I believe, has to begin now to be even more surveillant, more careful of what he does . . . has to do more and more to make it his own.

More and more, the director has to "write" his own films, even
if he uses a writer. And he has to "design" his own films. As a
designer, you can help him do that.

HARRY HORNER: The designer can create a mystery which allows
the audience to participate in a film a little more. I feel the
mystery that is created by the designer is like . . . de Chirico.
One should never be sure that around the corner is the influence
of another century, or the influence of another character.

# SIX
## The Costume Designer

In *The Parade's Gone By . . .* , Kevin Brownlow commends D. W. Griffith's "fine sense of period, and a historian's approach to his subject, which he managed to transmit to his players." He quotes Dorothy Gish: " 'We used to do our own [costume] research. We went down to the public library and looked up what we wanted.' " It is doubtful that many of Gish's silent-screen contemporaries shared her dedication to authenticity (few had directors who insisted on it), but until the mid-20s, after which time the studios had developed to the extent that they could support vast costume departments, many performers were at least partially the "designers" of their film wardrobes.

Hollywood's misemployment of its great costuming resources during the late-silent period and throughout most of the sound era has made the American cinema an easy target — and, on occasion, a source of great, giddy pleasure. Any museumgoer can tell you that history has frequently been ignored by American film costumes and any filmgoer with a sense of narrative logic has had his credulity assaulted by them. At the beginning of a career that has spanned many decades, Edith Head worked, along with several other designers, for "fifteen, sometimes eighteen months" researching period costumes for Cecil B. DeMille spectacles.

EDITH HEAD: But even then, we did not do authentic period costumes. DeMille wanted glamour and spectacle rather than accurate reproductions. And what DeMille wanted, we gave him. . . . We had a rule in early pictures that the actress *had* to be glamorous. I know I did a picture with Joan Bennett, who went across the prairies with a wagon train, and every time you saw her she had fresh white ruffles. They had rainstorms and floods and fires and Indian raids, and every day the heroine appeared with a new dress with fresh frills at her neck, and a fresh new hairdo and makeup.

The mandated glamour of the leading lady has also resulted in socioeconomically implausible and stylistically eclectic costumes. The wardrobes of the heroines in many thirties films (especially those from MGM) were improbably extensive and outlandishly luxurious, but they were said to take the audience's mind off of the Depression, which apparently hadn't affected the lives of the characters on the screen. The wardrobes of the career girls played by Doris Day in a series of romantic comedies in the early sixties are not quite as easy to justify. Films that scrupulously recreate the temper and the décor of another era have featured costumes that conform either in line or detailing to contemporary modes. Such "modernization" is usually the result of a performer's or a producer's (or, almost as likely, a director's) fear that total authenticity, which would make a popular star unrecognizable or "funny"-looking, might alienate the spectator. Even if the costumes in a period film are as true to the record as they can be, the hairstyles and makeup are apt to be updated. In the superbly designed *Bonnie and Clyde* Faye Dunaway wears authentic if stylized 1930s costumes, but her hair and makeup are done in the style of the 1960s. The *mélange* of styles in American period films is, of course, not unique to America or the film medium, Mlle. Clarion

having urged (in *Réflexions sur l'art dramatique*) her Théâtre
Français colleagues of the 1760s to avoid contemporary elements
in the costumes for Greek and Roman tragedies. Both stylistic
incongruities and modernization are comparatively absent from
the rash of American films of the 1970s set in the recent past.
Such films are relatively easy to research, flaws in them easy to
spot. And with audience nostalgia for times remembered or imagined as simpler and better running high, the differences between
contemporary modes of dress and grooming and those of two or
three decades ago are more likely to be exaggerated than understated.

Though beautiful clothes, worn well, provide undeniable satisfaction, the proper concern of the costume designer is the creation
of clothes that are not *merely* beautiful.

EDITH HEAD: A naked man or woman hasn't much identity. However, you can translate any man or woman through the medium
of clothes into practically anything you want. We costume designers try to translate human beings into something that they
really are not. Clothes are *identification*. My favorite rule is that
every man, woman and child has a dual fashion personality. I
think everybody in the world is a working person. Now that
applies to children who go to school — that's a job. Women in
factories, that's a job, women who drive cabs. A housewife has
a job, an actress has a job; even a woman with money who is
social has certain duties. Same thing for men. And when you are
on your job, I think then you wear what I call "the uniform"
which is correct and applicable to the job you are doing. When
you're out of uniform you can wear anything you want. What I
object to are secretaries, teachers — people who work in what
I call "costume."

THEADORA VAN RUNKLE: I'm not interested in clothes off the screen.
I'm interested in clothes only to the extent that they describe or
express feelings. In real life, how can you possibly have enough
clothes to express all of your feelings, and if this is what you're
trying to do with clothes, how can you possibly be successful?
. . . I missed out on doing *The Great Gatsby* because of a
scheduling conflict, but I dream of someday being able to do a

Faye Dunaway and Warren Beatty wear Theadora Van Runkle's costumes in
*Bonnie and Clyde*, directed by Arthur Penn. Dunaway's overall look is comprised
of a *mélange* of 1930s and 1960s styles.

picture based on a Fitzgerald novel on the same level I did *Bonnie and Clyde,* only with [the] knowledge [I've acquired since]. I'd love to translate his feelings, his moods into clothes.

EDITH HEAD: Years ago, we transmitted to the audience the mood of the character by the way we dressed the actor or actress. Many directors today want you to play against the mood. They say, "We do not want to telegraph to the audience that we're about to have a sad scene." Most tragedies — when people are going to be killed, they don't wear black. Because they don't know they're going to be killed. The designer has to get that from the director, whether you want to indicate the mood or whether you want to surprise the audience. . . . Before I discuss clothes with a star, I always discuss them with the director. What happens is that, naturally, I will have read the script. I have broken it down and made a costume plot. After that I talk to the director.

THEADORA VAN RUNKLE: I just read the script, and I'm so intuitive that I know exactly what I'm going to do as I'm reading it. If I don't get the inspiration at that point, then what I do afterwards is just what the director says he wants or, unfortunately, what the star wants. But all of my good work is done while I'm reading the screenplay. I see it all and then I draw it. I submit the drawings to the director, who makes selections or suggestions, and then I'll show them to the star and the star either accepts or rejects. After the star has approved it or made changes it goes into the workrooms, somebody makes a pattern, it goes into fittings. My great problem and my great ambition is to find directors who have as strong a visual sense as they seem to have had in the past, and who will grant me the freedom to do my work.

EDITH HEAD: I think fashion is a language and very few designers can communicate entirely by words. That's why we use sketches. Hitchcock says, in very few words, what takes me a long time to say. When I go to him and ask, "Hitch, what kind of clothes?," he'll say, "Edith, I really don't care; whatever the *script* says." Hitchcock loves certain colors, but as a rule says, "We'll pretty much go by the script; do me some sketches."

In *To Catch a Thief* Grace Kelly is one of the richest heiresses in the world. At a big costume ball on the Riviera, she had a golden wig, golden mask, golden fan, and she's all dressed in cloth of gold — little golden birds all over her dress and in her hair. Hitchcock had said, "I want her to look like a fairy-tale princess. . . ." A director can so easily give a word picture of what he wants. Such as, "In this scene I want a quiescent look; in this scene an aggressive dress is necessary."

THEADORA VAN RUNKLE: For *The Thomas Crown Affair,* Norman Jewison wanted that Safari look typified by the hat Faye Dunaway wears in her first scene. That's all he really stated.

EDITH HEAD: I did a picture with Martin Ritt which I thought was quite important — *Hud.* He wanted the clothes on Paul Newman to typify a very egotistical man, a very ruthless man. A man who's vain about his appearance, a bit of a braggart. And still — this, I think, is a particularly important thing — he said, "I want you to notice Paul Newman; I do not want to notice his clothes. I do not want to have anything like fancy cowboy boots or a trick belt or an unusually cocked hat. I want them to be honest clothes. I don't want them to be theatrical, but I don't want them to be poor or dull." I would bring in several kinds of shirts, two or three kinds of jeans aged in different ways, different hats. And we would do tests. Because no matter how good a designer you may be, until you actually see something on the screen you are not sure.

THEADORA VAN RUNKLE: Gene Saks had this idea that he wanted *Mame* to look very New York. At first it was very important to him to get a New York designer, which I'm not, but I convinced him that I didn't have to be, because you're dealing with another era and it's part of the universal unconscious anyway. We talked a lot about that particular era in New York, which was principally the beginnings of the great modern art movement in New York, placed importance on having great amounts of money and, of course, had a very definite style.

Grace Kelly and Cary Grant in *To Catch A Thief*, directed by Alfred Hitchcock.
Edith Head: "Hitchcock said, 'I want her to look like a fairy-tale princess.' "

In recalling her involvement with *Bonnie and Clyde,* Van Runkle suggests how importantly the ideas of the costume designer — working, in this case, almost independently of the other personnel whose work usually overlaps hers — can figure in crystallizing (or, possibly, determining) the director's visual conception of a film.

THEADORA VAN RUNKLE: It was my first job; I'd never done anything for the theater or films. Dorothy Jeakins recommended me. She was supposed to do it, but couldn't because she was going to Rome to do *Reflections in a Golden Eye.* I brought a lot of my drawings up to Warren Beatty's and met Arthur Penn there, and they liked my work. . . . I read the script. I drew at home and at an office at Warners for about three weeks. I never met the director of photography and I saw the art director only once. I didn't know enough to seek out the art director; I didn't know how movies were made. Then I made an appointment to show up at Warren's to show them what I'd done. Arthur Penn just leaped up — I'll never forget it — and grabbed me and we started dancing all around Warren's penthouse, and he said, "It's exciting, because *now* I know exactly what the movie's going to look like."

They all went to Texas on location while I prepared things at Warner Brothers and sent them on in big hampers. And the actors, with the exception of Estelle Parsons, who didn't wear any of my clothes, always wore just what I sent them. They didn't argue with me, or change what I had designed, they just wore what I sent. I got some beautiful things from stock for Estelle Parsons, really period and just right, and she didn't want to wear them because they were used. At that point I didn't have any time, so I had to go to shops — I went to the General Store in Beverly Hills, which was specializing in a classic look at that time — and got clothes for her.

The designer's clothes, however appropriate to the time, place, mood and characters of a film they may be, exist in limbo until they are worn by actors and actresses.

Paul Newman in *Hud,* directed by Martin Ritt. Edith Head: "He wanted the clothes on Paul Newman to typify a very egotistical man, a very ruthless man. A man who's vain about his appearance, a bit of a braggart."

EDITH HEAD: I design clothes to help translate actors and actresses into the parts they are playing. . . .

THEADORA VAN RUNKLE (With reference to *The Thomas Crown Affair*): I originally designed for an entirely different girl, a beautiful model named Astrid Hereen who eventually played one of Steve McQueen's girl friends in the film. The designs weren't altered for Faye Dunaway. They just worked because, in a sense, the character was strong enough.

EDITH HEAD: In many instances the director has to help the designer by saying, "I must get a certain feeling out of the actress. You've got to help me visually." I think that nine out of ten people with whom I have worked act differently when they are in costume from when they are rehearsing without costume. It seems to be an inner — I don't know what it is exactly. . . . When you talk with an actress it's a little like a doctor diagnosing a patient. You notice that they do this or that — different mannerisms. When I am working with a star with whom I have not worked before, I have a pretty clinical discussion. Everybody has built-in likes and dislikes. And within the framework of what I can do and what I have to do to satisfy the requirements of the film, I still try to take into consideration the likes and dislikes of the person. Because, psychologically, if an actor or actress is unhappy or uncomfortable, it does, in a way, spoil the characterization. I always show an actor or actress at least two, sometimes three sketches, all of which the director likes. (I do that — show a variety of sketches — with the director too.) And I think that way you make performers feel that you're designing *with* them and not *for* them. I give them a feeling that they are a part of the whole enterprise.

In the script of *All About Eve* Bette Davis is an actress who is in a foul humor. She is having trouble with her love life. She walks around the room and lights a cigarette and turns around and bites her finger — and throws down her cigarette. Now I worked this out with Davis. I gave her a fairly slim dress with panels that flew loose, sort of like a maypole. It's what you call an "action" dress. As she walked around the room the panels flared, but the dress underneath stayed shaped to her body. The panels were fastened onto a belt. When we had the fitting, Bette Davis would walk around the room and whirl and say, "That is good, it is going to help me do that scene."

After actresses become stars, it sometimes happens that they aren't as concerned that a costume fit the requirements of a character and the action of a scene as, say, Bette Davis was in the instance cited by Head. The star system of American films, which is based on the establishment and maintenance of an image, can work against the best interests, as the costume designer perceives them, of both the star and the film.

THEADORA VAN RUNKLE: I had some beautiful gauntlet gloves made for Raquel Welch to wear in *Myra Breckinridge* — white on top and red on the palms, with fantastic big flares beginning at the wrists. And she wouldn't wear them; she cut them off at the wrists. She wouldn't wear a lot of the clothes. She'd say, "I'm a tiny girl, I can't wear these things," not realizing — or refusing to realize — that she photographs like an Amazon; everybody thinks she's *enormous.* But her opinion of herself easily overrides my knowledge of how she photographs. Which is very frustrating.

I'm terribly nice and I'm trying to learn how not to be. . . . Do I sound negative? Maybe I'm down. When you're starting something you're full of fire; maybe my fire has dwindled. . . . I just spent nine months doing *Mame* with Lucille Ball. She's extraordinarily strong, she's an executive, a really formidable businesswoman, and that tends to cancel out, to a great extent, an aesthetic sense. She's used to running her own thing, she's used to telling people what to do and having people respond with, "Okay, okay, is this what you want, Lucy?"

It wasn't until the *very last goddam day* . . . She was putting on the most beautiful hat I've ever seen — I designed it, I don't know where it comes from. I looked through all the fashion magazines of the period — it's 1949 — to find out where I got the idea, I can't find it, it just came. It's black and a tremendous exaggeration of a Spanish bullfighter's cap — I call it the "Picasso" hat. She started putting it on the back of her head, so that she looked pretty. I said, "No, you're supposed to look elegant." She said, "Well, the mad hatter told me that's how it's supposed to go." The mad hatter is the woman who makes the hats at Warner Brothers, and she's a great hatter, but she didn't design it. "The mad hatter told me . . ." I said, *"I'm* the designer!," and she meekly said, "Oh." That's the first time I ever talked to a star like that. I learned after nine months that to get my work on the screen right, that's the way you have to be.

I designed Lucille Ball's face and hair as well as her clothes. We did a test of her with very understated lips, tiny mothlike eyebrows, very natural eye makeup with only one set of false eyelashes, hair flat on top and generally very restrained — that woman looked like Garbo in a dark wig. She looked about thirty-five because she has a beautiful bone structure and beautiful eye sockets. On the set the first day of shooting, the makeup artist was trying to follow what we had decided — I had given him pictures of Garbo — and she said, "I don't look like Garbo," and grabbed those crayons and started doing her own makeup, and so, she ended up with essentially the "Lucy" makeup. She told me later that she spent two nights watching TV to get the looks of people on TV — to get ideas for hair colors and hair styles and makeup. She was looking at *programs,* TV programs, *contemporary* programs — exactly what shade the blondes on the Dick Cavett show or whatever are — in order to feel connected with [contemporary] beauty. Instead of relying on me.

The purity of an idea becomes dissipated and corrupted when you get into egos and people who think they know. . . . Estelle Parsons got "creative" with the wardrobe woman on *Bonnie and Clyde.* There's one scene where she's standing on the highway stamping her foot. She's wearing a 1911 skirt, 1940s shoes, 1950s bag, and some kind of strange top. Maybe not that many people noticed, but *I* did.

The wardrobe man or woman, technically called the costumer, is charged with making sure that all the clothes to be worn in a film are ticketed as to player and scene and ready as needed. He or she sees that the costumes are dry-cleaned or laundered and is responsible for arranging fitting sessions with the actors and actresses. "I like to be at all fittings," Polly Platt says, "because sometimes a costume is made good by the fact that it doesn't fit — it's too tight, or too big." If a designer is not going to be present for fittings or on the set on a day-to-day basis during filming, establishing a rapport with the costumer and communicating the intentions of the designs obviously become important. A close rapport with the designer and a demonstrated ability to carry through the designer's ideas can result in the expansion of the costumer's role — and the solicitation of his or her own ideas. This is especially likely to happen in the case of a period film whose costumes are selected from available stores of clothing (and then, possibly, modified) rather than created outright. "If you know your girl," Platt says, "and if she's at all talented or creative, you can allow her to go through the racks herself and pull stuff that she thinks will be good for the picture." In recognition of the contribution made by the costumer Theadora Van Runkle has worked with on her last several films, and to better describe his actual function, the designer says that in the future she is going to try "to hire him under a different category, as an assistant."

The designer's executed creations are not only worn by actors and handled by the costumer, but photographed by a cameraman against décors created or selected by the art director.

EDITH HEAD: "A good job" is when the art director and the set decorator and the cameraman and the designer all work together and show each other sketches and have discussions. We used to, up until economy set in and we have smaller budgets, make actual [preproduction] photographic tests — film tests — of the stars in the costumes on the sets.

THEADORA VAN RUNKLE: Before *Bonnie and Clyde* I had been working as a commercial artist at home, by myself — the artist as exile! — and I carried it into movies. Later, it dawned on me: Wait a minute, I can get from those people, I can give to them.

On *Mame* I showed the director of photography swatches — everybody had an illustration of all of the costumes. We had no surprises: if they were going to have to shoot blue, they knew they were going to have to shoot blue.

The choreographer and I worked very closely. For instance,

Lucille Ball dances on a piano top in *Mame*, directed by Gene Saks. Theadora Van Runkle: "The fact that it was a musical influenced the choice of materials for the costumes as well as how they were constructed."

Mame's first costume, which I feel is much too flamboyant, went through several working designs. (Of course, the ultimate design was twice as hard to dance in than the one projected in the first place.) I did things with bugle beads, which we couldn't use, because what if one should come off while Lucy was dancing and she slipped on it? The fact that it was a musical influenced the choice of materials for the costumes as well as how they were constructed.

I worked very closely with the art director on *Mame* — we *attempted* to work very closely, but we were both so busy. . . . But we *did* read the same script, and imaginations *do* run in the same channels — especially if they're guided into the same channels by the director.

Van Runkle feels that "a designer's strength lies only in his ability to recreate the past," but says that she does little research in preparation for her period film assignments. "I'm constantly reading about the past in my everyday life, so to a great degree I just draw on that and supplement it with additional, specific research as needed. The only thing I got from Warners [for *Bonnie and Clyde*] was an idea of what the Okies should wear."

Edith Head recalls the considerations that figured in her work on William Wyler's *The Heiress*, "possibly the most perfect picture that I have ever done." Her pride in the perfection of her contribution to the film is somewhat tempered by her belief that designing for a period film isn't really "pure" designing: "All you are doing is interpreting something that's been done before."

EDITH HEAD: Willy Wyler said, "I want this to be a completely honest, authentic costume job. I think the clothes are tremendously important." I went east and worked in the different costume institutes, particularly the big Brooklyn Museum. . . . *The Heiress* was one of the easiest pictures I ever did because I had a blueprint. I knew exactly how many ruffles there were in the petticoats; how many stays in the corsets. . . . It went in two periods. It went from crinolines to bustles, which is a slightly different silhouette.

I worked very closely with the production designer and set decorator. Harry Horner, the production designer, chose the colors of the sets. The art director, who has bigger areas of color to work with, has to consider more than a single costume. We would have meetings to discuss the salon, or Olivia de Havilland's bedroom.

Olivia de Havilland, in the early parts of the film, was an awkward girl. She was never an ugly duckling in terms of clothes, because her father, Ralph Richardson, was very wealthy, but you had the feeling she wasn't quite put together. That no matter how much money she had she never looked *soignée*. That was what we tried to get in the early part, that she wasn't at ease in her clothes.

In the film this man, Montgomery Clift, betrayed her; she was ready to elope with him and he found out she didn't have as much money as he expected and left her. Years pass. Her father has died. She's now an heiress, a fantastically wealthy woman. The man comes back and she pretends to like him still. So she repeats the elopement scene. He knocks at the door but she won't answer. Here she is, looking as feminine and beautiful as she was awkward and ugly in the early part of the film. Here is a woman who now has everything: money, beauty, position — poise. She is sure of herself. She walks up the stairs to the sound of her lover pounding on the door. Wyler said, "I want her to look so beautiful, so feminine . . . she can have him now. She can have anything she wants. And she doesn't want anything anymore." He wanted a light dress because it was evening and all you saw was a woman going up the stairs carrying a lighted oil lamp. I asked Olivia, "What color would you like for this?" Any pastel would photograph a soft misty white in this black-and-white film. She said, "I would love a soft mauve." And Wyler said, "Surely, why not?" because — mauve is a lovely period color.

❖

THEADORA VAN RUNKLE: The two pictures that never "happened" from the costume standpoint were *The Reivers* and *The Arrangement*. Maybe it was because I was doing them at the same time. *The Reivers* also had some beautiful sets which I thought weren't taken full advantage of. . . . But the play's the thing.

Montgomery Clift and Olivia de Havilland in *The Heiress*, directed by William Wyler. Note the creases in the bosom of de Havilland's dress. Edith Head: ". . . you had the feeling she wasn't quite put together. That no matter how much money she had she never looked *soignée*."

My designs should never dominate. They should be there, they should be seen, but they shouldn't be the only things you see.

EDITH HEAD: The human ego is hard to squelch, and I think that every art director — I'm married to one, Wiard Ihnen, so I know — every designer of costumes, every cameraman wants to do something beautiful. It's pretty hard for me not to want to do a beautiful dress and have people admire it. And it's pretty hard for a cameraman not to want to do a lovely shot. And that's why the director is so tremendously important. He is the captain of the ship, and if he lets all of us get out of hand we could very easily handicap a film. A good director does not permit it to happen. And good technicians don't do it.

A sketch of Olivia de Havilland's costume for the final scene in *The Heiress*, directed by William Wyler. Edith Head: "Wyler said, 'I want her to look so beautiful, so feminine . . .'"

# SEVEN
## The Script Supervisor

One of the areas of moviemaking that is seldom explored and little understood is that of the script supervisor. This field, one of the few that has traditionally been allowed to females, is almost entirely preempted by women: The title script girl is still used widely in America and exclusively in France. But in the passage of time and the evolution of responsibilities, the contemporary title of script supervisor is both more accurate and more meaningful.

Frequently and, often, rightly referred to as the director's right (or left) hand, an extension of the director, or his *functioning* assistant, the script supervisor is defined by both Karen Wookey, whose background in the field is in American films, and Hannah Scheel, who has served European and American productions, as a liaison between the director and the editor.

In *La Script Girl*, one of a series of manuals published by the

French Institut des Hautes Études Cinématographiques, Marie-Thérèse Cleris suggests another function of the script supervisor when she labels her "the memory of the film."

The script supervisor, who is physically present throughout the shooting of a film, keeps a series of logs which relate to the technical and the administrative aspects of her overall role in filmmaking. The logs vary in number and form from country to country and from studio to studio, and according to the preferences and dislikes of a given combination of editor and script supervisor, and they are called by different names. The technical logs, for the editor's use, comprise: a basic description of the action and camera setups, with notes on the individual takes (Hannah Scheel refers to it as the master script, Karen Wookey simply as the editor's log); a lined script indicating the camera coverage on a scene, and a daily shot list. A daily log, prepared for the producer or the front office, serves an administrative purpose.

HANNAH SCHEEL: I keep what I call the master script, which is the script I work from on the set every day. And then, at the end of every day, I transcribe the notes that I have made pertaining to the individual takes, type them up in duplicate and draw the lines. I then make a lined script for the editor which indicates the coverage on a scene — full, medium, close shots, reverses and whatever — plus the additions to or deletions of the dialogue in the shooting script.

The lined script is not as detailed as to the action during the scene as the master script, because the editor has that in front of him on the moviola. So, when in my master script I write, "Actor crosses camera right, picks up cigarette," that information I don't transcribe to the editor's first script, what I call the lined script. The lined script is basically for his use during shooting, to get rushes together. At the very end of the shooting, the editor gets what I have referred to as the master script. So he has, at the end, two scripts, the lined script and the master script.

KAREN WOOKEY: [In the film editor's log] one can make either diagrams or word pictures — in any case, descriptions of what the shots are, what the individual setups are, so that the film editor is able to go through your notes and see what the company is shooting. It isn't always done that way, but it is ideal if you can establish a strong liaison between the director and the film editor. Some pictures are arbitrarily shot. The dailies are seen and then, months later, they're turned over to an editor in New York who wasn't aware of the production procedures at all. He is simply brought in as film editor, as a mechanical addition to the company. Because of the pressures that are now exerted on the director, most directors cut as they go along. But there is the occasional exception. These descriptions become even more important [in such cases] because the film editor hasn't been kept up with what's going on on a daily basis.

HANNAH SCHEEL: I also keep, because I tend to pamper my editors, a daily shot list in which I just write down, in continuity, scene numbers and action — very, very briefly described — and what takes were printed. In case he doesn't have the lined pages yet, he has that as a reference.

KAREN WOOKEY: Very often you shoot [a scene from] four or five different [setups], so it helps if the dailies can be arranged in continuity so that you don't jump back and forth — although you might have during the shooting day.

HANNAH SCHEEL: You keep the so-called daily log, where you note down calls, when you started blocking or rehearsing, when you got your first shot, when you broke for lunch, when you resumed shooting, when you wrapped, how many pages were covered that day, how many scenes, the scene numbers, how many setups. All this is bookkeeping for the production office.

KAREN WOOKEY: Some studios require more paperwork than others. There are arbitrary forms which are used, and at one time, we were to report how long it took to light a scene, how long it took to build the dolly track. It added a curious element to the job. I called it a "rat log." I took the position that if there were delays it was up to the assistant directors, who were more familiar with the mechanics of the crew, to make note of

Following are three types of records prepared by Karen Wookey for one scene in *The Parallax View*, directed by Alan J. Pakula.

The handwritten entries in the "Film Editor's Log" record scene numbers; indicate the running times of the take, whether they were completed, and if they were printed (circled take numbers); briefly describe the action of the scene, the equipment and effects used in its execution, etc. This material is transmitted to the film editor on a daily basis, sometimes before the lined script reaches him, to aid in the assembling of the daily rushes.

The typewritten "back pages," or the "legend," elaborate on the material in the film editor's log, and include the director's — perhaps the script supervisor's own — comments on the takes. The abbreviations "nga" and "ngd" stand for "no good action" and "no good dialogue," respectively. Dialogue or fragments of dialogue reported as "lost" (inaudible as recorded) in Scenes 850A, 850C and 850D were improvised and thus do not appear in the lined pages of the script. The "sighs" mentioned in reference to unprinted Takes 6 and 8 of the same scene were also improvised (by Warren Beatty, in the role of Frady). The back pages, or legend, correspond in substance and intent to what Hannah Scheel calls the master script.

The lined script pages indicate who — or what — was covered by the camera in each of the eight setups used to shoot Scene 850 of *The Parallax View*. As noted, Scene 850 is "wild," that is, at the time it was shot, it was not known exactly where it would fit in with the overall narrative. It is not a continuation of the previous scene and does not anticipate the following one. It is possible that in the released version of *The Parallax View* the order of the dialogue and action in Scene 850 will be altered, or that bits and pieces of both will be deleted.

This material is reproduced with the kind permission of Paramount Pictures and Alan J. Pakula.

FILM EDITOR'S LOG       PROD. # 10670

DAY: FRIDAY

DIRECTOR-PRODUCER:       DATE:  6/1/73

ALAN PAKULA       LOG PAGE:  99

| SCENE # | TAKES AND PRINTS | DESCRIPTION | SHOT AT: | SET UP |
|---------|------------------|-------------|----------|--------|
| 850 | 1- 240 Com | A CAM 180mm | 4⁰⁰ | 1 |
| | 2- 2³⁵ Com | MF dark room Best: cross on | bed | |
| | 3- 2⁵⁶ Com | Frady enters + puts bag on | | |
| | 4- 242 Com | dresser, turns as unseen | | |
| | 5- 132 Inc | Jack (on bed) speaks. Frady | | |
| | 6- 2⁵⁰ Com | puts light bulb in LT. CHANGE | | |
| | 7- 2⁵¹ Com | crosses to chair, moves to | | |
| | 8- 1⁵¹ Inc | door, crosses to window & | | |
| | 9  1¹⁰ Inc | sits in chair near Jack on bed | | |
| | 10  1³⁵ Inc | | | |
| | | | | |
| 850A | 1- 2²⁵ Com | A CAM 180mm | 6²⁵ | 2 |
| | 2- 2²⁰ Com | Frady enters for MCL Frady | | |
| | 3- 2⁰⁷ Com | Dolly to full Frady | | |
| | 4- 2⁰⁷ Com | | | |
| | 5- 1⁵¹ Com | | | |
| | 6- 1⁵⁸ Com | | | |
| | 7  1⁵⁸ Com | | | |
| | 8  1⁵³ Com | | | |
| | 9  1⁰¹ Inc | | | |
| | 10  1⁵⁸ Com | | | |

DAY: *MONDAY*

DIRECTOR-PRODUCER:         DATE: 6/4/73

ALAN PAKULA            LOG PAGE: 100

| SCENE # | TAKES AND PRINTS | DESCRIPTION | SHOT AT: | SET UP |
|---|---|---|---|---|
| 850 B | 1 - 2¹⁵ Print 2 - 2¹⁵ ③ 2³⁰ ④ 2⁴⁰ ⑤ 2²⁰ | A CAM 100 mm. FS Jack resting on bed LT. CHANGE ? | 9¹⁵ | 1 |
| 850 C | ① 2²⁵ ② 2³⁰ | A CAM 180 mm CU Jack resting on bed | 9⁵⁰ | 2 |
| 850 D | 1 - 3⁰⁷ 2 - 3⁰⁵ 3 - 3¹⁰ 4 - 3²⁵ 5 - 3⁰⁹ ⑥ 3²⁹ 7 - 3²⁵ ⑧ 3¹⁰ ⑨ 3²¹ ⑩ 3²³ | A CAM 180 mm close tracks Tracks sits for med 2 Jack + Ttrack | 11⁰⁰ | 3 |
| 850 E | 1 - 3¹⁰ 2 - 3⁰¹ 3 - 3⁰⁵ ④ 2⁵⁵ | A CAM 180 mm Tracks x L to R CU Jack (LOCKER) | 12²⁰ | 4 |
| 850 F | 1 - 1³⁰ ② 50 ③ 10⁰ | P.U. 850 E | — | |

850   6/1/73                          A CAM:   180 mm.
1  -  2:40 Comp. quite nice          MF dark room; boots in light cross on
2  -  2:35 Comp.  gd.                bed.  Frady enters and puts bag on
3  -  2:56 Comp. indicatey at        dresser, turns as unseen Jack (on bed)
      start; delayed ent. gd.        speaks.  Frady puts light bulb in (LT.
      otherwise                      CHG.) and crosses to chair, moves back
4  -  2:40 Comp. nga                 to door, crosses to window and sits
5  -  1:32 Inc. ng lt. chg.          near Jack on bed
6  -  2:50 Comp.  PRINT best at
      dresser; not so menacing
7  -  2:51 Comp.  PRINT
      long time with bulb
8  -  1:51 Inc. gd. 1st part PRINT
9  -  1:10 Inc. ngd
10 -  1:35 Inc. ngd

850A  6/1/73                         A CAM:   180 mm.
1  -  2:25 Comp. PRINT               Frady enters for MCL Frady; dolly to
2  -  2:20 Comp; long stall with     CU Frady
      bulb
3  -  2:07 Comp.  PRINT
4  -  2:07 Comp. nga
5  -  1:57 Comp. lost "sorry to
      hear it"  PRINT
6  -  1:58 Comp. sigh at door, crazy
7  -  1:58 Comp. messy
8  -  1:52 Comp. ng sigh, hey, you know
9  -  1:01 ngc
10 -  1:54 Comp.  PRINT

850B  6/4/73                         A CAM:   100 mm.
1  -  2:15 Comp. rpt.                FS Jack resting on bed  LT. CHANGE
2  -  2:15 Comp. PRINT DIRT IN
      APERTURE - PRINT ANWAY
3  -  2:20 Comp.  PRINT DIRT IN
      APERTURE - PRINT ANYWAY
4  -  2:40 Comp.  PRINT
5  -  2:20 Comp.  PRINT

850C  6/4/73                         A CAM:   180 mm.
1  -  2:25 Comp.  PRINT              CU Jack resting on bed  LT. CHANGE
2  -  2:31 Comp.  PRINT              (X cam. for walk to window)
      lost "I'm sorry to hear
      that."
      "So were we."

850.    INT. FRADY'S HOTEL ROOM    NIGHT                    850.

THE ROOM IS DARK. WE DIMLY SEE A PAIR OF BOOTS BEING
CROSSED ON THE BED. JACK IS HALF-LYING, HALF-SITTING
ON THE BED WAITING IN THE DARKNESS FOR FRADY.

850A MCU    850B FS FXX    850CC CLOSE JACK

FRADY ENTERS CARRYING A BROWN PAPER BAG. HE CLOSES
THE DOOR AND STARTS TO TAKE A FEW THINGS OUT OF THE
BAG AND PUT THEM ON THE DRESSER.

                    JACK
        I'VE GOT THE RESULTS OF YOUR
        TESTS.

FRADY WHIRLS AROUND TO FACE THE VOICE IN THE DARK. HE
HAS JUST TAKEN A LIGHT BULB OUT OF THE BAG.

                    FRADY
        HOW'D I DO?

                    JACK
        WE'VE ALREADY RECEIVED AN OFFER
        FOR YOUR SERVICES. 25,000 A YEAR.

                    FRADY
        WHO FROM?

                    JACK
        MANUFACTURERS INTELLIGENCE GROUP.

                    FRADY
        NEVER HEARD OF THEM.

                    JACK
        THEY WORK OUT OF THE HAMMOND
        BUILDING IN ATLANTA.

                    FRADY
        WHAT DO THEY WANT ME TO DO?

                    JACK
        WELL, THEY'RE INTERESTED IN HAVING
        YOU WORK IN THEIR SECURITY PROGRAM.

FRADY STARTS TO SCREW THE LIGHT BULB INTO A WALL FIX-
TURE RIGHT ABOVE THE DRESSER.

                    FRADY
        SOUNDS GOOD TO ME.

                    JACK
        GOOD. JUST ONE MORE THING.

                    FRADY
        WHAT'S THAT?

                                    CONTINUED

850D  6/4/73                          A CAM:   180 mm.
1  -  3:07 Comp. nga                  Frady crosses to window for CU Frady
2  -  3:05 Comp. ok                   and sits for Med. 2 Jack (on bed)
3  -  3:10 Comp. down                 and Frady (on chair)
4  -  3:25 Comp. lose thanks
5  -  3:07 Comp. look at one
      another
6  -  3:29 Comp. PRINT  down
7  -  3:25 Comp. way down
8  -  3:10 Comp. laughy
9  -  3:40 Comp.  PRINT
10 -  3:20 Comp. PRINT very good
      mush "indecent"
11 -  3:22 Comp.  PRINT


850E  6/4/73                          A CAM:   180 mm.
1  -  3:10 Comp.  eyes?               CU Jack.  Frady crosses L to R
2  -  3:02 Comp.  gd."invaluable"     for Jack's look CR
      PRINT
3  -  3:05 Comp. bobble ex FBI
4  -  2:55 Comp. PRINT


850G  6/4/73                          A CAM:   180 mm.
1  -  2:40 Comp.                      Frady sits in for CU Frady
2  -  2:35 Comp. PRINT
3  -  2:15 Comp.  PRINT   simpler
4  -  2:30 Comp.
5  -  2:51 Comp.
6  -  2:45 Comp.
7  -  2:55 Comp. PRINT solid
8  -  2:34 Comp.  PRINT
9  -  1:10 Inc. ngd
10 -  30 plus 2:50 Comp. gd.
      start  PRINT
11 -  2:54 Comp. nga

850.   CONTINUED                                          850. CONT.

FRADY FINISHES SCREWING IN THE LIGHT BULB AND THE LIGHT
GOES ON.

                    JACK
          WHO ARE YOU?

                    FRADY
          WHO AM I?

                    JACK
          YOU'RE NOT RICHARD PALEY.
          YOUR SERVICE RECORDS DON'T
          CHECK.

                    FRADY
          THEY DON'T.

                    JACK
          THERE WAS A RICHARD PALEY
          IN THE FIRST AIR CAVALRY, BUT,
          AMONG OTHER THINGS, HE'S DEAD.

FRADY CROSSES TO THE CENTER OF THE ROOM.

                    FRADY
          I DON'T HAVE TO TELL YOU A THING.
          YOU'RE NOT A COP (THE POLICE).

FRADY MOVES TOWARD THE DOOR.

                    JACK
          I WAS GETTING KIND OF ATTACHED
          TO YOU.  I WOULDN'T STEP OUT-
          SIDE THAT DOOR.

FRADY LOOKS AT THE DOOR AND THEN CROSSES TO THE WINDOW,
PULLS THE BLIND ASIDE AND PEEKS OUT.

                    JACK
          WE SIMPLY HAVE TO KNOW.

FRADY SHRUGS AND MOVES TO THE CHAIR AND SITS.

                    FRADY
          ALL RIGHT.  MY NAME IS RICHARD
          PARTUN.

                    JACK
          WHY DID YOU WANT US TO THINK YOU
          WERE RICHARD PALEY?

                              CONTINUED

850D   850E
TITE 2   CLOSE JACK
850G

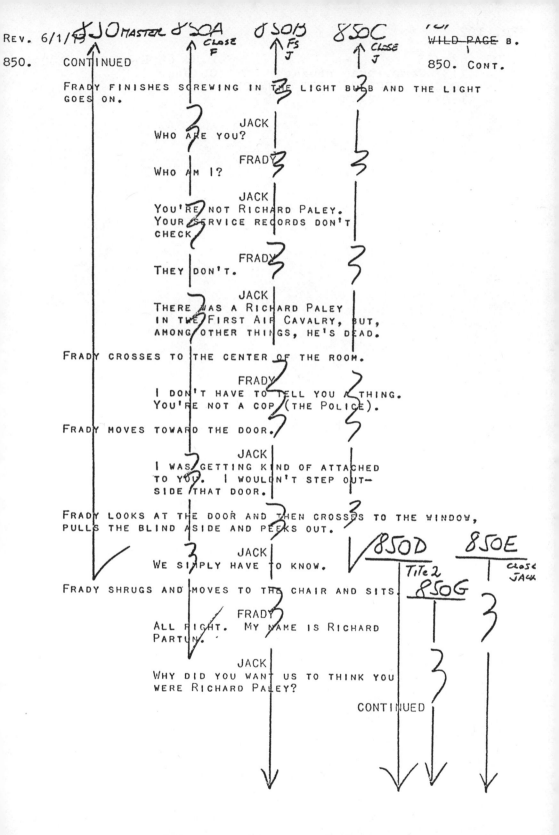

Pg. 102.

850F  6/4/73                          P.U. 850E   A CAM: 180 mm.
1  -  1:37 Comp. nga  repeat          CU Jack
2  -  50 Comp. PRINT SHORT VERSION
3  -  1:07 Comp. PRINT "       "

850D    850E    850G 102  WILD PAGE c.

TITE2    CLOSE J    CLOSE F

FRADY
LOOK — I NEEDED A JOB A FEW
MONTHS AGO IN EL MONTE, I GOT
INTO A LITTLE DIFFICULTY.

JACK
WHAT KIND OF DIFFICULTY?

FRADY
(EMBARRASSED)
IT'S NOT IMPORTANT.

JACK
IT IS IMPORTANT.

FRADY
I WAS DRINKING IN THIS BAR —
I USED TO DRINK A LOT — THE
NEXT THING I KNOW I'M RUNNING
AROUND A LAUNDROMAT ONLY I DON'T
HAVE ANY CLOTHES ON. SOME OLD
LADY CLAIMED I WAS TRYING TO —
YOU KNOW — MOLEST HER.

JACK
WERE YOU?

FRADY
I DON'T KNOW. I DON'T REMEMBER
ANYTHING — HOW I GOT THERE, WHY,
WHAT, NOTHING. ALL I KNOW IS
I GOT ARRESTED FOR INDECENT EX-
POSURE — AND — I DON'T KNOW —
A THING LIKE THAT FOLLOWS YOU
AROUND. YOU TRY TO GET A JOB —
SEX OFFENDER. I'M NO SEX
OFFENDER.

JACK
I'M SURE YOU'RE NOT.    850FPU 850E

FRADY
WHAT I THINK REALLY HAPPENED
IN THAT BAR IS THEY PUT SOMETHING
IN MY BEER THAT MADE ME TAKE MY
CLOTHES OFF.

FRADY IS HANGING HIS HEAD, MORTIFIED.

CONTINUED

850D 850E 850F 850G
↑ TiT@2  ↑ CLOSE  ↑  ↑ CLOSE 103.
          J              F
                              850. CONT

JACK
- IF THAT'S ALL THERE IS TO IT,
WE'LL CHECK IT OUT WITH THE EL
.MONTE POLICE. THERE'LL BE NO
PROBLEM.

FRADY CAN'T SAY ANYTHING.

JACK ·
RICHARD, I'VE TRIED TO BE A FRIEND
TO YOU, HAVEN'T I?

FRADY
YEAH - YOU HAVE.

JACK
-YOU SEE SINCE WORKING AT PARALLAX
I'VE FOUND THAT PEOPLE WHO'VE .HAD
REAL TROUBLE IN THEIR LIVES, SO-
CALLED ANTI-SOCIAL PEOPLE, IF I
CAN EARN THEIR LOYALTY - I CAN GIVE
THEM A SENSE OF THEIR OWN WORTH -
AND THAT'S VERY REWARDING, BELIEVE
ME. I HONESTLY THINK THAT WITH -YOUR
NATURE - YOU'LL BE MORE RELIABLE FOR
SECURITY WORK THAN ANY SEMI-RETIRED
EX-FBI AGENT THAT THEY COME UP WITH
IN A RISK SITUATION - I BELIEVE YOU'LL
GO RIGHT DOWN THE LINE. THAT'S
SOMETHING MONEY CAN'T BUY.
     (PAUSE)
YOU'RE INVALUABLE, RICHARD.

them in their reports. I basically feel that changing the setup, a time-consuming activity, is the director's prerogative . . . . Ideally, it's most interesting for me if my function relates directly to the director.

The script supervisor's administrative record-keeping is probably responsible for the school of thought that regards her as the producer's secretary, or, even more denigrating, as the producer's "spy." (Indeed, many script supervisors in the past have risen from the ranks of producers' secretaries, according to Wookey.) Her technical record-keeping has probably given rise to the popular misconception of her as the director's secretary. Though the large proportion of her total working time that is devoted to administrative and technical logs lends some measure of justification to her old, but occasionally still employed American title — script clerk — even under the least fortuitous circumstances, the script supervisor is far more than just a clerk, just as the most restricted film editor is more than just a "cutter."

On the set, on a day-to-day basis, the script supervisor is responsible for timing the individual takes and scenes, for "screen direction looks," continuity, and the fidelity of the dialogue to the script, or the coordination of the dialogue.

The script supervisor is also responsible for "screen time" in the sense that her running estimates of the number of minutes or seconds that the scenes, as shot, will play are the basis of the film's projected running time.

KAREN WOOKEY: The master shot [usually a medium or long shot of a scene played through from beginning to end] will, in dialogue terms, give you a fairly accurate estimate of what a scene will run. But when there are intercuts of other kinds of action — crosses, entrances and exits — I think it's up to the script supervisor to estimate what time will "hold." We can be used to pretime a script, and there are script supervisors who specialize in pretiming. Usually, a production office will engage someone to pretime a script on the pretext that it is too long, or the reverse. It's really roulette, because until you know a director and the physical aspects under which you'll be shooting, you can't really give an accurate timing. An entrance and an exit out of a hotel in Monaco may read one way, and you allow so much time for it, but if there's some extraordinarily interesting thing happening on the steps, naturally the director's going to take advantage of it, and it extends the time.

Whether or not a script has been precisely pretimed, the producer and director have made some prediction of the length of the film it will yield. Advance calculations may suggest that a 120-page script will provide a two-hour movie. Once shooting starts, if the script supervisor estimates that the first (presumably typical) forty pages filmed will result in sixty minutes of scene time, it is possible that some of the scenes already executed will be deleted or shortened or, more likely still, that yet-to-be shot scenes will be dropped, compressed or paced faster.

KAREN WOOKEY: In other cases, where a film is running short, additional scenes are written. But as a general rule, very seldom do you expand; the tendency is to shoot more than you need.

In covering a single piece of action from more than one vantage point, the changing position of the camera *vis-à-vis* the actors, who remain stationary or moved within a fixed and consistent area from setup to setup, can result in setup-to-setup discrepancies in the actors' "screen direction looks" — the side of the screen they face — and destroy the geographical unity of the scene as a whole. The script supervisor is responsible for the uniformity of screen direction looks from setup to setup.

HANNAH SCHEEL: If in the master shot, Actor A is camera right and facing in one direction and Actor B is camera left and facing in the other, when you go in to do your coverage shots — angle shots, individual close-ups, and so forth — you can't place the camera so that Actor A, who is camera right in the master is now camera left. His "looks" and his physical relationship to Actor B would be wrong — different from the relationship originally established in the master shot. If you did you would be crossing what we call the "stage line," that all-important, imaginary line [which, once crossed, violates previously established spatial relationships and] makes it impossible for the editor to cut [together shots of one piece of action taken from more than one point of view].

Crossing the stage line is one of the things I'm a stickler on. I just finished a feature with a first-time director. He didn't understand, I couldn't make him understand [that, in one instance, he had crossed the stage line]. The cameraman didn't help me because he didn't want to change his composition — he loved what he had. I said, "You may love what you have here, but it's going to be impossible when it gets into the cutting room." Ten years ago, I would have been a bitch and staged the scene; that I don't do anymore. I tried to illustrate what they were doing wrong, and they could not see it, so all I could do was say, "Okay, but I told you," and make a note in the script that the stage line had been crossed. You can be very, very bitchy and note "S.U.P." — shot under pressure — but that I reserve to protect cameramen, who are sometimes forced into doing shots that they don't approve of.

A lot of new directors, because they worked on or have seen a lot of television commercials, in which you can do practically anything you want, say, "But it's done on television all the time." It's one thing in a television commercial and another in a situation where you're trying to sustain a relationship, because it's confusing to both the eye and the mind when you hop from one side of the screen to another.

It is in her capacity as the watchdog of the continuity of a film that the script supervisor functions as its "memory." If an actor pronounces either as eye-ther and accents the first syllable of despicable the first time he speaks the words, then, barring a motivated change in pronunciation or inflection, he must do so throughout a film. If an actor's necktie is slightly askew and his cigarette smoked halfway down in the last frame of one segment of a continuous sequence, his necktie must be slightly askew and his cigarette smoked halfway down in the first frame of the next segment of the sequence, which may be filmed many days or weeks later. The script supervisor relies on notes, Polaroid snapshots and her own powers of observation and recall to insure against verisimilitude-destroying lapses in consistency and continuity.

Obviously, it is humanly impossible, even with the help of *aides-mémoires*, for the script supervisor to remember *every* nuance of the action, the pronunciation and inflection of the dialogue, the décor and the accessories in a film. Marie-Thérèse Cleris stresses the importance of developing a "sense of values" which, judiciously applied, result in a "hierarchy" of details. Hypothetically, she says that it is far more important to remember that an actress wore a radiant smile as she left an exterior garden setting than the fact that she carried her hat in her left hand. If the actress were to enter a studio-set house in an immediately following but separately filmed scene with her hat in her right hand, it would far less disastrous than if she were to be frowning. "When you've been doing it for a while you begin to realize what to look for, rather than to look for everything," Karen Wookey says.

With regard to the part of the script supervisor's job that is concerned with the fidelity of the spoken dialogue to the written dialogue, Karen Wookey says, "If specific dialogue is to be used, then we are responsible for seeing that it *is* used." In carrying out this responsibility, the script supervisor is increasingly called upon to run lines with the actors prior to the shooting of a scene and to read, during shooting, from an off-camera position, the lines to be spoken by other actors whose parts of the scene will be filmed at another time. The services of a separate dialogue director, who traditionally cued actors and read off-camera lines, are less frequently employed in American feature filmmaking today.

KAREN WOOKEY: A lot of people think there should always be a dialogue director on a film, but I enjoy that part of it, I think it's part of our function.

HANNAH SCHEEL: I did a picture last year where we had a dialogue director, and that was a boon to me. Though born in Paris of Danish parents, if anything I have a British accent, and it's very difficult for me to cue actors on lines, because actors very easily pick up an accent. It's also very difficult for me to read off-camera lines to actors, because they do get thrown by what is very definitely an accent.

Films in which improvisational techniques are used "change the role of the script supervisor," according to Scheel. "Improvisation makes the script more challenging to us."

The script supervisor must note all extemporized verbal additions in her script, deleting or revising at the same time the written but unspoken or partially spoken dialogue. In cases where all or a portion of the action was also improvised at the moment of shooting, the script supervisor is wise, according to Hannah Scheel, to "forget about the dialogue. The one thing you concern yourself with there is the action, the pauses and when they do this, that or the other thing. You take down a key word — let's say that four gentlemen were sitting there and on a certain word one would cross over and stand camera right — and the action in each and every take. You can always have [the rest of] the dialogue played back." If, basically, this sounds no more "challenging" than conventional stenography, it must be remembered that the content of the improvised dialogue, if not surveyed closely, can result in contradictions to the narrative and discrepancies in character. The actors, says Karen Wookey, "can't extemporize out of context, and sometimes it becomes necessary, if they vary in some way from the continuity of the dialogue, to intercede."

The script supervisor may be invited by the director to intercede or assist in other areas or to include her own opinions on the footage catalogued in her notes to the editor.

HANNAH SCHEEL: I did a picture earlier this year with a director who came out of the editorial ranks and, therefore, was unbelievably good in staging scenes and covering them for the cutting room. So, before we started the picture, he said, "Hannah, do me a favor. Don't worry too much about cutting, because I've already cut the picture in my head. But," he said, "watch the acting for me, because I feel weak there." It was basically an action film, but there were a couple of intimate dramatic scenes. He said, "When we get to those scenes, concentrate on the acting and let other things ride if necessary. I want your very honest opinion." I don't think it's fair to this director to divulge his name, because he's a man who makes his living as a director. I don't think it's fair to him to reveal that he had the guts to tell his script girl that he feels a little weak in the dramatic department.

KAREN WOOKEY: The notes for the editor include comments made by the director about each take. Alan Pakula [with whom Wookey worked on *The Parallax View*] annotates the takes in a very specific way: "The first part of the scene was good, the last part fell apart." I try, whenever I can, to use his exact words, so that, later, when he looks at the footage, it'll be easier for him to recall it. Mr. Pakula is an example of somebody who seems to enjoy hearing other people's opinions and listens to them. He's very open; he's willing to accept help from the people who are there to help him. As a result, you can make known your opinion. John Frankenheimer [with whom Wookey worked on *The Iceman Cometh*] is a different kind of director, a different kind of personality. He's a very flamboyant kind of leader-director, and, personally, he is very dramatic. The result is that he dominates and smothers the reactions of the people around him. . . . In general, I'm expected, and I think I'm free to include in the editor's notes whatever I can that may not have been noted by the director. The observations that I make might be about things the director had not noticed or was not looking for, for example, an actor rises too soon or sits too soon. Or, if I am particularly enthusiastic about something I will so state; I am not consciously influencing. I think it's a contribution, which the director can weigh and either accept or reject. . . . As with so many other jobs, the responsibility varies depending on the combination of people.

Script supervisors, like other movie personnel, claim that for the most part the range of their responsibilities depends on the "personality" of the director. Yet, as is the case with other types of movie artists and technicians, the personality of the individual script supervisor and the relative strength or weakness of other members of the filmmaking team also play a part in expanding or contracting her role. Marie-Thérèse Cleris exhorts the script supervisor to be authoritative yet diplomatic; she must not be intimidated by directors whose responses to interruptions and corrections aren't likely to be favorable, but must avoid criticism if she has nothing positive — no alternative — to suggest.

Karen Wookey says, "Some directors work in such a way that they have either people they've worked with in the past, or a pattern that they work in, that I feel doesn't utilize the script supervisor to the fullest extent. They rely on their familiarity with a particular assistant director or a particular system." She recalls that in the case of *Flap*, Sir Carol Reed's assistant director "had his ear, so to speak, so whatever notions or ideas Sir Carol had went to the assistant director, who hopefully disseminated them to the company. And their relationship and their rapport was the pillar which supported the whole company."

Wookey suggests that the assistant director or directors ordinarily render more assistance to the production office than they do to the director. "Every once in a while," she says, "an exceptional assistant director who really understands that he is assisting the director will come through. But for the most part they're operations officers. It's just the way the industry is set up." For this reason and because, as Hannah Scheel points out, "the assistant director rarely gets to direct," Wookey feels that working as a script supervisor is "much better training than the sort of structured and ritualized assistant director's route. As a script supervisor you can learn in a much shorter time what a director does, without involving yourself in the production problems that surround becoming a director through the prescribed channels." She adds that "once you're a director you should be free of those production problems; they are handled by someone else — the assistant director!"

Ironically, Hannah Scheel predicts that the second assistant director, who is now responsible for some of the script supervisor's traditional administrative tasks — "when the extras were called, when they were released, when the first shot was made, when you broke for lunch" — will be eliminated from film crews in the future, and his responsibilities will revert to the script supervisor. The first assistant director, too, may become "a thing of the past." Scheel says that it is altogether likely that his current responsibilities will be assumed by the production manager.

Writing in 1964, Marie-Thérèse Cleris notes with satisfaction that in Mexico, apprenticeship as a "script boy" has become "a more normal channel for aspiring directors than that of assistant."

Since part of the script supervisor's responsibilities relate to the producer, her relationship with the producer, especially if he is closely involved with the film while it is before the cameras, can be instrumental in determining the perimeters of her function. Rick Rosenberg, of the TV-movie production team of Christiansen and Rosenberg, says, "The script supervisor on our last picture came in and rewrote half the script. A couple of her ideas were very good. Even for two of those ideas, it paid to give her that freedom by saying 'Hey, what do you think?' "

The script supervisor is more likely to play a part in what Marie-Thérèse Cleris calls the "literary" aspects of the film if her entry into a project is early, while the script is still in preparation. Rather paradoxically, the stenographic and typing skills which Cleris insists are essential to the script supervisor's job are apt to facilitate her early entry and to be heavily relied on during the preproduction stage. Yet it is at this time that the script supervisor is best able to establish a harmonious relationship with both the director and his project and to play, or lay the groundwork for playing, a creative role in it. By acquainting herself with "the nuances of the subject, the transformations it undergoes, the controlling idea and the precise intentions of the authors," she is better equipped to remind the director of these at a later stage, when they might be temporarily forgotten in the heated confusion that attends the shooting of the film. And, during the preparation, "it is not prohibited that the script girl give an opinion, suggest an idea, make a personal contribution to the film."

At the time Marie-Thérèse Cleris wrote *La Script Girl*, American crews were usually larger than French crews. (This is not necessarily the case now.) Consequently, she says, American film technicians — the script supervisor included — are more specialized and confined to their specialties than French film technicians, less apt to "give an opinion," etc. Hannah Scheel was associated with Orson Welles during the preparation of *Touch of Evil* in 1957. And it is just possible that *because* she was not the functioning script supervisor on the film, but rather, as she insists, the director's "Gal Friday," her recollections of working with Welles refute Cleris all the more dramatically.

HANNAH SCHEEL: Welles wrote each and every word. The way you work with him on preparing a script is that he has an idea, and he may or may not discuss it with you. When he did discuss it, what would usually happen was that he would give me a scene, ask me to read it, then come back and say, "Well, what do you think?" And if I just said, "Oh, that reads fine," he'd be very upset. "It either reads great," he would say, "or there's something wrong. What do you mean, 'It reads fine.'" Then I would say, "Well, for me, that doesn't ring true," or, "for me, that doesn't work." And he'd say, "You're right," or, "you're wrong." But he was interested. He didn't need you, but he used you as a springboard or bouncing board. Not for new ideas; new ideas he would just take and run with. And if you had told him it would never work, he couldn't care less, because when he got a new idea it completely took hold of him and he would be the one who discarded it. The respect that man has for the audience is incredible. The audience is a very, very revered monster. And let's face it, I do approach a story basically from the point of view of the feminine audience.

At one point he came into my office, where I was clean-typing some pages, yanked the paper out of the typewriter, and said, "Don't ever let me catch you just sitting typing. If you've got nothing else to do, you just sit and think. You're too valuable to be a typist." For that you'll work, willingly work, around the clock. Because he relies on you, you stretch and you perform ten times better than when you're working within a given set of rules, where you're only allowed to do this, that or the other thing. Working with him was a learning experience of tremendous importance not only technically, but also storywise. He challenges you — "challenge" is the operative word — and will not accept the statement "that's not possible." He dares you to use your imagination. He makes you part of it regardless of how you're involved in it. It may be an Orson Welles picture, but during the making of it he makes it clear it's everybody's picture.

# EIGHT
## The Editor

Karel Reisz begins his definitive *The Technique of Film Editing* by quoting V. I. Pudovkin's *Film Technique*: "Once more I repeat, that editing is the creative force of filmic reality, and that nature provides only the raw material with which it works." In editorial and other terms the earliest films were very close to nature — theatrical nature. Even the most sophisticated efforts of the Lumières and Méliès suffered, as Reisz writes, "the limitations of theatrical presentation." He notes that in Méliès' *Cinderella* (1899):

> . . . each incident — like each act in a play — is set against a single background and is self-contained in time and place; scenes are never started in one place and continued in another; the camera . . . remains stationary and outside the scene of the action — precisely as does the spectator in the theatre auditorium.

The American Edwin S. Porter advanced the art of film beyond the stage of what Reisz calls "motion *tableaux*" by creating "an illusion of continuous development" in *The Life of an American Fireman* (1902) and linking parallel action by "continuity of idea" in *The Great Train Robbery* (1903). Individual scenes in the early films of D. W. Griffith were photographed from more than one camera setup, and the resultant footage cut together to lend emphasis to the details the director wished to point out. By the time of *The Birth of a Nation* (1915), Griffith had managed to achieve on film the density of detail that had previously been the primary preserve of the novel. His use of montage in *The Birth of a Nation* and, especially, in the following year's *Intolerance*, strongly influenced the Russians Pudovkin and Eisenstein, who drew from and expanded upon Griffith's techniques and used the result — a startling and, according to André Bazin, in Volume 1 in *What is Cinema?*, "synthetic" juxtaposition of images — to score dramatic and ideological points. Though there are many silent directors who did not rely heavily on editing to achieve their effects (Bazin's impressive examples are Stroheim, Murnau and Flaherty), the opinion is often expressed that film editing reached its apogee both as an art in itself and as a determinant of a film's style and substance in the late silent era. Writing in 1953, Reisz laments that the "tradition of expressive visual juxtaposition, which is characteristic of the best silent films, has largely been neglected since the advent of sound." Early sound-recording equipment, by limiting the mobility of the camera, reduced the number of camera setups possible — the film medium returned to theatrical nature, one might say — and, therefore, the film editor's options. But even after technological improvements once again allowed extensive camera coverage, the latitude enjoyed by the editor of silent films was not fully restored. The sound-film editor functions within the framework imposed by recorded dialogue.

DANIEL MANDELL: I think cutting was more sophisticated [in silent film days] than now, because the film was much more flexible and you didn't have sound to explain things. You didn't want to cut to title [cards] every other foot or every other second to explain things. As a matter of fact, most directors tried to

avoid using titles by staging scenes or constructing the story
in such a way that [the] action was understood not so much
through the words, but by the manner in which the people
acted. [But] you could change the story with titles. Instead of
a man being a girl's uncle, he could be her father; instead of
being her brother, he could be her second cousin. . . . The [title-
card] dialogue was changed . . . and sometimes a scene would
be given an entirely different meaning. I've worked on pictures
with title writers, and between us we'd reconstruct the whole
story. It happened very often, but most of the time the director
had the final say.

Bazin minimizes the differences between silent- and sound-
film editing style, arguing that:

> . . . history does not actually show as wide a breach as might be
> expected between the silent and the sound film. On the contrary
> there is discernible evidence of a close relationship between certain
> directors of 1925 and 1935 and especially of the 1940's through
> the 1950's. Compare for example Erich von Stroheim and Jean
> Renoir or Orson Welles, or again Carl Theodore Dreyer and
> Robert Bresson.

And Reisz acknowledges, in the Enlarged Edition of his book,
published in 1968, that developments in world cinema in the late
50s and afterward have largely invalidated his putdown of sound-
film editing. Ernest Walter (among others) isn't quite as impressed as Reisz is by these developments. In *The Technique of
the Film Editing Room*, Walter writes that "some of the most
modern techniques are merely variations of old systems, using
up-to-date materials." Daniel Mandell describes the materials in
use at the beginning of his career in the silent era.

DANIEL MANDELL: Reels, the rewinds, a pair of scissors and your
eyes. We had no moviolas. . . . Moviolas came in . . . I would
say about 1925. You got so that you could by jerking motions
pull the film through your hands and almost be able to watch
the action. There were editors, of course, who would use a
magnifying glass — you know, to [insure that the position of

an actor's hand in a long shot matched its position in a close shot]. . . . The splicing machine came in not long after [the moviola]. Before that we used to scrape the film with a razor blade and then put cement on one piece and then . . . stick the other piece to it. And you'd see every splice at almost every cut like a little jump.

. . . It was more of a hit-or-miss proposition. You would have it spliced together and then take it to the projection room. If there were any errors or mismatches you'd take it back and have another try.

Reisz asserts that in the silent days the director and editor were "usually the same person," and Walter claims that the "early (i.e., silent) filmmaker (presumably the director) did everything himself — photography, chemical processing, editing, titling, even to the extent of eventually becoming the projectionist." Today . . .

FREDRIC STEINKAMP: A director has a script which a writer has done or which he has worked on with the writer. He shoots that script, and the editor cuts it with the director. Now, a director could write his own script and he could edit the film — actually, it's possible. The editor, who is an extension of the director's arm, is also a specialist — like a writer. . . . [The director] gets an objective point of view from him.

Whoever the film editor might be and whatever else he might do, the person who edits a film was, and is, responsible for the selection of the pieces that make up the whole, and their assemblage. The extent to which the editor of record in modern films exercises his own discretion in the selection and assemblage process "must," according to Reisz, "necessarily vary from one unit to another." The latitude enjoyed by an editor depends on the editor himself, on the producer, but, according to David Bretherton, "more on the director."

The following pages, consisting primarily of opinions and professional recollections provided by five film editors, explore the functions of the editor during the preproduction, production and postproduction phases of filmmaking and examine the editor's relationships with the director and other contributors to film.

The Model UL-20-S Moviola editing machine is typical of facilities used for many years by editors in viewing and marking cuts on 35-millimeter film footage.

DAVID BRETHERTON: You read the script and you say, Can I do it? . . . I had a chance to do *They Shoot Horses, Don't They?* I was quite depressed myself at the time, and the combination of that and the depressing subject matter — it would have overwhelmed me, it would have been a detriment to my work. The version of the script I read — though they said it was going to be revised and lightened — was so unrelenting.

I start with a picture, hopefully, a week or two before it starts shooting. That way I can really absorb the script, see what the director's trying to say. You try to figure out in what way the director — is he Sidney Furie, or George Stevens, or is he Michael Crichton, [who] knows how to write, God knows that, but doesn't know much about making films. [Bretherton served as film editor on *Westworld,* Crichton's directorial début. — D.C.] The nuances lost — maybe you can contribute there. . . . When I read the written word, I envision the whole picture — literally. I can see that some things will not transpose well onto the screen. They're either too "articulate" or too strong. . . . I'd love to have more preparation time.

FREDRIC STEINKAMP: It's better if a film editor can go with the company two or three weeks before they start shooting because he can be of great help in the editing of the script before you even shoot. You can critique the script from an editor's standpoint and present the director with [options] or problems. You might say, "I don't really understand what the motivation of this character is; it isn't indicated in the dialogue, and I can't see that it is ever brought out visually, subtly or otherwise." Or you can say, "Here's one paragraph that says 'Indian fight' that is probably going to be expanded into an eight- or ten-minute sequence. Isn't this going to put the picture over in terms of running time?" And then you might suggest that, in order to bring the film closer to a previously estimated, or manageable, running time, sequences that seem redundant, or redundancies within sequences, be deleted. Now, the director can take this critique and throw it away — but at least he had another person, with another point of view.

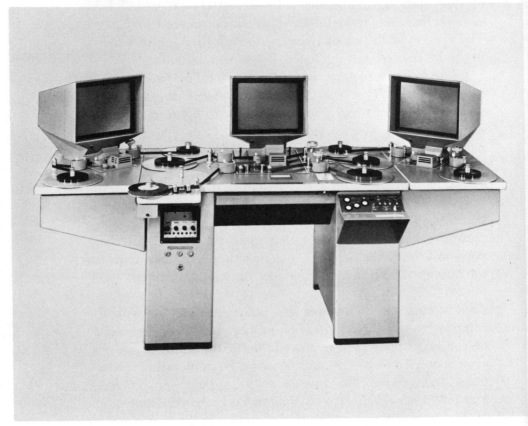

A Kem editing table with three picture heads. Multiple picture heads facilitate the assemblage of footage of the same scene shot from different points of view.

DANIEL MANDELL: Sometimes if a scene ran too long and there was more dialogue than necessary to make the points, I would suggest to Mr. Goldwyn to have the scene rewritten. It was pretty tough to get him to do anything like that because he always hired writers with big names and . . . he probably had more confidence in them than in me. I wouldn't say anything if I could see the cuts, see that I could make the cuts in the film. But sometimes dialogue is written in such a way that one line is a lead into the next, and that is a lead into the next line, and so on. If you try to drop a couple of lines, you find — the scene, it doesn't make sense. You could, as a film editor, delete whole scenes you felt could be left out and not be missed, but in many cases you'd find that there'd be dialogue that was a plant for something that came later. So you'd have to find a way to incorporate those things in other scenes. In a case like that, you'd suggest a rewrite.

DAVID BRETHERTON (With reference to working on *Westworld* with Michael Crichton): "Isn't this scene too slow?" I might say. "It reads beautifully," he'll say, "But it plays too slow." "Well, what do you do?" "Well, drop this line, drop that line, they're redundant. Either you show it or say it; don't do both. . . ." And he'd ask, "Why didn't I see that?" "Simply because you aren't experienced in the film medium. You'll learn!" And it's wonderful to experience that; then you feel you're contributing something.

When the art director or a continuity-sketch artist is extensively involved in the preparation of a film — "storyboarding" it to "help the director get in and out of scenes," as Gene Allen puts it — he may take over or share the preediting task.

DANIEL MANDELL: I did a picture [*The North Star*] with Lewis Milestone, and he [laid out] all the continuity sketches and said, "Now, this was my intent." It usually went together pretty well . . . by following . . . the original idea.

Once a film starts shooting, the editor, ordinarily under the guidance of the director, begins selecting and assembling pieces of film.

FREDRIC STEINKAMP: You're with the director every day, running dailies of the previous day's shooting. . . .

FRANK KELLER: Generally, a director and I discuss sequences ahead of time, so I have a pretty good idea of what he has in mind. . . .

FREDRIC STEINKAMP: You discuss the sequence — its values, its point of view, having the point of view of the whole script in mind already. . . .

FRANK KELLER: And in cases where he has two or three different takes, he usually tells me which take he likes the best and we decide if it will work matchingwise. . . .

FREDRIC STEINKAMP (With reference to working with John Frankenheimer for the first time on *All Fall Down*): He'd be very specific. He'd say, "I don't like that reading, I don't want that in the picture," or "That angle I'm in love with, I want that in. . . ."

DANIEL MANDELL: William Wyler would print three takes, and in many cases he'd want you to use a piece of each take, and then sound tracks from something else in another take. . . .

FREDRIC STEINKAMP: Obviously they always pick the takes, and you always agree. And if you don't agree, you have a discussion and you usually lose. . . . Then I'd just go to work. When I haven't worked with a director before I am terribly nervous until I run a cut sequence with him. Even though we've discussed, intellectually, what the point of view of the picture is, how the characters are playing and how he wants them played. . . .

FRANK KELLER: Peter Yates and I would run the cut sequences [of *Bullitt*] together. He sees how the picture is coming along. . . . If you have a dialogue sequence which is typed in script form and you get various angles of that dialogue sequence — individual close-ups, two-shots, master scenes, and all of that —

then it is up to you, based on your own instinct and experience, to know where you think you should come into a close-up, or whatever. . . . I get the rhythm by instinct. Sometimes your instinct will be wrong, and the director will tell you what his instinct is. . . . In several cases, Yates said, "I would rather you use close-ups in this area." I try immediately to do that, before I continue with my assembly of the film. I try to get the things he has seen in an altered form, so that they will be acceptable to him in the first cut. Then you put that aside, and try to catch up editing the film which has been shot subsequently.

FREDRIC STEINKAMP: John Frankenheimer shoots it upside down and backwards — that's his style. John loves crazy set angles, which he does fantastically, but, because he doesn't move his camera, it's difficult to put his footage together. You have a lot of film, and there are a lot of ways to go, which makes decision-making very difficult, even with the specific instructions or suggestions Frankenheimer might have offered. When I worked with him on *All Fall Down*, which was the third or fourth picture I'd ever cut, somehow we just hit it off. . . . It's luck or talent or feeling — or whatever that enables good film editors to get inside of a director and still be able to put their own values into, or get their own values, their own feelings out of a film.

DAVID BRETHERTON: When we had the luxury of time, which we no longer have, George Stevens used to shoot "around the clock," as we call it. He would shoot his master scenes from three, six, nine and twelve o'clock, as it were [i.e., from four vantage points corresponding roughly to the 90-degree, 180-degree, 270-degree, and 360-degree points on a circle]. Then he would shoot corresponding close-ups for each, so you had in effect four different pictures. Then he would say, "I want a bit of this and a bit of that and a bit of that." A man like George Stevens gives you so much. He has tremendous talent, which is sometimes frustrating: everything he shoots is brilliant, or it is George Stevens, it is a brilliantly enacted thing. But it does go on, and in some way you have to condense it into usable footage for people to view. . . . Yet if I were to edit a picture for a man who camera cut, à la John Ford, that would be absolutely no fun at all, because he would have already predetermined what the film was going to look like. I would function on a mechanical level — and I would hate that. Hopefully, I could make one or two contributions, but not as many as I would want. . . . Neither one is the ideal way to work.

DANIEL MANDELL: It was more difficult to cut a picture for William Wyler [than for Billy Wilder] . . . because he used to shoot about four or five times as much film as Billy Wilder. . . . I've worked on things with William Wyler where he'd go through with a sequence halfway and change his mind how it should go. . . . Billy Wilder . . . knows what he wants. You don't have any of that . . . vacillating with him. When he likes something he doesn't change his mind.

During the course of production, the film editor sometimes resumes his preproduction role of script editor by suggesting to the director that scenes be deleted or compressed on the one hand, and expanded on the other. In suggesting that scenes be expanded, the editor may recommend additional dialogue or action to clarify or amplify a character or a dramatic situation, or he may simply ask for more coverage — more angles — on a scene that has been — or is to be — filmed essentially as written.

DAVID BRETHERTON: I haven't had to suggest additional footage so much lately. But I used to work with a brilliant man at Fox, a writer-producer-director named Philip Dunne. We did *Ten North Frederick,* which was probably the best-edited picture I ever made. Because Phil didn't want to show his sentimental side, he would underplay things. We used to talk together every day after shooting; we used to go to Gary Cooper's dressing room and have a glass of champagne and sit and talk. I would say, "When you have this kind of a relationship between this kind of a person and that kind of a person, wouldn't *that* happen, wouldn't you want to feel that tenderness? Isn't there a look he can give her when he comes through the door that makes it a little more special, not just a guy coming through another door?" And Phil'd say, "Hmmm, I'm going to be in there on that set tomorrow, I might pick that up."

Many directors resent an editor's request for more extensive coverage because they suspect, sometimes rightly, that the editor is a mouthpiece for a nervous or devious producer who wants additional (usually "safer," more conventional) coverage to facilitate the recutting of the film to his own specifications after it leaves the director's hands. In light of William Wyler's reputation for extensive coverage, and the fact that by the time of *The Westerner* (1940) he and Samuel Goldwyn had enjoyed a fairly long and very fruitful association, Goldwyn's reason for dispatching editor Daniel Mandell to the Tucson location of the film is somewhat surprising.

DANIEL MANDELL: I was on the set almost all the time. I'd stay on the set for about three, four days and then fly to Hollywood, run through current days' rushes with Mr. Goldwyn, and then go back to Tucson. . . . Just watch the way things were shot to make sure that when we got inside [on studio sets] things would go together, just make sure everything was covered. Most of the time I'd just watch and . . . occasionally I'd venture a suggestion. But if things were going as I thought they should, mechanically, I'd just remain quiet. Unless I was asked.

Mandell assigns an important role to cinematographer Gregg Toland in determining the coverage — and therefore, to a significant extent, the editorial style — of the Samuel Goldwyn productions on which he and Toland served William Wyler.

DANIEL MANDELL: . . . Some directors stage a scene so the actors are positioned and the camera movement is such that the scene can play completely through without a cut. Where a close-up is required, they plan the scene so that the camera sneaks close to the actors at not precisely that moment, but a little before — so as not to be too obvious. Gregg was very good helping on those kinds of scenes. . . . He invented setups and moves so that a whole scene could be covered in one shot without going to separately filmed close-ups to point up different things; he was always experimenting with lenses. His deep-focus technique obviated the necessity of going to close-ups. . . . I don't mean to say that Gregg Toland had anything to do with the staging of the scene, but he used to say to the director, "If you have this character in a little closer, I won't have to move. And we'll save one move." . . . If the scene played well, what's the sense in going to close-ups? I was never for jumping around, just to be cutting. I always liked to feel I had a reason for cutting from one shot to another.

I remember one fellow referred to us [Wyler, Toland, and Mandell] as a team. I hadn't thought of it until then, and I thought, By gosh, that's right. You know, we did work together. Gregg Toland would talk to me and ask me what I thought and I'd — I'd confide in him too. "Look, I was thinking maybe we could do so-and-so. Why don't you talk to Willy?" We really worked together. But it's funny, I never considered ourselves that way until it was pointed out to me.

David Bretherton's appraisal of the cinematographer's contribution is somewhat less enthusiastic than Mandell's.

DAVID BRETHERTON: I think that Laszlo Kovacs is a very fine, very inventive new young cinematographer, and to the extent that we were involved with each other on *Slither*, we had a fruitful association. A cameraman can help a director, especially an inexperienced director, just as I can. My pet peeve is the cameraman who, when working with young or new directors, interferes and undermines their confidence instead of building it up. Give the kid some help; not this "boy-do-you-need-me" attitude. You don't do that to a guy who's on his way up.

Let's just respect each other and do our jobs. Now, Geoffrey Unsworth [with whom Bretherton was associated on *Cabaret*] — there's no pretense about him. He just says, "I know what you want. You want this, you want it sketchy, you want a flare down there, I know how to do it." No big show.

Mechanical and other "practical" problems are often referred to the editor while a film is in production, and if he is successful in solving them, he is temporarily looked upon as a kind of savior.

FRANK KELLER: [In shooting] the very end of the chase [in *Bullitt*], where the cars are coming down the hill and one breaks loose and hits the gas station, a phony car with dummies . . . went off ahead of time. It tripped the wire that set off the gas station, so the gas station went up in flames before the car ever got there. You never see the car hit the gas station. The scene was covered by four cameras and you could see in every one of the four angles that the station went up in flames while the car was still en route. . . . I remembered that a few days earlier Yates had done a zoom shot toward the gas station from a moving car. I asked the production manager to give me a full-frame explosion against black — the black gasoline barrel. So, when the car is coming down and it is already released and is in mid-air, I cut right down to the frame before the one in which you can see the reflection of the flames. It was the last frame with the auto going toward the gas station, before you could see that the place was already burning. What you saw was about one foot of zoom and one foot of explosion spliced together, and then back to the car. It worked.

DAVID BRETHERTON: One day, at the time we were doing *Peyton Place* at Fox Studios, Mark Robson called the cutting room and said, "We shot something yesterday" — I had not been on the set — "and you've got to cut it right away. It's the rape of Selena [Hope Lange] by her stepfather [Arthur Kennedy]." I said, "What's the matter?" and he said, "Don't ask questions, just do it, because the front office doesn't like it." So they rushed me prints at about ten o'clock in the morning, all this film and a sound track they didn't even allow time to code so that it would be in sync. So I cut the rape scene — the train going by, and all you see is the headboard of a brass bed and hands grasping it. I cut that in an hour and five minutes, and the sequence — from the attack to the end — was never changed. The reason I had to do it was not so much the performance by the actors, but because you couldn't see all four corners of the screen. That was the whole big deal. I cut the damned thing, I'm soaking wet, and I find out they're worried about how the scene will project in the drive-in theaters of the country. At that time, the studio head said, "You must, because

I've got this chain of four hundred drive-ins, see everything." Well, of course, they couldn't see everything in this scene. All they could see was the head of the goddam brass bed, hands grasping it, and occasionally a glimpse of a face. Afterwards Mark Robson came to me and said, "It's exactly perfect; the answer print, don't let them change it, don't let them, I don't want it any lighter." And I said something like, "It will not be changed, I promise thee, O Chief."

After a film has finished shooting, the editor assembles all of the sequences he was not able to put together previously and melds them with the footage cut earlier in preparation of what is known as the editor's cut. If the film editor is allowed a measure of autonomy at this stage of his work, and if a relatively large number of sequences have not been assembled during production and reviewed (and possibly altered) by the director, the terminology is apt. This version of the film is alternately called (mostly by film editors) the first cut; for other purposes, the version of the film presented to the producer by the director, after the editor has submitted his cut to the director and the director and editor have worked together on refining it, is the first cut.

HAL ASHBY: Now, as a director, I let the guys go through and get their first cut on it. What I'm always trying to do, because I've been an editor, is free them and have them work as I did as an editor, and that was to please myself. I always went for that. But it's very, very tough to find [editors] who give a damn. Many will say [to the director], "Well, Jesus, you shot this, it should be in the picture."

FRANK KELLER: The first cut, that is where you are able to put your own creative touch on the film. I think that the way Yates and I work together is the best way. . . . He leaves me alone for the first cut.

DANIEL MANDELL: I had to submit everything that I did to Wyler, and he'd approve or give me suggestions for changes. . . . Of course, he couldn't be ignored . . . because I had too much respect for him. After all, he is a *great* director. Why? Because he points out things; I find that he points out interesting things to an audience. [Physically,] he stayed out of the cutting room, though. . . . Sometimes I'd call Billy Wilder into the cutting room. I'd say, "Take a look at this on the moviola and see what you think of it." He'd never walk into the cutting room of his own accord.

DAVID BRETHERTON: I never look at it scene-by-scene, as some editors do. I never look at it until I have the whole picture together, or as much of it as I can. Then I look at it, I'm as critical as anybody would be, I censure myself horribly. I might change eight cuts out of ten in a single sequence. I can do that because there's no personality, there's none of my ego involved. When the director comes in, after having shot the whole thing, hopefully having envisioned the whole thing in his mind, he knows why he shot that shot. Many times I shortchange him, as it were, because that pan shot that took four hours to light doesn't mean a damn thing to me. It means a four-foot cut instead of a twenty-four-foot cut, because I'm trying to go by the story. A week or so after we've finished shooting, I'll give the director the picture as I see it. He might take one part of it, ten parts of it, all of it.

FRANK KELLER: After we had the first cut of *Bullitt* Yates worked very closely with me. After I put the chase scene together for the first time we had something like the normal way of seeing the action. It was mainly from the outside of the car with short cuts to the inside. Yates said, "We are not getting the most out of this." He mentioned that when you are inside the car you have to stay with it long enough to get the roller-coaster effect. So we found a couple of cuts where Steve McQueen was turning the wheel fast and we used it twice. We used it once from the inside and once from the outside. It was the same footage.

Working with Yates [as Keller has now done on five films] is great because, as time goes on, you become more relaxed and you don't think that you are insulting him when you tell him that a certain scene isn't very good. In any case, I found that you do have to be honest with a director or a producer or whoever is controlling the picture. If you intend to help the picture you have to express what you think about it. Otherwise you are nothing more than a technician.

DANIEL MANDELL: With some directors I'd listen very respectfully to whatever suggestions they had if I thought they merited attention and I'd follow them. Otherwise, I'd ignore them and take the initiative — that is, *after* the ["cut" guaranteed directors by an agreement between the Directors Guild and the producers]. . . . [In] *Pride of the Yankees* . . . Sam Wood wanted to expand and dramatize the final scene of the picture, Gehrig's farewell, Gehrig Day. Well, that didn't need anything. Look at that newsreel — that had more drama than anything I ever saw. So I threw out all the film that he made to elaborate it and cut it like the newsreel — as close as I could. Of course, it made him angry, but I went to Goldwyn and I won out.

FREDRIC STEINKAMP: In every picture there have been things I've had to fight for. There's [usually] more than one thing or more than one area or more than one point that I will feel so strongly about that I will fight for it. I'll hold off on the fight for a point until a propitious time: when everything is together and I'm seeing the film as a whole and I'm thoroughly convinced that I *have* a point, I fight for it. I say "fight," which it isn't really. And if the director or the producer, or whoever's got the say-so, says, "No, I know what you mean, I know exactly what you mean, I know how you feel, but I'd rather have it this way," all you can do is say okay. Frankenheimer used to say, "Okay, kid, you won *that* one, I'll give *that* one to you," but it was just friendly jest. It doesn't go into an "I'll-give-you-this-if-you-take-that" kind of thing.

In speaking of his Academy-Award-winning work on *Cabaret*, David Bretherton explains how he worked both on his own and with the director, Bob Fosse, and suggests the rationale behind decisions that substantially altered the structure of the film and enhanced it overall.

DAVID BRETHERTON: We finished shooting in Germany, and Bob
  Fosse — everybody — had to leave because there's a tax structure in Germany which says that after six months, if one member of a foreign production company stays behind, the company
  must pay something like twenty-five percent of the cost of the
  production in Germany in taxes. So everybody bailed out. Bob
  Fosse went to London and I flew to New York. My German
  assistant — apprentice,   actually — packed   up   all   the   film
  helter-skelter in boxes and shipped it on to New York.

  Bob Fosse showed up in New York about two weeks after I
  had arrived there, and it was kind of . . . desperate. Fosse was
  appalled that I'd cut any film at all. Basically, we shot all the
  interiors set in the club first. Consequently, I cut those things
  first, as I got them. Bob was so busy concentrating on concept
  and performance that he didn't know what I was doing, no idea
  I was cutting it at dailies every night. He would say, "You
  might do this or do that," or, "I like this take better than that
  take, that dance step is better," but these remarks (he thought)
  were mainly for future reference. Well, I was up to what he had
  shot, except for the film that was still in the labs in Germany
  and that was late in being sent over to me. He said, "*Why* did
  you cut it?" I said, "It's my job." He said, "I'd better see it."

  And he was amazed that I knew how to cut film without him
  saying how it should be cut. God! After all, isn't that my function? That's why I was on the set, that's why I used to creep in
  — without intruding on him, I used to creep in and watch him
  in rehearsals. I'd hear him say, "I want a little more out of you
  and a little less out of you, and why don't *you* try to pick up
  the tempo." I'd hear him telling the actors what he wanted, and
  even though sometimes they didn't accomplish it on film, in [a
  single] angle, you knew that you could accomplish it when you
  started editing the film. You could get the reaction of Liza
  Minnelli to Marisa Berenson's line, knowing that you could
  condense Marisa's speech overall.

  Bob would shoot scenes of Joel Grey, and when I saw them
  I'd say to myself, My God, I can't use it there. Where the script
  says the scene should be, it takes too much time, it stops the
  flow of the story. So you say, Where can I use it where it'd be
  beneficial? And in the middle of a car ride you put in a cut of

Joel Grey in order to keep alive that horrible, nasty degenerate feeling you established in Reel One and that you're going to end up with in Reel Ten. It's like a thin thread you weave through the picture.

The intercutting of the dances with what was going on outside the cabaret — the dead dog being thrown on the doorstep. The dance didn't hold up; it was a musical number you couldn't afford. But if you cut the thing with the dog into the number, it makes it stop, true, but it makes it larger in scope, because suddenly you're telling a different but somehow related story.

This was unconventional — or it was unplanned. One of the cameramen, under the tutelage of Geoffrey Unsworth, took a handheld camera and, during rehearsals of the club scenes, would shoot the crowds [which served as the "audience" in these scenes]. And from that I got some of the greatest gut reactions during the mud fight. As I said, those weren't planned — there were no key lights, nobody was following them with a lamp. We printed them at every density we possibly could so they would integrate with what was happening on the stage. Now, these stolen shots were also used for other dance numbers to get that kind of strange, distorted, degenerate I-love-to-see-somebody-hurt feeling that would keep the [film's] audience uncomfortable with and disturbed by what was happening on the screen. It wasn't meant to become more important than the numbers, it was just a comment on how the people in the club were looking at the people on stage.

Eighty percent of what Bob Fosse saw cut, which was perhaps eight reels out of ten, he loved. Twenty percent he probably loathed with a passion, though he never said that. He's not that kind of a guy. We had a very good rapport, because I admired him tremendously. After this we worked together. But, basically, my work on the first assembly is the time I make my greatest contribution.

There was a song in *Cabaret* called "Tomorrow Belongs to Me." A young German boy sings it [before a crowd of people who, stirred by its nationalistic-militaristic fervor, rise one by one, then in progressively larger groups, and join in the singing]. One day — not even one day — of rehearsal and one day of shooting. I used every piece of handheld camera footage of the crowd. I made a cross chart of about twenty people on bits and pieces of films — ten feet, five feet, six feet — and I wrote down lyrics that might fit in their mouths. When Bob saw that he flipped, because he didn't have time; he didn't have rehearsal time, the kid wasn't good, the panoffs weren't good, the people were "acting," as many novices will. Bob didn't feel he had anything special and he was so despondent. But when he saw it he flipped. He said, "Come on, let's do this. Let's get this guy to stand up then, can we do that?" I said, "We can try. We'll look through this cross chart. We'll find some guy that stands up on this line and we'll put him over here." He said, "I don't care what the juxtaposition is, let's just get a piece where this happens and that happens." It was like a wonderful chess game or a crossword puzzle, and it all worked together. And we didn't have more than twenty frames of film left when we finished the number. These beautiful innocent children being led — from that I got the idea of inserting the face of Joel Grey there. I wondered about it, and Bob said, "Play it, play it, play this guy." We had stolen that from a scene in which he was backstage and sticks his tongue out at a girl, a scene that came about five minutes later. It gave an idea of that threat, of what was going to happen later on.

A significantly large number of films employ more than one editor. The credits for *The Diary of Anne Frank*, for instance, include two editors in addition to David Bretherton, and Sam Peckinpah's *Pat Garrett and Billy the Kid* made some kind of history by utilizing the services of six (credited) editors. Putting to the side for the moment cases in which the work of the first editor to tackle a film is unsatisfactory or incompatible with the director's (or producer's) vision and additional editorial talent is enlisted to complete or revise the task, Fredric Steinkamp indicates why and how two or more editors might work on a film simultaneously.

FREDRIC STEINKAMP: Because Richard Rush wanted to be totally involved in the editing of *Freebie and the Bean*, we didn't cut at all as he was shooting. This is my first experience in working this way. Now, because the film has got to be put together within a certain time period to fulfill contractual obligations, there are two of us editing the film. In a sense, we've got two teams going. One cutter is working on the Kem — a new European table-type editing machine — and Dick sits right with him and watches. I started out that way, but with somebody watching — even though your heads are going the same route, your hands don't do the same thing — it was very slow. So, I'm working as I normally work: I will run and review all the film on a sequence with him on the Kem, then cut the sequence myself in a separate room while he's working with the other cutter. When I finish a sequence I'll go in on the Kem and do any recutting he wants, with him watching.

*Grand Prix,* on which four editors are credited, was a unique situation. John Frankenheimer had no time. The picture had a prebooked première date the day before Christmas, and John Frankenheimer didn't finish shooting it until the middle of October. We were based in London, and I spent three months there, during the shooting, trying to organize the whole thing. Because of the amount of film shot, the time came when it was necessary to hire another editor. We gave him a race — the Spa, Belgium, race — and in the meantime I was working on the British Grand Prix and doing dialogue sequences whenever Frankenheimer would say, "We've got to see some dialogue sequences, we've got to . . ."

So we came back, and Saul Bass, who had shot a lot of second-unit work with Frankenheimer, started working on the main title. I was concentrating on getting the story together — the dialogue sequences — but we still had two, actually three, big races to cut. We hired another editor, another team in a sense, who put the Dutch Grand Prix together — very stylized, all panel work. Then Hank Berman came in and cut the Monza race — the last race shot, with miles of film on it — and basically did just that and a couple of dialogue sequences. One of the film editors, Stew Linder, who got credit didn't do that much cutting, but he literally held the whole operation together. We had twenty-five or thirty people working in postproduction on the film, and the personnel coordination, plus the technical coordination, plus cutting, was an incredible job. Without him we couldn't have done it.

Whatever film we worked on, we worked on with John. He supervised each team. In working out the complicated main title design, Saul Bass would come to John with a concept, and he and John, like a writer and a director, would kick around this concept, and then Saul would go off on that; the same, really, with all the cutters who worked on the film.

*Grand Prix,* in my opinion, was enhanced by the different styles of the various editors who worked on it. Motor racing is, to me, quite dull — nothing happens, they just go around in circles. Doing it alone, you'd say, Oh, Christ, here comes another car race. We'll go around in circles and cut to faces and cut to the wheels spinning — I've got to think of a new way to cut this race! For one person — if I had to do the whole thing, it would have taken me two years. What really made that picture was that more than one person had his head into it; it needed that visual uniqueness that each editor brought to it. And I think Frankenheimer would agree with that.

Throughout the production and postproduction phases of his work, the film editor has at least one assistant.

FRANK KELLER: At the beginning the assistant editor gets the dailies and syncs the sound to them. Then he takes them down to a coding room. Later, he breaks each scene down and identifies it as to scene number. Normally, when I am making a first cut I splice it. As the picture progresses, the assistant keeps measurements on it. He does all the ordering of the opticals and makes sure that the orders are filled correctly.

FREDRIC STEINKAMP: He breaks the film down into rolls in order to facilitate construction of scenes on the moviola. He files and catalogues the trims so that when you want to put a piece of close-up in where you had a long shot, he gets it for you. He coordinates all the postdialogue recording — the looping; he coordinates getting that material ready for the loops to be made, and in some studios he actually makes the loops himself.

[There have been instances in which the film editor has "directed" the actors in looping sessions, either at the behest of the director or because of his absence. — D.C.] He is with you when you're with a director in the projection room and takes notes; he may express an opinion in a director-editor or producer-director-editor session. And for me, he's the greatest sounding board in the world when I'm cutting. I'll say, "Come here and look at this, what do you think?" and he'll offer an objective opinion. He does, absolutely he does [advance ideas and make suggestions]. He's an integral part of the whole thing.

FRANK KELLER: It is nice if you can keep an assistant with you. But if they are good they usually get the opportunity to move up to cutting.

FREDRIC STEINKAMP: For me, one of the greatest things is to have assistant editors, whom I've in a sense raised, working on their own as top film editors.

The script supervisor, whose self-described function is to serve as liaison between the director and the editor (see Chapter 7), is seen from the editor's standpoint.

FRANK KELLER: I really lay out the film from the script supervisor's script. It is very helpful when you have any kind of matching problems to confer with the script supervisor. I have had occasions when directors on films dream up scenes that they thought they had shot but never really got around to. I would be looking for these scenes and I would go back to the script clerk and ask him [or her] if there was such a scene. A good script clerk can answer yes or no quite quickly.

FREDRIC STEINKAMP: Script supervisors can be a great help and they can also make it so we can't find anything. A good script supervisor records the takes so that we can find them and describes the scenes so that we can understand what it is and what it was intended for, often amplifying or expanding upon what the director has told the editor. There are script supervisors who will number the speeches in a scene and make detailed notations on the readings in the various takes. This is very helpful when you go back to print footage that wasn't originally printed, to look for better readings. Otherwise, you can print eight takes looking for one line. A good script supervisor is probably more valuable to us than she is to the director, I would think.

Whether the length of the cuts in scenes backed by music is determined by the length of the musical pieces, or vice versa, depends on the function music is to perform in the scene and, to an extent, on the point at which the composer writes his score. In the majority of cases involving nonmusical films the composer begins his work with a look at the completed rough cut of a film, so to a significant extent he is subservient to the editor from the outset. But that does not rule out compromises and concessions by both editor and composer, or heated conflicts between them at the later stages of postproduction.

DANIEL MANDELL: Sometimes a composer would ask me if I could give him another second, two seconds or three seconds on a score. And if I could I would, but that's about all it ever amounted to.

DAVID BRETHERTON: On *Peyton Place,* the composer, Franz Waxman, would ask me to change cuts, and I'd say, "No, absolutely no. It's a great picture; you're to complement it. Don't ask me to change one cut, because I won't do it." Franz would get furious with me. He'd say, "You cut here because I want to do something here." I'd say, "I'm terribly sorry, but *I* want to do something here — pictorially. No, Franz, don't do that to me."

FRANK KELLER: *The Hot Rock* has a scene where Robert Redford comes out of a bank and walks down Park Avenue. I had several different scenes of this. We had to cut it to music rhythm. Each cut had to be on a musical beat.

FREDRIC STEINKAMP: In editing *They Shoot Horses, Don't They?* I worked very closely with the director, Sydney Pollack, and the composer, John Green. I had to. [See John Green's account

of his work on this film in Chapter 9, The Composer. — D.C.]
For instance, a record runs two and a half minutes and you
can't change it; sure, you can repeat a bar, but since the music
was well known — modern classics — you'd notice it right
away. They had a playback machine, and, when they were
shooting, they'd start the playback at the beginning of a sequence so that the performers could get the rhythm. And that
sequence was timed, even in the close-ups, to coincide as
closely as possible with the length of the musical piece. Still,
you never knew until you got into it how long a person was
going to talk in a close-up — how long it was going to take Jane
Fonda to get a line out — and how many reactions you're going
to have, silent reactions that will stretch the sequence and make
it longer than the record. So I had to block out all those dialogue sequences. I would take the record — or tape, a mag of
the sound track — and run it in my synchronizer so that I knew
at any time how I was doing in terms of the duration of the
piece of music. There were some sequences that just got too
long, so they had to stop playing one song and start another in
order to give me a chance to realize all the dramatic values in
the sequence. But, basically, I had to stay within the framework
of that two-and-a-half-minute record — or however long it was.
I would say that there were no dramatic values lost because we
were locked into this framework. The film wouldn't be different
without it, but my job would have been a hell of a lot easier.
It was a huge problem.

DANIEL MANDELL: In a number in *Ball of Fire* Gene Krupa's band
. . . hardly ever [gave] exactly the same [visual performance
from setup to setup and take to take]. So, many times you
couldn't cut just at the place that you wanted. You'd have to find
a place where the [prerecorded] music and the picture matched.
In a number in *Wonder Man*, starring Danny Kaye, I had to
stretch the music two bars here, four bars there — in other
words, repeat the track — in order to keep the cadence [of the
editing].

On *Guys and Dolls* . . . Mike Kidd, the choreographer,
directed all the musical numbers. I never had such an easy time
as I had with him. The musical numbers that look like they

might be the most difficult [to cut] were the easiest I ever did because he planned everything so well.

Perhaps it is the basic affinity between musical composition and film editing that is responsible for the occasional hostility of editors required to cut within the framework imposed by a musical piece, and of composers required to provide music for a precut scene. Many editors are frank in stating their preference for cutting to a musical beat. But because the composer's score is usually not yet available to provide it, they resort to temporary tracks — music not expressly written for the film.

DAVID BRETHERTON: Ninety percent of film editing is rhythm, and rhythm is musical. In editing *Westworld*, I lay in pieces of music. Fred Karlin was to write the score for the film, but we were going to preview with my track. I'd used scores from three different pictures — full scores, small scores, piano rolls. They're all pertinent to what I'm showing, but I have nothing thematic going for me, I don't have to conform to anything. But they've been a tremendous aid to me in cutting this film.

There's a barroom fight that goes on for four minutes. I was cutting this thing and it was getting shorter and shorter, and I stopped to ask myself, What am I trying to prove? I didn't have any idea of what I was going to do, so I asked my assistant, "Have you got any kind of music that's kind of corny, distorted, weird — anything," because it's not a real fight. It's a fight between robots and humans, so it's got to be not real. So he went to a picture called *The Wild Rovers* and got a twangy thing with guitars that seems to slow down in the wrong places, almost as if it were done through a very bad recorder. . . . He gave me this piece of music, I looked again at this thing which I thought was a disaster, and I saw the comedic value of the music he had given me. There was a trumpet fanfare, and at that time I would cut to my hero as he was taking a drink out of a bottle — just for a flash, it would only be, like, a foot and a half. Then there'd be fifteen or twenty feet or more of something else, and then I'd cut back to my hero again and repeat the trumpet piece. And now he's lying flat on his ass, laughing like a clown because he's just been knocked down.

Music gave me a form to cut the damned thing in. You can cut with a click-track — this thing that clicks every twelve frames — but it has no emotion, no feeling. . . . Now, when Fred Karlin writes his score to fit [the scene] hopefully he will use whatever accents — like the hits in the fight scene — are inherent in it.

But many composers (see Goldsmith, in Chapter 9) are violently opposed to working within the framework of accents provided by music they didn't write. The use of music in editing *The Thomas Crown Affair* benefited the editor without restricting him and, at the same time, did not slight or impinge on the composer of the film's score.

HAL ASHBY: We had already shot *The Thomas Crown Affair,* but I said [to director Norman Jewison], "Let's just get Michel Legrand and have him write music, and we'll do two or three wild sessions, whatever it is." And we did. I ended up with an hour and twenty minutes of music, and most of it wasn't even written to specific cues. It was all done wild; while cutting, I'd just listen to that music constantly and say, Gee, I think this will get it on here and this will get it on here — work that way. As a result, I believe, there was just one twenty-second segment of the film that was "scored to picture," and this only as a sweetener. All other music in the film came from the wild sessions.

The editor may but is not likely to be involved with the director of photography during postproduction. He will also have some degree of contact with the sound effects and music editors.

FRANK KELLER: [On *Bullitt*] the director of photography would be there for the running of the dailies [during production]. But other than that, unless I had some occasion to go down to the set, I normally wouldn't see him any other time. He is not generally in on the editing at all. As a courtesy, the director might invite him to come and see the picture just as it is finished, to check if the color printing [timing] had been done properly at the lab.

FREDRIC STEINKAMP: I have something very strong to say about that. With the twenty-eight or twenty-nine pictures I've cut, there have been only two or three where the director or the producer *hasn't* said, to the director of photography, "We'll contact you as soon as we get this all together. You come to the lab and we'll run the work print and talk about the timing of the answer print." Many times cameramen are busy working in some other part of the country where you can't get to them, but they have almost always, on the productions I've worked on, been considered, and, always, we've done anything we could to have them there for the timing of their photography. . . . Nowadays the director, or director-producer usually follows a film all the way through, but there have been times when [because] the director has gone off to do another picture, the cameraman is unavailable, and the producer is doing something else, all of the postproduction work falls under the jurisdiction of the editor. And when it comes to the lab timing, you are the one who says, "That scene is too dark," or "Conceptually, we'd like to have it darker because we're doing a time lapse." But it almost always involves at least one run with the director of photography.

DAVID BRETHERTON: I can contribute until the end. I try to contribute in the dubbing room. You can say, "No, that's not the right sound; you can do better than that."

I've worked in just about all the countries in Western Europe, and professionally, on the set, the Americans are the best. In postproduction I would have to say the French are the best. They follow through. In other words, the film editor in America cuts the picture. Period. Then he turns it over to a sound effects editor, who turns it over to a music editor, and somewhere along the line it gets lost until we all end up to synchronize it all together. In France, the editor is not only the film editor, he is in a sense the sound effects editor and the music editor. The French are so passionately involved in everything they do. When I say passionately, I mean to the extent that you'll fight with someone, as the French do when they're dubbing a picture — putting dialogue and music and sound effects together. They'll scream and beat their heads and storm out of rooms because they believe — emotionally believe — in what they've done. There's no animosity, but they do express themselves. Here, in America, nobody expresses himself unless he's asked. We have a protocol. In France it's like a family. I worked with a wonderful sound effects man named Maumont on *The Train*, who performed miracles for me working with the invention of a guy named Neny. It's a unit and you work and you do your damnedest to make the best picture you know how. This is more likely to be the case on a United Artists picture, wherever it's made, than with other studios' pictures. UA doesn't interfere.

The often influential role of the producer or production company in editorial decisions has been suggested at various points in this chapter. Mandell, Keller and Bretherton confront the subject of the editor's relationship with the front office directly.

DANIEL MANDELL: When I first started to work for Samuel Goldwyn, he stayed close — in fact, I thought he stayed too close for comfort. I mean, sometimes you wished he'd leave you alone — so you could get some work done. . . . In later years he very rarely made any suggestions or found fault with how it went together until he saw a first cut of the whole picture. Then he had his suggestions. Samuel Goldwyn's instructions were general. He'd say, "I think this scene moves too slowly," or, "I think you're featuring the wrong person," or, "I'd try to feature the other person, because I think he's more important in the scene," or, "There's not enough preparation; see if you can point things up a little more in this area." Those kinds of instructions. And then, most of the time he'd rely on me to invent something if it wasn't already there.

I would suggest something once to Mr. Goldwyn, and if he'd turn it down I'd suggest it again a few days later. The best example I can think of was on a Danny Kaye picture, *The Secret Life of Walter Mitty*. We had a sequence in his imagination. Danny was a rebel in the Irish Rebellion, and . . . he sings a song, "Cockles and Mussels." I thought the whole thing was out of character, and it ran about seven, eight minutes. So I suggested [deleting] it. Mr. Goldwyn didn't like the idea. A week

later I suggested it again. He said, "Let me think about it."
About a week after that I was in his office and somebody came
in — one of the writers, I forget who — and Mr. Goldwyn said,
"Listen, I've got an idea. The last thing we see is so-and-so, and
then, instead of going to this, we leave out the . . . number."
The visitor's comment was, "Not a bad idea, not a bad idea." I
said nothing. About a week later, Mr. Goldwyn asked me what
I thought. I had already had the picture mounted in such a way
. . . that all we'd have to do was to leave the reel out of the
picture — the sequence was mounted on a separate reel. That's
how sure I was that he'd come around.

. . . Mr. Goldwyn and Wyler very often didn't see eye-to-eye
about things, and you might say I was in the middle. I had to
please both of them. . . . I used to try to get them together and
let them fight it out. . . . I used to cut it the way I thought it
should be and then have them look at it. And if they disagreed
about anything I'd just sit there and let them fight.

The first cut of a film is supposed to be the director's according to the Directors Guild agreement with the producers.
But beyond that, we'd do as . . . as we thought best.

FRANK KELLER: After the director's cut, the producer often takes
the film and makes changes if he wants to. But you usually find
that the director and the producer will work together. . . . Also,
in Peter Yates's case, he is allowed to have two previews of his
cut. The final decision about the release version of the film is
pretty much made out here in Los Angeles. When *The Hot
Rock* was at that point, we had Elmo Williams, who was head
of production for Twentieth Century-Fox sitting in with us. We
had the picture in what we considered to be pretty final form,
but because Elmo was interested in the picture personally, we
had him come in. As an ex-film editor, he had quite a few
constructive suggestions for little alterations.

DAVID BRETHERTON: When you work for MGM — MGM here, I
worked for MGM in Europe and it was different — you're nothing. The director is nothing, which is even more disastrous.
Whom do you work for? For [studio executives] Aubrey . . .
Netter . . . Melnick . . . Jack Haley, Jr.? You can't please them

all. You're supposed to please your director and your producer.
So the director is so-and-so and the producer is so-and-so, but
then you've got all these other people to please, and it just can't
be done.

Though it is to be hoped that all major changes in the substance
or sequence of a film will be made prior to or during production,
such revisions may be effected during postproduction phase. The
decisions that result in these alterations to a film as conceived and
shot may involve the director or writer-director in varying de-
grees, or not at all. They almost invariably involve the producer or
financier of the film, who may either determine the changes and
supervise the editor's execution of them or lend him a relatively
free hand. As Fredric Steinkamp indicates, he had virtual *carte
blanche* in his reediting of *A New Leaf*, the results of which
were the basis for one of the most heated director-studio
conflicts of recent years.

DANIEL MANDELL: Universal fired Erich von Stroheim and hired
    Arthur Ripley to supervise the editing of *Foolish Wives*. And
    he gave the job to me. The studio wanted a two-and-a-half-hour
    show [from thirty-eight reels, or approximately twelve hours of
    film]. Now there was a case of . . . combining sequences. There
    were three different nights in the Monte Carlo casino which
    were all combined into one. There were such things done like
    taking a telephone conversation that was originally between
    von Stroheim, who played the heavy, and the American am-
    bassador's wife, and making it a conversation between von
    Stroheim and one of the phony countesses he was living with.
    Arthur Ripley was very clever as a story constructionist and we
    had a very clever title writer [in] Marian Ainslee. But basically,
    the story was about the same.
        [With reference to the change in story sequence in *The Best
    Years of Our Lives* made during the postproduction editing of
    the film]: As I remember, we had a conference, decided on
    certain things, and I went ahead and made the changes. Mr.
    Goldwyn, Wyler, and myself. The author [Robert E. Sherwood]
    wasn't there. Earlier, he had come out from New York at the
    request of Mr. Goldwyn — two or three weeks before we fin-

ished shooting on the picture. So we'd still have the cast if he should suggest some retakes. He was very pleased with what he saw and went back to New York. Everything was fine — for him. . . . But most often we'd stick to the original continuity. We did more juggling in the silent days.

FRANK KELLER: After we got *Bullitt* in first cut we saw that the ending — a priest giving the last rites to the dead person at the airport — was a pretty flat ending to such an exciting picture. Also, I strongly felt that we should see Steve and the girl back together again. So, the picture ends with the scene where he comes up the stairs and sees the girl in bed. Then he puts his gun down and goes to wash up. That sequence belonged way back in the middle of the picture. It was to have gone after they had stolen the body out of the hospital and loaded it into the ambulance. If you look very closely you will see that the wardrobe doesn't match.

FREDRIC STEINKAMP: One picture which I redid completely was Elaine May's *A New Leaf*. I had total control of that. Elaine May is a tenacious, very talented person. She and an editor in New York had been cutting the film for a year and they weren't getting anywhere. Contractually, I think, her time ran out after a year and Paramount, in a sense, took the picture away from her and called me in to doctor it, to see what I could do to make it work. I met with her — she was still with it, she hadn't left it — and she was fantastic — to a point. I said, "I don't want to see her version at all. I would rather start from dailies." So we had the film reconstructed; we ordered reprints of the original dailies and I just started from scratch with my version of it, the way I interpreted it, without talking to her about it. She was just there.

I got about three sequences finished and I ran them for Paramount. They just loved them; they couldn't believe how they came together. I ran them for Elaine and she just loved them. She said, "How can that be? You're fantastic!" So, I was given the green light and went through the film and did with it what I thought was right: the best I could get out of the film, all the values I could get out. It's one of the toughest things

I've ever cut, because the film did have a lot of inadequacies.
. . . Now, I'm not saying that Elaine May is inadequate, because
she is a brilliant writer, and I thought she was really terrific as
an actress in *A New Leaf*. . . . As long as I could find the words
she had written in the midst of all the ad-libbed material (they
just went crazy), as long as I could get it and weed out all of
the extraneous stuff and get to what she had written and what
she and Walter Matthau played, it really worked. . . .

After I cut the whole picture, we ran it with her. The second
half of the film didn't work in my opinion and it didn't work in
Paramount's opinion. There were three premeditated murders
in it and it just didn't work because we'd established such a nice
love story between Walter Matthau and Elaine May. Plus it
was endless, it just took forever. Elaine May, however, thought
she had a black comedy and that it was working. Paramount
made a decision to go with my point of view — I figured out a
way to change the second half of the story and make it a love
story without any premeditated murders in it — and at that
point she left. Until then she was elated, she was really elated.
We had a terrific relationship, and I would say that we still do.
It's just that she felt her original concept hadn't been given a
chance. But it had been given a chance for a year, and then I
gave it everything I could give it — [relatively speaking,] it
took me much longer to cut the last part of the picture — and
it still didn't come out.

I went ahead and recut the end of the picture, got it all
together, and Paramount said, "That's fine." Then Elaine May
sued Paramount, saying they had twisted her story around and
taken away her black comedy. So there was a Steinkamp version
and a May version of the film that went into court, I had to file
a deposition about the whole thing, it was decided she had no
case, and they released my version; I shouldn't say that — it's
Elaine's film. And subsequently, she did another film, *The
Heartbreak Kid*, which I think is just sensational; beautifully
directed, acted — and edited!

Elaine May has since made her third film as a director. Its title
is *Nicky and Mikey*, its principal actors are John Cassavetes and
Peter Falk, and its trouble-plagued shooting, which proceeded in

two stages, from May to August 1973 and January to March 1974, is said to have been responsible for the most acute cases of executive jitters at, yes, Paramount since *A New Leaf*.

In spite of the many changes likely to be imposed on an editor's cut of a film by the director, the producer, the composer *et al.*, it sometimes happens that the editor's version of key sequences or of a film as a whole has been the one released.

FREDRIC STEINKAMP (With reference to the first elimination derby in *They Shoot Horses, Don't They?*): Sydney Pollack is a terrific director; he gave me fantastic film, *lots* of film. The two of us really didn't know each other that well, so I just took the film and locked myself in the cutting room for three weeks.

The amount of wear on the characters at various points in the race and their positions relative to one another — it was, very, very difficult to get consistency and show the progression in that race because there were so many different angles and takes. In some of the takes that were intended for the beginning of the derby, Pollack had run [the actors] so much that they were shot down and stumbling — or just happened to stumble and fall — and I'd take those out and save them for later [in the race], as it progressed. It was a matter of digging and sifting and shifting around, and staying within the framework that Sydney had written and shot.

I'm not sure, quite frankly, whether the coincidence of story time and playing time — ten minutes — was planned. I know that Sydney, when he was planning it and shooting it, said, "Well, this will come out to probably eight, ten minutes; it's got to take that long to show all that I want to show and to make it real — without any kind of dissolve time lapses." There were certain points in the derby where Rocky [Gig Young] would note the time, and as I got into it I noticed — He said, "Three minutes left!" Well, I was at seven minutes!

After three weeks' work on this material I did what we call a temp dub — we just took some shouting, adding that extra excitement of the sound track — and ran it for Sydney. What he saw, with the exception of one or two short eliminations, is what you saw — literally, a first cut.

DAVID BRETHERTON: [On *The Diary of Anne Frank*] we'd done
footsteps of Germans. Should we have a pace and a half, or
should we have a two-and-a-half-frame cut of this? Not literally,
but it was almost that. George Stevens would dwell on them.
. . . We'd run two projectors at the same time, trying to figure
out which projector was running that piece of film and what did
he particularly like. There was one sequence in *The Diary
of Anne Frank* — the Chanukah sequence — that he never
touched one frame of. He'd always put it off by saying, "I'll
work on it tomorrow," or, "Let's work on it last." He supervises
everything, but circumstances being what they were — the time
element and the preponderance of film, 250 or 300 thousand feet
of it — he always put it off.

It was my proudest moment as an editor that, from the day I
cut the sequence to the day the film was released, he never
touched the Chanukah sequence. He said, "Just let it go, let it
go the way it is." He just said, "We'll let that go, it works okay."
Not to be self-congratulatory, but to me, the sequence was
probably the second most tender moment in the whole picture.
The beauty, the simplicity of that sequence, of this young girl
distributing her gifts to her fellow confinees.

Ernest Walter, in *The Technique of the Film Cutting Room*,
says that, "No two editors, given the same film, will produce the
same result." However, editors, like cinematographers, are divided
on the question of whether or not they have a personal style. It
would seem that the nature of the material, the director, the
zeitgeist, the historical-technological background against which
the editor gained his experience of the medium, the demands of
the editor's own aesthetic — all contribute unequally but significantly to the editorial style of a film.

FRANK KELLER: I edit according to the picture. I have heard that
some people think they have a style, but it seems to me that
each picture is different. I think you have to go by what the film
tells you.

DAVID BRETHERTON: As an editor, you don't have a style. I used to
work with one of the most brilliant editors of all time, Bob

Simpson, who cut musical numbers in which you couldn't see a cut — absolutely fabulous, smooth, silken. I worked with another man named Louis Loeffler, who could cut a trial that would make you sit on the edge of your chair. Now, had Bob Simpson cut the trial it would have been smooth and silken — and not exciting. Had Louis Loeffler cut the dance number, it would have been a horribly static or jumpy kind of thing. We're talking about twenty years ago now. You can't have a style any more.

FREDRIC STEINKAMP: I think I have a certain style, as do Sam O'Steen — he's brilliant — and Ralph Winters.

DANIEL MANDELL: . . . I think my style of cutting has changed in the past, let's say the past twenty-five, thirty years. I think I used to make the mistake of cutting too often. . . .

FREDRIC STEINKAMP: Quite often, I'll tend to overcut a sequence. Take a sequence that has maybe ten or fifteen angles. In those various angles, there will be values that in my mind — and in the director's mind, everybody's mind — are really terrific, but they're hard to get to. In other words, there might be in the close-up the best reading and the best visual performance of the beginning of a scene, but in the construction of the scene that close-up just won't work; coming at the beginning, it'll be off-tempo, out of rhythm. I'll strive to rearrange things so that I can get to those values and will tend to, on a first cut, be too "cutty." I'll go for the jugular vein right off and get all of the values out, and then, I'll sometimes have to go back and simplify it. . . .

DANIEL MANDELL: . . . In my case, cutting too often rubbed off from the silent days. With the absence of sound you cut to everything to illustrate.

DAVID BRETHERTON: The kids who constitute the great majority of the film audience — actually, all people today — have been subjected to so many facets of life and experience that they won't sit still for the kind of setbound, talky movie that used to be made, the kind of movie that is, in a strange way, naïve. The kids, especially, are into faster situations, faster scenes. They don't want nuances. They experience in high school what we didn't experience until we were thirty. The type of beauty that lies in, say, watching a flower grow from a seedling — they don't want to see it. They want to see the bud and they want to see the bloom; they don't want to see the in-between. And that's the way you cut today. You don't cut with the long dissolves, as someone falls into someone else's arms. They say, "Oh, that's bullshit, that's old-fashioned. Crazy, I mean, man I meet you and I like you and now we're in bed and now we're in love." All the hand-kissing and the conventional I-love-yous are deleted, and it gets down to the real nitty-gritty of what life is about. It progresses from A to B, and how it gets there is really not important; it's just that it does and here's the end result: if you go from A to B you'll end up with C. That you did it is exciting enough — in one cut, as opposed to twenty, or a montage. I think it's terrific: you see the problem — the situation — and the answer, with none of the bullshit in between.

FREDRIC STEINKAMP: What I aim for is to get the most out of the piece, without having it look like it's obviously been cut to achieve this. You have to dig into the various takes of various angles to get the pieces of film with the best performances, the greatest amount of nuances, the most potent dramatic values, and then assemble them so the scene is seamless and fluid. The picture as a totality should create an illusion of reality.

❧

DAVID BRETHERTON: I believe in what I'm doing, I love what I'm doing. I want to be the best film editor in the world. I don't want to be the second best director, I don't want to destroy someone else's — a writer's — work.

DANIEL MANDELL: Yes, I consider it an art. To some people, it's just being a mechanic. It depends on who the film editor is.

# NINE
## The Composer

The history of motion picture music begins some three decades before the advent, in the late 1920s, of the sound film — that is, the film with recorded dialogue, effects and music integrated with the visual image in a permanent and nonincidental way. A film presentation of the Lumières in Paris in 1895 was accompanied by a piano, and the films of Georges Méliès, which also predate the turn of the century, had piano scores especially conceived and timed to mimic the action on the screen. Anticipating the large-scale involvement of "serious" composers in film work by approximately twenty-five years, in 1908 Camille Saint-Saëns wrote his Opus 128 for strings, piano and harmonium especially for the Charles Pathé-Le Film D'Art production of *L'Assassinat du Duc de Guise*. Consisting of an introduction and five tableaux, each part of the score was carefully cued by the film.

In the following decade the scores of such composer-arrangers

as Dr. Hugo Riesenfeld, David Mendoza and Major Edward
Bowes were played by symphony orchestras in the big downtown
movie palaces of the United States, and subsequently rearranged
for the "Mighty Wurlitzer" organs in the neighborhood houses and
the single piano of the small-town movie theater. Reliable sources
indicate that the scores of Riesenfeld *et al.* made liberal use of
noncopyrighted concert music. So, too, did Joseph Karl Briel,
whose score for D. W. Griffith's *The Birth of a Nation* was a
pastiche which included borrowings from the works of Grieg,
Wagner, Verdi, Rossini, Liszt, Tchaikovsky, and the songs "Dixie"
and "The Star-Spangled Banner," in addition to original music.
(Griffith, who had studied music, was one of many silent directors
who employed musicians to play on the sets of his films as an
emotional aid to the actors.) The "authorship" of silent film scores
is complicated by another factor. As Earle Hagen points out in the
introduction to his *Scoring for Films,* the silent-movie-house
pianist was also in a sense a "composer" — he rarely played a piece
of music the same way twice. It wasn't until the last years of the
silent era, and the introduction of sound systems combining either
cylinder or disc records with visual projection, that a film's musical
score — whatever its derivation — was heard in the same version
at every performance of the film.

Contrary to belief, music scoring was no more exempt from the
insecurities resulting from the advent of the all-sound film than
other areas of moviemaking. With few exceptions, in the earliest
nonmusical talking films music is used continuously, as it is in
silent pictures, or is almost nonexistent. By 1936, however, the
basic pattern of what is now called the "traditional" or "formal"
sound film score was set, and some of the greatest names in music
— Honegger, Shostakovich, Prokofiev, Walton, Thomson and
Auric among them — were composing for films. Copland, Amram,
and other composers whose primary achievements are not in the
motion picture field, wrote film scores in subsequent years. But
the strongest and most abiding influences on traditional sound
film scoring are the men who have from early in their musical
careers devoted themselves either substantially (as Erich Wolf-
gang Korngold, Miklos Rosza and Bernard Herrmann have) or
entirely (as Alfred Newman, Max Steiner, David Raksin, Bronislau

Kaper and Dmitri Tiomkin have) to film work. Against the background of radical shifts in the theory and practice of film music in recent years, Elmer Bernstein, John Green, Alex North and Jerry Goldsmith have adapted and kept alive the traditional form of motion picture scoring.

Before examining how the film composer works, and exploring his relationships with the director and other film personnel, it may be useful to focus attention on some of the potential functions of motion picture music.

ELMER BERNSTEIN: Cecil B. DeMille believed in music as a story-telling part. . . . That was his greatest talent, he told a story. He believed that every individual and emotion in a film should have a theme. In the case of *The Ten Commandments*, there was a theme for Moses, there was a theme for God, there was a theme for evil, there was a theme for the exodus. His concept was: if two characters are in a scene at the same time the themes for the two characters should be intertwined and used as the background for this scene. DeMille believed in this Wagnerian theory, and I think that in the terms in which he made his pictures it was very successful for him.

You might decide that one of the things you want to do with music is to tie a picture together. You find some central theme, a kind of glue. You might make up one motif and really bang away at it all through the film, to help unify the thing. If you work with Wagnerian leitmotif on a . . . fragmented film, with quick cutting back and forth and back and forth . . . you get a very humorous effect. I did that in *Thoroughly Modern Millie*, where I purposefully did that sort of thing for a comic effect.

Music can be used where it helps establish atmosphere . . . in a geographical sense. The music of the locale. In *The Magnificent Seven* I used a lot of local instruments, Mexican instruments. But if it becomes an end in itself as a piece of exotica, it gets to be a bore after a while.

Music can be used in a purely kinetic way. It steps up the pace of the picture, or it's part of the pace of the picture. In my case, the most obvious example of using music in this way would be *The Magnificent Seven*. My reaction to the picture

when I first saw it, if I said, Well, what contribution can I make
at this point? . . . I felt I wanted to get up and ride the picture,
I thought it was a little slow-moving. What it lacked most to
me was a sense of getting on with it.

There are other ways to use music kinetically. For instance, if
a man is riding a horse across a field, you may use music in such
a way that it underlines the image. In other words, you pick up
his actual pace. That's the last thing you should have to use
music for in a film. If the image isn't strong enough to support
itself it shouldn't be there in the first place. What the music can
do, perhaps, would be to develop some emotional aspect behind
the scene. In other words, where is the man on the horse going,
what's his state of mind? What music can do in a film is to
create an emotional ambience. That is its greatest use and its
most valid use.

In discussing the use of music to create an emotional climate
for a film, Bernstein cites three examples from his own work that
vary somewhat as to method and intent:

In *To Kill a Mockingbird,* which was reasonably subtle,
musically, I went for something very simple, basically the magic
of the child's world, represented by the various bell-like kinds
of sound I used.

There was a scene in *Birdman of Alcatraz* depicting the first
birth of a bird in this prison. What I was saying in the music,
which is somewhat contrapuntal, was, Here's a fantastic, beautiful, miraculous thing happening in this terrible place. And
nowhere in the music is there a hint of this terrible place.

In Anthony Mann's *Men in War* there was a platoon of men
cut off from the main body of troops, and they had to get back.
There's a scene in which they're marching through a forest with
death all around them; the whole thing is mined. Something
which has always fascinated me about war is the death and
destruction going on in the midst of the beauty of the forest
and the birds [singing]. So I played a very, very gentle kind of
rustling music that dealt only with bird sounds and the kind of
quiet, tense beauty of the forest that surrounded [the soldiers].
It was contrapuntal to the scene, it was another element.

Bernstein suggests that it is possible for basically utilitarian film music to transcend its function ("I generally try to incorporate it into a bigger scheme of things") and aid in the creation of an emotional ambience.

In scoring *Raintree County,* John Green says that he "decided on the leitmotif approach — hanging themes on the various characters and locales — to peg them for the sake of the viewer, or comprehender if you will. I felt that I could enhance the impact and clarity of the dramatic action." Still, the theme of Nell Gaither (Eva Marie Saint), whose relationship with Johnny (the film's protagonist, played by Montgomery Clift) deteriorates when he becomes involved with Susanna (Elizabeth Taylor), does more than just identify or define a character. "Nell's piece was used as a figuration," Green explains. "Whenever I felt that, dramatically, one had to be reminded of this other relationship, this music played."

And the film's main locale theme — the main theme of the score, which subsequently became known as the song "Raintree County" — accommodates emotional resonances. As Green says, "It endeavors to give the impression that Raintree County was a part of the characters. There was a little enclave somewhere in Indiana that was their lives." The theme for the swamp, the locus of a mythical raintree sought by the idealistic Johnny, also alludes to more than a geographical entity. Green attempted — successfully — to insert a feeling of "spaciousness" and "heighten the emotional content" of the dialogueless scene in which Johnny goes through the swamp.

When Johnny falls into the swamp, the music underlines the action. "This is the point where I may have come dangerously close to the border of 'mickey-mousing,'" Green admits. "Some people criticized me for that. They said that it was too representational. I figured that the swamp was the kind that you fall into when you get too preoccupied with looking for some ephemeral, spiritual thing . . . when you fail to realize that the spiritual thing is found by the way you live from hour to hour and minute to minute."

Just as Green's use of leitmotif justifies itself many times over by the larger ends it achieves, Alex North's jazz composition for the initial meeting of Blanche DuBois (Vivien Leigh) and Stanley

Kowalski (Marlon Brando) in *A Streetcar Named Desire* has an emotional rationale that exceeds in importance the logical, or practical explanations for its existence. "Source music" in the sense that the music is presumed to emanate from a club advertised by a flickering neon sign in the background of the scene, North feels the piece "underlined that particular scene." But the arrangement and instrumentation ("a saxophone solo, smoky-sounding piccolos, with the only percussive beat from the piano") play *against* the scene in an emotionally suggestive way. The "comedy" scores of the Frenchman Georges Auric for the British films *Passport to Pimlico* and *The Lavender Hill Mob* subtly punctuate the often wildly improbable action on the screen, but at the same time they comment on it, usually by the infusion of Gallic elements into the music. David Raksin's monothematic score for *Laura* is utilitarian in the sense that it cannily excites interest in the title character in the early stretches of the film, when she is absent from the screen, but it is successful in this regard only because it manages to suggest the emotional significance Laura has for the characters whose lives she has touched.

In "nine cases out of ten," according to Alex North, the composer's work begins after a film has been shot and is in its rough assembly; there are only four instances in a career spanning almost a quarter of a century in which North's involvement began at an earlier stage.

ELMER BERNSTEIN: For years and years producers didn't want to call to consult with me earlier; they were afraid they would have to pay me for a day. I hated that. After a while, I said, "No, I don't want to make deals by the week anymore, I make only flat deals, so that we don't have this nervousness about who gets paid when."

Elmer Bernstein also says that at an earlier time, when the major studios had large, well-organized music departments, "the director never got into the discussion of who the composer was going to be, and the producer rarely did. The head of the music department made the selection." Today, whether the selection of a composer is made by the director or the producer, or both, depends in large part on the relative degree of strength or influence each enjoys in a filmmaking situation. Jerry Goldsmith reports that producer Arthur P. Jacobs hired him to do the score for *Planet of the Apes* before Franklin Schaffner was engaged to direct the film. Yet following the time-honored pattern, Goldsmith didn't begin his work until filming was completed. In the case of combination producer-directors, such as Otto Preminger, things are obviously less complicated: one man makes the choice.

After his selection for a particular assignment, the composer examines a rough cut of the film.

ALEX NORTH: I like to look at a film by myself and make notes, so that I am not inhibited by the presence of the director or the producer or whoever else is involved creatively. I have a better feeling of concentration and prefer to make my own analysis as to where the music should be used and what purpose it serves. . . .

JERRY GOLDSMITH: It sometimes happens that when you see a film the director has gotten bored with it. So he puts in track music to keep his interest up. You're stuck with this somehow, and psychologically, it works against you; I find myself working down to that level. I've adopted the policy that if there's temp music in it I won't watch it.

ALEX NORTH: . . . Then I like meeting with the director if he is available (he may be off on another project). . . .

When Jerry Goldsmith began work on the score of *The Don Is Dead*, the director, Richard Fleischer, was already involved in the preparation of another film. Goldsmith's only contact with him consisted of a telephone conversation; decisions involving the music in the movie were arrived at in a series of discussions with producer Hal Wallis.

JERRY GOLDSMITH: Ideally, I like to go over my notes and discuss my point of view and the director's point of view in terms of whether music should be used in a particular scene. Also, we discuss what contribution the music makes, if any. Then you agree or disagree and compromise.

ELMER BERNSTEIN: You have a discussion, and you say, "Well,
listen, I have a better idea, listen to my idea." And then the
director listens, but it's the director's decision, it is the director's
prerogative to make the wrong decision, even. The composer
has got to do one of two things. If he's dishonest he may go
ahead and do what he wants to do anyway. If he isn't, then he
will set about to try to find a way to achieve what he wants in
the framework of the director's desires. And if he's *really* honest
he may say, "I can't do it." I don't know anybody, though you
might find somebody like that. . . . I did a picture a couple of
years ago called *True Grit*. Although it was very "western" in
an old-fashioned way, having John Wayne as the star, there
was something slightly hip about the picture. The dialogue was
kind of quick — I found it a very interesting picture. I wanted
to score it in a more modern way and I spoke to Hal Wallis, the
producer, about that. He didn't want that. He wanted to stay
reasonably traditional. And we did in the scoring of that picture. That was his choice. . . . Anthony Mann, the director of
*Men in War,* was a marvelous guy. He never said anything to
me about the music. He never said a word. . . . It's interesting —
in my desire to talk I make people uncomfortable; I think I
make some directors and producers terribly uncomfortable because they don't want to make those decisions.

JERRY GOLDSMITH: John Frankenheimer did not have a great
knowledge of musical instrumentation. On *Seconds,* I had the
idea of using just organ and strings. I wanted a certain purity in
the music, along with . . . a certain irony — a quasi-Baroque
approach. I wanted the massiveness of the organ. I told John
the idea, and he said, "I *hate* organ, I *hate* it!" At that time I
had an organ at my house, and I said, "Come over, we'll take a
listen to what I have for the opening of the picture." I played
it, and he said, "I love it!" But there had never been a great
in-depth discussion. . . . Franklin Schaffner is one of the few
directors I've worked with who has a true understanding of
music . . . a knowledge and awareness of the dramatic value of
music. So it's easier to communicate with him, and there's a
constant dialogue that goes on between us.

Arriving at an overall idea of the function of music in a film —
whether by decree, consensus, or a unilateral decision on the part
of the composer — is probably accomplished with much less strain
than "spotting" it, that is, determining which scenes, or sections of
scenes, are to be scored.

ELMER BERNSTEIN: Usually, the director wants all the weak scenes
scored, and the composer wants to score all the good scenes,
because they're the most stimulating ones.

JOHN GREEN: The original roadshow version of *Raintree County*
for which I wrote the score was over three hours long. I wrote
and recorded exactly two hours and eighteen minutes of music,
of which two hours and eight minutes remained in the release
print. That is one hell of a lot of music. As released, the picture
ran a little under three hours, so the proportion of music went
up. There were one or two spots for which I was asked to
write music and refused because I felt that these spots were
dramatically complete and did not require the added element
of music. The music that is in the picture resulted from my
"spotting" it and from my discussions with the director, Edward
Dmytryk; the writer, Millard Kaufman; Sidney Franklin, the
great director-producer who was involved in the editing of
*Raintree County*, and the studio head, Dore Schary. The ultimate amount and placement of music resulted from a meeting
of the minds.

ALEX NORTH: In the area of scoring or not scoring certain scenes,
you may argue with the director, but very often, for various
reasons — the acting didn't quite come off, the pacing was slow,
or whatever — he wants music to try and help. I tried to "help"
in scoring *Who's Afraid of Virginia Woolf?*, where there were
two scenes that I felt should not have been scored, but Mike
Nichols thought music could add another dimension to the
scene and action. I confess his judgment proved correct. Mike
is unusually music-conscious . . . and I'm happy I furnished the
extra music.

It occurred to me when I saw *A Streetcar Named Desire* after many years, that I would not have scored several scenes because the music level was so low. This is exasperating and annoying and reminds me of Muzak — and is better without any music. Looking back now on an early scene in which Karl Malden meets Vivien Leigh, I was surprised to hear a lush piece for harp and high strings. I don't remember having written this, but I now realize that it was much too early in their relationship to establish a motif that would or could tip off the fact that some sort of romance would eventually materialize between them.

JERRY GOLDSMITH: A director may sulk, but if he's halfway human about it, he'll say okay. The greatest example of that is John Huston. On *Freud,* we kept running a scene over and over, and I said, "Well, let's try some music in it." And John said, "No, why should you spend your time and effort and energy writing something that you don't feel and that probably won't work anyway. Forget it, let's go on."

After a film is spotted, cue sheets — basically, written descriptions of the scenes to be scored, which note their duration down to one-third of a second — are drawn up.

ELMER BERNSTEIN: The composer at this point becomes a hermit; you go home and you do your thing. . . . Sometimes it's difficult, you know, to be all alone in a medium which is not basically a lonely medium. Some of the composers currently working in motion pictures bring a moviola into the house and run the film on the moviola. I have a very good memory, so I've never felt that I didn't remember what the picture looks like.

ALEX NORTH: I try to chart the music out for the entire film in advance. This is dictated by the story conflict, whether it involves one person, two, three, or whether it is a spectacle, [for which I do what] I refer to as "exterior" or "objective" composing: the music is not necessarily making a personal comment or statement, but a purely visual or physical one. I like to start from a melodic point of view and treat that melody with em-

bellished rhythmic and contrapuntal variations as the particular story develops, enhancing the dramatic content. An example
is the simple varsovienne, the Polish theme that Blanche —
Vivien Leigh — keeps recalling in *Streetcar*. It is used in its
barest form and also within the [context of a] large orchestra.

In dialogue scenes, very often you have to make sure that the
actor's voice and the music do not conflict or defeat each other's
purposes. For example, with Orson Welles in *The Long, Hot
Summer*, with his great resonant bass voice, I had to make sure
that the register of the orchestra was above the range of his
voice.

ELMER BERNSTEIN: After having been given much too little time to
write the score . . .

JERRY GOLDSMITH (Uncomplainingly): Oh, one never has enough
time. I usually have about five weeks.

ELMER BERNSTEIN: . . . you come back with an orchestra and the
music is recorded while the film is running on a screen. Usually,
everybody on the scoring stage is enthralled . . . because it's the
only thing in films that happens fast.

ALEX NORTH: The composer is very fortunate in the sense that he is
the one to contribute the final element or ingredient to the film.
If the director comes to the recording and dislikes what you've
done, if you agree, you can perhaps make a change then and
there. But it is very unlikely that money will be spent to bring
the orchestra back to record a new piece. Naturally, [the direc-
tor] is not able to listen to the score in advance, but if I have
respect for [his] taste and judgment in music I [will] play a
theme or two on the piano to placate his anxieties.

JOHN GREEN: My approach to the musical sound of *Raintree
County* was a lush approach. . . . I thought that was the right
approach. Perhaps a drier, cooler approach might have been
better, but so far nobody has suggested that to me. When I
recorded this romantic, soaring swamp sequence, the orchestra
applauded and Sidney Franklin came running out of the sound

booth to congratulate me. Film editor Margaret Booth sent
two dozen American Beauty roses that were at my home by
the time I arrived there from the recording session. I confess
that I fell in love with my concept . . . and, of course, that *can*
be dangerous.

There are cases, however, in which the dialogue between the
composer and the director doesn't really begin until the score is
recorded. In other cases, discussions between composer and director resume at this point or later, at the dubbing or re-recording
stage, when the music, dialogue and sound effects tracks are integrated.

JERRY GOLDSMITH: Many directors say, "I don't know anything
about music, but I know when it's right." That one really drives
you up a wall, because it often isn't true. But in Robert Wise's
case, it was true. There was one scene [in *The Sand Pebbles*],
the first time you see the boat going up the river. It was so
enormous: this huge screen was filled, and the music was really
blasting away. He said, "I hate it," and I said, "What's wrong?"
He said, "Well, it's too big. Here's this crummy little boat going
up this great big river through the countryside. You're playing
the countryside, not the boat." I said, "You know, you're absolutely right." The boat was a character in the film too, but at
that instant it was not that large and noble. The nobility came
later in the film.

Franklin Schaffner has the ability . . . to bring everyone's
interest out and to know what their contribution is — what *he*
wants them to contribute to the film, what *they* want to contribute to the film. . . . On *Patton,* he was on the stage the entire
time we were recording. In one scene, the slapping incident,
what I wanted to do was to create sympathy for Patton prior
to the scene. As he was going through the hospital, you could see
the man was really torn apart. He had been riding in a jeep and
the wounded men were marching past him and a soldier makes
this comment that he overhears, "There's Old Blood 'n' Guts."
Someone replies, "Yeah, our blood, his guts." This weighs
heavily upon him. So I tried to create — to bring the audience
to a very sympathetic attitude toward Patton, and try to soften

their feeling toward him so that when he finally did slap the soldier you were shocked by this savage outburst. This was something I had discussed with Franklin, and he said it made sense to him. But I did it too well, and only when we were in the dubbing stage, with all the dialogue and the effects, and got the total feel of it did I realize that it was a disaster. I thought it worked so well that you wanted to applaud him for hitting a soldier. You believe that he's absolutely right and justified in what he did. Certainly there are enough people who believe that without my music. Franklin spent a great deal of time and thought on this, and he had to agree with me in my feeling. But he said, "Maybe there's a way we can still accomplish something and save the music." We spent almost a day starting it at different places, bringing it in later, taking it out sooner, eliminating this part of it. Finally I said, "Franklin, it just isn't going to work. Take it out and be done with it." There was no music. That's the way *we* resolved it. But Franklin, because of his respect for me and what I was trying to do, believed there was a validity in my [original] theory, that it was worth trying to make it work.

ELMER BERNSTEIN: The filmmakers usually get terribly nervous [during the dubbing]. They suddenly get full of a tremendous sense of eternity, and the most commercial film suddenly becomes the Taj Mahal. It's a terribly tense process, with basically little give-and-take — which is unfortunate. I have had producers who have allowed me to sit in on dubbing sessions to control effects, because that is very musical in character. There are certain things which are inimical to music, such as a windstorm. If you're going to have a windstorm there's no point in having music. Let that be the score. In recent years I've chosen not to go to dubbing sessions most of the time, which results in a tremendous loss to the music that I do. I used to go to the dubbing room and fight a lot, but I kind of lost my taste for that.

ALEX NORTH: Fortunately, Kazan was at the re-recording of *A Streetcar Named Desire* and *Viva Zapata!* If the director is not there to support your music it can be drowned out by horses' whinnies, or anything the sound effects men put on the track. I

was so frustrated at the preview of *Streetcar* by the generally
low level of that score that I walked out. The [studio] music
department head, Ray Heindorf, walked out with me. I told
him that if the music was going to make a contribution, then it
has got to be heard. I think that music is obtrusive only when
it is wrong. I think you should be aware of it, if it is the right
music.

Ironically, North had hoped to end *A Streetcar Named Desire*
very quietly and very tenderly, but was overriden by studio executives. "The picture had to have a loud ending; that was the pattern
of scoring at the time."
The observations that follow concern those comparatively rare
situations in which the composer began his work before shooting
on a film was completed.

ELMER BERNSTEIN: DeMille had me on *The Ten Commandments*
from the day he started. He would call me on the set when he
was shooting scenes, and he'd say, "We have a situation with
this — Charlton Heston has to walk across the way and back
and I'm going to follow him. I really don't know how long it's
going to take. I'll run a rehearsal for you and I would like you
to tell me whether you think that this is something where music
will function, because this will have an effect on how I stage the
walk." You could say, "I don't know"; that was perfectly all
right with him. Or you could give him a precise answer: "I
think yes, that's perfectly fine" or, "No, we won't have any
music here, so don't depend on my music."

JOHN GREEN: When I first read the novel *Raintree County*, and
then found out that MGM was going to make it, I knew that
I wanted to write the score. I envisioned the picture in black-
and-white, at normal program length and not as a spectacle.
. . . I also initially envisioned [a score on a corresponding scale].
When I found out how Dore Schary saw the picture I was
worried. He saw the film quite differently: in color . . . as a
spectacle, an epic . . . a sort of latter-day *Gone With the Wind*.
Thus, the film was mounted in what initially seemed to me to be
an overblown frame. Actually, the novel is a psychological

study . . . a searching journey into the psyche of this poor be-
nighted girl from the South [i.e., Susanna, played by Elizabeth
Taylor]. As the film was done, it emerged as an intimate psychological study rolling around in a frame too big for it. But I
was still beguiled, trapped by my determination to do the
score. I am not attempting to alibi the score; I think it is a very
decent job and, frankly, I like it *very* much!

When I read the script, before I had seen a foot of film and
before we started shooting, I wrote the following themes: the
theme of the locale, the love theme and Susanna's "mad" theme.
I had previously determined that the mad theme would be
serially constructed. I already knew that I was going to use
strange bell-like sounds mixed in with it . . . antique cymbals
of varied pitches.

Green reports that he saw the daily rushes on *Raintree County;*
was then given a black-and-white dupe of the rough cut on which
he "worked closely" with the director, Edward Dmytryk; and subsequently worked with a color dupe while Sidney Franklin and
Margaret Booth "as his lieutenant" supervised the fine-cutting of
the film. Apart from the themes written after he read the script,
Green composed the score during these various stages of production and postproduction. Green notes that *Raintree County* was
"one of those rare instances" in which the making of the sound
effects track was delayed until the musical score had been recorded.

JOHN GREEN: [During the shooting of] *They Shoot Horses, Don't
They?* . . . I was with the director, Sydney Pollack, every
minute. . . . Music was a constant and vital part of the whole
ambience of the picture; it was going all the time. We were
locked into the necessity of musical sound (since the entire
action of the film took place in a big dance hall). That dance
band was right smack on camera, and . . . we were locked in
by what the band was playing. We preselected all the songs,
and also predetermined the tempo and the general sound of
the arrangements. In terms of the scene that would be playing
in front of the music . . . to the degree that we could possibly
do it . . . we preanswered such questions as, "When the camera

comes by and 'sees' the band, will the brass be playing? If so, will the brass be muted or open? Will the reeds be on clarinets or saxes?" Then, Al Woodbury and I made what we called sideline scores, and this was throwing darts seventy percent in the dark. Who knew how long Sydney Pollack was going to shoot in a given setup? Who knew after he shot this angle, that angle, this reverse, that close-up, that medium shot, how he was going to put it all together? And all of those factors determine musical length, of course. Sydney gave me time to rehearse the sideline band for every one of these scenes. A piano was set up on a dolly and rolled out in front of the band, and I played. The musicians didn't make any sound, but they had in front of them a quasi-orchestration and mimed playing. They all had the melody line and, in addition to that, the bass, the piano and the drums had a rhythmic indication. On all the parts, in red, was a dotted-line indication of who was playing in any given bar. Ultimately, Sydney made his rough cut . . . but, from that point onward, we had to cut the picture together, as a team. To the degree that he possibly could, Sydney molded every cut, every angle that he used to the metric pattern of the music. We then postscored the actual music to the final cut of the picture.

ALEX NORTH: I worked on *Spartacus* for a year and a half. It gave me an opportunity to write reams and reams of musical ideas. For the training sequences and the battle scenes where the two armies opposed each other, I wrote a temporary score for two pianos and percussion. Stanley Kubrick is exceptionally musical, and so is the man who was editing the picture, Irving Lerner. They would say, "Let's try something. Let's use this temporary score with its impacts, its pulse and its rhythm. . . ." They tried to cut certain sequences according to my music. The temp music was done to a click-track — metronomic tempo — so that when it was rewritten to the final cut it was mathematically accurate. . . . [Apropos of the interdependence of music and film editing, in *The Film Sense* montage-minded director Sergei Eisenstein recalls that in some sequences of *Alexander Nevsky* "the shots were cut to a previously recorded music-track," in other sequences "the entire piece of music was written to a final cutting of the picture," and in still other sequences "both approaches" were used. — D.C.] Having that much time to score a film is a rare luxury, and when I saw the final cut I was able to compose a much more sophisticated score.

I knew I was going to do *Who's Afraid of Virginia Woolf?* about two months in advance of shooting. I approached that complex musical problem three ways. First I wrote a jazz version [of the score] and felt that wasn't right. There was so much action, so much dialogue in the film that the accents would possibly hit an important syllable in a word and thus clutter the track and made it unclear. Next I attempted a serial approach, which I gave up because I felt it was too abstract. . . . [I] finally ended up with a quasi-Baroque style, avoiding sentimentality, but at the same time hoping it would convey a feeling of a love story. . . . It is only against such a background that . . . quarreling [of the kind indulged in by the characters in the film] has any deep significance. The things we do to the people we love — and can *only* do to the people we love.

JERRY GOLDSMITH: I found that in the one instance where I was brought in early [Otto Preminger's *In Harm's Way*] it was a total loss. The only contribution you could make — he'd be shooting a scene and he'd ask, "Would you like me to make this scene a little longer so you can play a little more music here?" What can I say? I haven't composed the music, I don't even know if I'm going to compose music for that scene until it's all put together. Putting music in a film is not an arbitrary thing. There's a form and a shape, an overall pattern of where you put music in. I can't even write a theme for a picture from the script, for the simple reason that we are dealing in a visual medium. I am making an attempt to comment on the emotional elements that are not visible on the screen. You can't get that from a script because you have no idea what's going to appear on the screen. I have to wait until I see it. "Give me a few more feet so I can compose some music there!" It may be on the cutting room floor, maybe it won't even be in the picture. You can't really give in a situation like that. . . . Unless someone is doing something very specific with a rhythmic quality to it that's going to be cut to the beat of the music. But that's still done in the editing stage. So I really think that's idealistic non-sense. The composer really just sits [on a film set] — nothing really concerns him. His function is strictly a postproduction function.

The serious composer who does film work on a regular or exclusive basis has probably always been involved in some kind of artistic self-abnegation. To begin with, there are the requirements of time-composing, writing in segments that are, at most, a few minutes in length.

ELMER BERNSTEIN: You develop that technique and you get very, very good at it. But I think the measure of any artist's achievement is his ability to sustain and develop a line or an emotion over a long period of time, in terms of a larger form. And this, I think, the film composer tends to lose to his own detriment and, eventually, to the detriment of anybody for whom he works.

Once a composer decides to devote the bulk of his time and energy to motion picture music, necessity often forces him to accept inferior assignments.

ALEX NORTH: There are very few films that I have been involved in where I had that so-called inspiration. I mean, *Willard* was about rats. So where does my inspiration come from? There was a scene where the rats were chewing up a man, so you try to write a piece of music that lends something to the scene that isn't there. . . .

And sometimes there are fluky extrinsic considerations that dictate alterations in the composer's work for those rare films to which he feels a commitment, which "inspire" him.

ALEX NORTH: There was one scene in *A Streetcar Named Desire* where Brando was calling Stella [Kim Hunter] who was upstairs visiting her friends. When she slowly comes downstairs, apparently unable to resist the physical attraction of her husband, [there was] a piece of music for saxophones, muted trombones and light percussion. The film was shown to that [Roman] Catholic organization in New York that rates films. Their reaction was that this particular scene . . . was "carnal" because of the music. I was obliged to rescore it with strings and a French horn solo.

Developments since the early 1950s have increased the film composer's generic pessimism. The decline in feature film production after the advent of television forced many talented men into accepting TV work. For example, Leonard Rosenman, whose film credits include *East of Eden* and *Rebel Without a Cause*, now provides the music for *Marcus Welby, M.D.* In the July 1972 issue of *High Fidelity* magazine, Gene Lees writes:

> In these days of low-budget quickie TV movies or one-hour shows, a composer may be given ten days in which to come up with a score, and sometimes only six days for forty minutes of music. If you've ever seen one of the composers working against such a deadline . . . you will know immediately why movie composers get bugged, and why so much film scoring in TV movies, even by gifted writers, is crushingly trite.

Though complaints against the "commercialism" of the American film date back to nickelodeon days, considerations of the marketplace began to affect the composer in a new, more direct way in the late 1950s with the burgeoning sales of motion picture sound track albums.

JOHN GREEN: While there are notable exceptions, nowadays the musical treatment of dramatic motion pictures has been taken over by the record companies. . . . The *former* barometer was, "What does the music on the sound track of this film do to enhance the dramatic and emotional impact, to heighten the interest and entertainment value of this film *in the theater* where it is being seen and heard? However, the barometer *today* is, "What will make a good single record? What name group can come up with something (with a title that coincides with the title of this film) that will sell a million singles or a half a million albums?" That potential, record-selling "smash" having been found, it then gets "shoehorned" into the film.

A comparatively recent, and even more disconcerting trend is the use of a collection of original or preexisting songs in place of a traditional, or formal, film score, thereby obviating the need for the film composer altogether.

ELMER BERNSTEIN: Unless a film is specifically designed for the use of lyrics — in other words, unless you've left some elements out which the lyrics are going to take up — I really don't see why you should resort to lyrics in a film, I really don't. . . . I thought it worked beautifully in *The Graduate* and I think that Mike Nichols must have consciously shot the picture knowing that he was going to use those songs. I think he left some of the mood to be created strictly by the lyrics rather than by other things.

JERRY GOLDSMITH: A formal score would have been much better, I think, would have said much more. I think Nichols was planning to use a formal score, but put those songs in as a guide track to cut to and then kept them as the score. . . . There's . . . a song in *The Don Is Dead,* but it makes a story point. It's not extraneous. A character in the film writes a song, and then later on it's heard.

The pervasive cynicism of the postindustrial, postassassination, post-Watergate era is also thought to have had an adverse effect on film scoring and the status of the film composer.

ELMER BERNSTEIN: We are being dehumanized in so many ways that it's staggering. . . . What does this do to music? We're embarrassed, we really are embarrassed if we hear a soaring line. We reject the soaring line. We reject the strong musical statement. We want to do things in relatively unemotional ways.

Bernstein also says that the widespread recognition since the 1960s of the director as the key figure in filmmaking has so inflated many directors' egos that they minimize the potential importance of the composer's contribution and, consequently, are unwilling to spend much time communicating with the composer. Yet American filmmaker Brian DePalma has acknowledged his indebtedness to Bernard Herrmann for the role the composer played in the realization of *Sisters*. And would anyone, least of all Bernardo Bertolucci, deny the value of Gato Barbieri's jazz-Latin rhythms to *Last Tango in Paris?* It could be that films like *Last Tango,* which are augmented by the composer's work, and directors like DePalma, who credit it, will make good Jerry Goldsmith's prediction that "ten years from now we may be sitting around and saying about today, 'Those were the days.'"

# TEN
## Special Effects/Special Surprises

The term special effects conjures up cinematic images of fires, explosions, storms on land and sea, over- and undersized human and animal mutants. The greater part of the special effects artist's work is devoted to the artificial reproduction of natural and unnatural phenomena which, after a moment's reflection, the reasonably informed spectator is likely to recognize as artificial reproductions — special effects. A somewhat different category of special effects, though equally concerned with illusion, is less known and its creations more difficult to identify. That is why space is devoted to it here. Yet the special effects artist who contributes to a film by simulating a tidal wave is by no means less a collaborative associate of its director than the one who aided Howard Hawks in executing the scenes involving the leopard in *Bringing Up Baby*, Stanley Kramer in carrying out the grand-finale plaza sequence in *It's a Mad, Mad, Mad, Mad World* and

Orson Welles in realizing his vision of many scenes in *Citizen Kane*.

LINWOOD DUNN: After the first day's shooting on *Bringing Up Baby,* they found that the trained leopard was not so well trained. So the scenes in which the leopard appeared had to be done with the help of trick photography.

[To accomplish the scene in which Cary Grant and Katharine Hepburn ride in the front seat of a car and the leopard is a back-seat passenger] the leopard was processed [photographed separately] in front of the moving street background, seated in a mock-up of the rear half of the car. Then the film [of the leopard and the street] was back-projected behind [Cary Grant and Katharine Hepburn] in the mock-up of the front half of the car. So, everything behind the two people is on a screen.

Here's an example of the use of a simple split screen: Charlie Ruggles's reaction [upon seeing] the leopard . . . [and his terrified flight were filmed in one shot]. Then . . . [in a separate shot], the trainer . . . got the leopard to turn his head to follow Ruggles's exit . . . [and] the two scenes [were] later composited.

In the scenes of the leopard walking between Katharine Hepburn and Cary Grant [such as when Grant walks down the hallway of an apartment building followed by the leopard, which is followed in turn by Hepburn], we utilized all the space that was available between the [actors] for the mattes [of the animal]. We shot the leopard first, and timed his walk. Then the actors walked at about the same speed. We then put the two scenes together on the optical printer [by] using a mechanical wipe-off device. . . . This wipe-off is motor driven, so we drove the wipe-off device at about the speed Grant was walking and we kept adjusting it until we found the correct speed to follow him through the scene. The speed of the leopard and [Hepburn] were about the same. It wouldn't have mattered if they had varied slightly as long as they didn't run into the matte. It's just a matter of checking the action through the optical-printer-viewing camera. The setting and blending of the two mattes is really not too difficult.

Dunn reports that he worked on Stanley Kramer's *It's a Mad,
Mad, Mad, Mad World* for close to a year. His involvement with
the film began with a conference in which Kramer and fifteen
key members of the film company participated. Using a storyboard breakdown of the climactic plaza sequence as a reference,
the feasibility of each segment of the sequence was discussed from
the points of view of the various artists, craftsmen, and technicians
who would be involved in its realization. (According to Dunn, one
of the advantages of the studio system of moviemaking, with its
fully staffed and continuously operating departments, was that
conferences of the kind held by the independent producer-director
Kramer were a matter of course. An employee writer, he says,
wouldn't include a scene requiring out-of-the-ordinary or obviously difficult special effects in a script until a resident special
effects expert had been consulted.) Kramer had previously indicated how strongly he would rely on Dunn's abilities by telling
him that the plaza sequence had "to top all of the other stunts
in the picture. If it doesn't top them, we don't have a show."
Dunn recalls that various effects in this vitally important sequence
were accomplished by:

Integrating, by means of matte processing of twenty-one exposures, shots of a four-story set erected at Universal Studios
with a painting, action elements, and footage of a real street
several miles away;

The use of stuntmen wearing masks made from the faces of the
principal players;

Miniatures of various portions of the set with three sizes and
types of figure models taking the place of stuntmen; and

Salvaging, through a traveling split-screen technique effected
on the optical printer, a scene in which a moving truck topples
a water tower which in turn knocks over an outhouse. The wire
mechanism triggering the collapse of the outhouse was set off
too soon, and the camera recorded it collapsed before the tower
had actually hit it.

LINWOOD DUNN: The art director will give you a sketch of what
he has in mind. Then, later, when they're building or rigging

the set, you look at it with the director — in this case, Stanley Kramer — and he locates the camera setup for you. Then you plan all aspects of the scene and start to generate the elements you need. The great day comes when you have two thousand extras on the set and you now have the procedure all worked out. You set up the camera where [you] previously agreed [it would be] and then Kramer — and he's not unusual in this respect — might say, "You know, on second thought, I think I'd rather have the camera over here, about twenty-five feet to the side." Then what do you do? It's very hazardous now to change from that original setup because of the preliminary planning. You just call for another camera and set it where he wants the new angle. And so you're still protected with the initial shot — and sometimes you end up using the one he picked out first anyway. You must do two things: you've got to protect yourself so you will end up with a good shot, and at the same time give the director what he wants and do so without making a big deal out of it.

A small amount of fuss, based on a misunderstanding, preceded Dunn's mutually beneficial association with Orson Welles on *Citizen Kane*. "When Welles, with the help of his editor, Robert Wise, discovered what could be created on the magical optical printer, he began asking for anything to enhance his show."

LINWOOD DUNN: I would sometimes say, "No, we can't do that," because I really didn't think it was practical from the cost standpoint. He'd be very polite and return the next day and say, "What do you mean, it's not possible?" I'd say, "No, nothing's impossible. It's just a matter of time and money." Then he'd come back again and say, "You've got the time and the money's okay." So then I'd go up to the front office for a confirmation of this. "Yes, he has complete autonomy on the show — up to a certain point." So then we did many unusual and difficult shots. There are all kinds of scenes in *Citizen Kane* that were modified on the optical printer while the picture was being edited.

There was no statue on [the library] set. Upon Welles's request, [it] was added later. The scene started at the base of the statue in the library. So we had to shoot the statue as a separate miniature, two feet high, and on the optical printer make a downward traveling split screen and matte it onto the production scene.

In the opening sequence, the glass ball is in Kane's hand when he's lying on his deathbed. The ball shot was made with the camera angle cutting at about his elbow. During the editing, Welles said, "I'd like to start up inside the ball." I said, "The quality won't be any good. I'd have to make an optical zoom that would take me this far in, and then another one that would take me that far, and . . . by the time I have made a dupe on top of a dupe and so on, to get that much of a zoom in, the grain and definition would be very bad. It just wouldn't be any good." He was very polite and said. "Would you mind trying to do it?" I said, "Of course not." So I made the dupe with all of the zoom dupes on top of each other. When finally the printer moved up inside the ball, it looked just like I'd warned him. He then said, "Let's double-expose some more falling snow inside the ball." We did this, and that smoothed out the excessive grain; and once we started the pullback motion, the definition problem was greatly alleviated.

"Rosebud," too, at the end — that long move down to the name Rosebud was done in great part on the optical printer. Welles couldn't get in far enough on the set during the actual shooting, so the optical printer completed the move.

We put ceilings on the sets. We put walls in. That room with all the junk and boxes [piled up] — there's a wing on the side, like an adjoining room. There was none when they shot it, and then Welles said he wanted the wing in the scene. We just blocked out an area of the scene on the printer, made a painting of the wing, and matted it in.

There's a shot where Welles is standing in the doorway in the distance down a hall and Dorothy Comingore is in the foreground. She is leaning against a door and he is way in the distance. There is only the door beside her and the door frame around him. That's all there was to the real set. Everything else in between them is a painting. The walls, the whole set, even the reflection of him on the floor was painted. You now have a great depth of focus in that scene. Gregg Toland, in the beginning, did some of that type work directly in his camera. He was doing some things that were more difficult to do in the camera than on the optical printer. After he'd done two or three of these shots, I said, "Why don't you let me put the elements together on the optical printer?" Toland said, "I don't like dupes in my pictures." I said, "I don't like some dupes either. Bad dupes are bad, and good dupes are good. They've got to be the best dupes. Let me just do a couple for you." So we did this and, from then on, we composited several such scenes for the film.

Dunn contrasts working with Welles on *Citizen Kane* with his overall experience on major studio productions. At a major studio, "you have too many people to please. You can't possibly satisfy them all." On the other hand, "there are times you get a producer-director with the authority Orson Welles had, and you then don't have to check with anybody else for approvals. Dunn corroborates statements made by Charlton Heston, Polly Platt and Hannah Scheel about working with Welles. "I learned a lot," he says, "because I hadn't had just that kind of creative opportunity before. I was more of a practical man as were many of my colleagues at RKO . . . and then along came this boy genius. . . ." It is a pity, and perhaps an indictment of the powers-that-were, that Welles was never allowed to go ahead with his film version of Joseph Conrad's *Heart of Darkness*. Dunn's description of a preproduction test and his recollections of Welles's technical aspirations for the film ("He didn't want to use film cuts, so that, at the end of every scene, with the help of the optical printer, the action would continue right into the next one, except when the script called for a new one.") suggest that it might have been one in which both men stretched themselves even further than they did in *Citizen Kane*.

Though the importance of lengthy and rigorous preplanning in filmmaking has been insisted upon time and again in these pages, some of the medium's most special effects owe their existence to happenstance — serendipity. In the chapter on the actor, Ingrid Thulin calls at least part of her performance in the wedding scene of *The Damned* an "accident of the moment." She attributes her

overall bearing and the rejection of Dirk Bogarde's supportive arm
to the hostile distress with which she responded to Visconti's
inappropriate (she felt) and inflexible conception of the scene.
Though actors' improvisations are comparatively deliberate in the
sense that they are usually preceded by a conscious decision to
extemporize, the results of improvisation, either before or during
shooting, often fit the category of happy accident. Accident and
design are intermingled in the approach of William Wyler.

HARRY HORNER: In *The Heiress* he [shot a great many takes of]
the scene in which Olivia de Havilland, dressed to go out and
carrying a little bag, comes down the staircase and unexpectedly
finds Montgomery Clift. She came down the stairs wearing the
taffeta hoop skirt and carrying the bag and she was surprised
and she wasn't shy and she was and did all of the things she
was supposed to be and do. He shot it and he shot it again and
he shot it again. Since Wyler doesn't communicate particularly
well, he works by subtracting or reducing what he feels is
wrong. He might say, "Don't shake your head" after one take
and don't do something else after the next. She went on with
this thing for thirty takes, and by that time she was so relaxed
or so tired or so nervous that she accidentally dropped her
little bag as she saw her lover standing there. It slid down her
taffeta skirt, making a marvelous "ssss" sound. And Wyler said,
"Print it."

In another scene, Ralph Richardson comes home, is greeted
by a maid who takes his hat and helps him off with his coat,
and begins to walk into another room. They shot that many,
many times, and it seemed all right. She took his things in the
way a maid would and he would walk on. Then in one take —
take twenty-eight, maybe — the actress playing the maid didn't
time it well and hadn't gotten the coat completely off of him as
he started walking. She had to sort of follow him a bit to finish
the action and, again, this was the take Wyler printed. Wyler
waits for these accidents.

Jean Renoir, whose work probably shows less evidence of cal-
culation than that of any reasonably disciplined director, recalls

the circumstances surrounding the filming of a scene in *La Nuit du Carrefour*.

JEAN RENOIR: I remember it was an extraordinary adventure. . . . We occupied a kind of barn which was a little house at a crossroads, at the crossroads which is the title of the picture. We were sleeping on straw — we had brought plenty of straw — and we were drinking, we were — you know, I will never find it again. It was simply wonderful. We were a little drunk, and my nephew — he was just starting as a cameraman — rushed in and said, "Oh, now we have a nice patch of fog. Hey, let's shoot the scene." And we were all going outside and shooting.

Responsible for "moments" in *The Damned* and *The Heiress*, and the "weather" in a scene in *La Nuit du Carrefour*, chance has also played an important role in filmmaking on a more basic, conceptual level.

HOWARD HAWKS (With reference to *His Girl Friday*): . . . We were talking about dialogue, and I said that without a doubt the finest contemporary dialogue was Hecht's and MacArthur's. I had a couple of copies of the play *The Front Page*. There was a girl there who was a pretty good actress, and I said, "Read Hildy Johnson's part and I'll take the part of the editor." And while she was reading it I said, "My God, they are better lines coming from a girl than they are from a man." So I went off and bought the rights to the play, which had been filmed earlier as *The Front Page*, put Rosalind Russell and Cary Grant in it, and it was very successful. So, it really wasn't anybody thinking of it. It just happened that way.

HANNAH SCHEEL: Quite a few of the scenes in *Touch of Evil* — actually they were the best scenes — were written after we were in production. Mercedes McCambridge came to visit. She is an old friend of Orson Welles, and all of a sudden . . . the idea came to him to include her in the film. He wrote her scene — it was thought out and planned — but it was an addition, it wasn't in the original.

FEDERICO FELLINI: I shot most of the ending of 8½ with the train.
. . . But before the picture was finished I wanted to shoot a
trailer. So, I asked the producer if it was possible to call back
all the actors and all the extras who worked on the picture.
Just to shoot an extravagant trailer. So they came — two hundred people — and I asked for seven cameras — hand cameras
— and I said to them to go on the staircase and, when the music
started, to come down, to walk and talk. I said to the second
cameraman, "You do what you want. Take just the people because it is a trailer in which I want to use my voice." When the
music, the band started to play and all the people came down, I
was very moved by this scene and this atmosphere and I felt
that this was the right ending for my picture. So, I said to the
producer, "I have changed my idea. I don't want to use the
train. I have a new idea for the ending and I will shoot, more
precisely, the cast on the staircase."

Perhaps, in the final analysis, chance is the one constant, the
sole common ingredient in all filmmaking situations. "Visconti
didn't say one thing. He just smiled," Ingrid Thulin says. "A
director has to be ready . . . not to disturb that moment." The
director tests and, in a sense, redefines himself and his film by his
responses to various kinds of chance — the caprices of nature, the
fallibilities of man and machinery, the ideas of his collaborators.
Filmmaking is, to borrow a phrase from Norman Mailer, an
existential errand: a film's being is preceded by its becoming. At
what point does a film stop becoming?

JEAN RENOIR: You know what my preoccupation is in pictures?
When the picture is finished. It is that I would like the picture
to give the feeling to the audience that it is unfinished. Because
I believe that the work of art where the spectator, where the
re-viewer, does not collaborate is not a work of art. . . . If art
doesn't take us in as collaborators, art is dull.

# Credits

## Actors

Jack Benny has appeared in nineteen films. In addition to *To Be or Not To Be* (Ernst Lubitsch, director, 1942), they include *Man About Town* (Mark Sandrich, director, 1939), *Charley's Aunt* (Archie Mayo, director, 1941), and *George Washington Slept Here* (William Keighley, director, 1942).

Lynn Carlin made her film début in John Cassavetes's *Faces* (1968). She appeared subsequently in . . . *Tick* . . . *Tick* . . . *Tick* (Ralph Nelson, director, 1970), *The Wild Rovers* (Blake Edwards, director, 1971), and in *Taking Off* (Miloš Forman, director, 1971).

Leslie Caron's career as a film actress dates back to 1951, when she appeared in *An American in Paris* under Vincente Minnelli's direction. Minnelli directed her again in *The Story of Three Loves* (1953) and *Gigi* (1958). She also performed for Raoul Walsh in *Glory Alley* (1952); Joshua Logan in *Fanny* (1961); Bryan Forbes in *The L-Shaped Room* (1963); René Clair in *Three Fables of Love* (1963); Ralph Nelson in *Father Goose* (1964); René Clément in *Is Paris Burning?* (1966); and for Nanni Loy in *Il Padre di Famiglia* (*Head of the Family*, 1970).

John Cassavetes has appeared in *Edge of the City* (Martin Ritt, director, 1957), *The Killers* (Don Siegel, director, 1964), *The Dirty Dozen* (Robert Aldrich, director, 1967), and *Rosemary's Baby* (Roman Polanski, director, 1968), among other films. He has directed *Shadows* (1961), *Too Late Blues* (1962), *A Child Is Waiting* (1963), *Faces* (1968), *Husbands* (1970), and *Minnie and Moskowitz* (1971). Cassavetes collaborated on the script of *Too Late Blues* and, beginning with *Faces*, has written the films he has directed (he also acted in *Husbands* and *Minnie and Moskowitz*). *A Woman Under the Influence* (1974) is his latest directorial effort, *Nicky and Mikey* (Elaine May, director, 1974) his most recent film as an actor.

Peter Falk has acted in such films as *Wind Across the Everglades* (Nicholas Ray, director, 1958), *Murder, Inc.* (Stuart Rosenberg and Burt Balaban, directors, 1960), *Pocketful of Miracles* (Frank Capra, director, 1961), *The Balcony* (Joseph Strick, director, 1963), *It's a Mad, Mad, Mad, Mad World* (Stanley Kramer, director, 1963), *The Great Race* (Blake Edwards, director, 1965), *Castle Keep* (Sydney Pollack, director, 1969), *Husbands* (John Cassavetes, director, 1970), and *Nicky and Mikey* (Elaine May, director, 1974).

Nina Foch began acting in films in the mid-1940s and was, in her own words, "a B-Plus actress" in Columbia pictures for the remainder of that decade. *Johnny O'Clock*, one of Miss Foch's modestly scaled films of that period, was directed by Robert Rossen (1947) and another, *The Dark Past* (Rudolph Maté, director; 1948), emerged as an impressive sleeper. She worked subsequently in such films as *An American in Paris* (Vincente Minnelli, director; 1951), *Executive Suite* (Robert Wise, director, 1954), *The Ten Commandments* (Cecil B. DeMille, director, 1956), *Spartacus* (Stanley Kubrick, director, 1960), and *Such Good Friends* (Otto Preminger, director, 1971).

Henry Fonda has acted in roundly seventy films since 1935. His directors include Fritz Lang (*You Only Live Twice*, 1937, and *The Return of Frank James*, 1940); William Wyler (*Jezebel*, 1938); Preston Sturges (*The Lady Eve*, 1941); William A. Wellman (*The Ox-Bow Incident*, 1943); Otto Preminger (*Daisy Kenyon*, 1947; *Advise and Consent*, 1962, and *In Harm's Way*, 1964); Sidney Lumet (*Twelve Angry Men*, 1957; *Stage Struck*, 1958, and *Fail Safe*, 1964); Alfred Hitchcock (*The Wrong Man*, 1956); King Vidor (*War and Peace*, 1956); Franklin Schaffner (*The Best Man*, 1964); Don Siegel (*Madigan*, 1968); Sergio Leone (*Once Upon a Time in the West*, 1969); Joseph L. Mankiewicz (*There Was a Crooked Man . . .*, 1970), and Paul Newman (*Sometimes a Great Notion*, 1971). His seven pictures for John Ford are *Young Mr. Lincoln* (1939), *Drums Along the Mohawk* (1939), *The Grapes of Wrath* (1940), *My Darling Clementine* (1946), *The Fugitive* (1947), *Fort Apache* (1948), and *Mister Roberts* (co-directed by Mervyn LeRoy, 1955).

Charlton Heston has been acting in films since 1950. Heroic roles in period films became his specialty after *The Ten Commandments* (Cecil B. DeMille, director, 1956); he appeared subsequently in *Ben-Hur* (William Wyler, director, 1959), for which he won an Academy Award; *El Cid* (Anthony Mann, director, 1961); *The Agony and the Ecstasy* (Sir Carol Reed, director, 1965), and *Khartoum* (Basil Deardon, director, 1966). Heston's more impressive films not in this mold include *The Naked Jungle* (Byron Haskin, director, 1954); *Touch of Evil* (Orson Welles, director, 1958); *The Big Country* (William Wyler, director, 1958); *Major Dundee* (Sam Peckinpah, director, 1965); *Planet of the Apes* (Franklin Schaffner, director, 1968), and *Will Penny* (Tom Gries, director, 1968).

Robert Stephens's films include *The Prime of Miss Jean Brodie* (Ronald Neame, director, 1969), *The Private Life of Sherlock Holmes* (Billy Wilder, director, 1971), and *Travels With My Aunt* (George Cukor, director, 1972).

Ingrid Thulin has acted under Ingmar Bergman's direction in *Wild Strawberries* (1959), *The Magician* (1959), *Brink of Life* (1959), *Winter Light* (1963), *The Silence* (1964), *The Ritual* (1969) and *Cries and Whispers* (1972). She has also appeared to advantage in Alain Resnais' *La Guerre est Finie* (1966) and Luchino Visconti's *The Damned* (1969).

Jean-Louis Trintignant has acted in *And God Created Woman* (1957), *Les Liaisons Dangereuses* (1961) and *Nutty, Naughty Chateau* (English title for *Château en Suède*, 1964) for director Roger Vadim; *Violent Summer* (1961) for director Valerio Zurlini, and *The Easy Life* (1963) and *Il Successo* (1964) for director Dino Risi. His performance in Claude Lelouch's immensely successful *A Man and a Woman* in 1966 was followed by *Les Biches* (Claude Chabrol, director, 1968); *Z* (Costa-Gavras, director, 1969); *My Night at Maud's* (Eric Rohmer, director, 1970); *The Conformist* (Bernardo Bertolucci, director, 1971); *The Crook* (Lelouch, director, 1971); and *Without Apparent Motive* (Philippe Labro, director, 1972). In 1972, shortly after completing Yves Boisset's *The French Conspiracy* (English title for *L'Attentat*), Trintignant made Jacques Deray's *The Outside Man*, the first of his films shot in the United States.

Liv Ullmann's films for Ingmar Bergman include *Persona* (1967); *Hour of the Wolf* (1968); *Shame* (1968); *The Passion of Anna* (1970); and *Cries and Whispers* (1972), for which she won the Best Actress Award of the New York Film Critics. *The Emigrants* (1972) and its sequel, *The New Land* (1973), for director Jan Troell were followed by *Lost Horizon*

(Charles Jarrott, director, 1973) and *Forty Carats* (Milton Katselas, director, 1973), two Hollywood films. Ullmann and her fellow Scandinavian Troell then worked together again on *Zandy's Bride* for an American film company.

Jon Voight won the Best Actor Awards of both the New York Film Critics and the National Society of Film Critics for his performance in *Midnight Cowboy* (John Schlesinger, director; 1969). In 1970 he was seen in *Out of It* (filmed before *Midnight Cowboy*) and *The Revolutionary*, both directed by Paul Williams, and *Catch-22*, directed by Mike Nichols. *Deliverance* (John Boorman, director, 1972), *The All-American Boy*, filmed by director Charles Eastman in 1970, but released in 1973, *Conrack* (Martin Ritt, director, 1974), and *The Odessa File* (Ronald Neame, director, 1974) comprise Voight's more recent credits.

# Cinematographers

Conrad Hall débuted as a cinematographer in 1958 with shared credit for *Edge of Fury,* directed by Robert Guerney, Jr., and Irving Lerner. He has been associated with Richard Brooks on three films, *The Professionals* (1966), *In Cold Blood* (1967) and *The Happy Ending* (1969), and won an Academy Award for his contribution to *Butch Cassidy and the Sundance Kid* (1969), directed by George Roy Hill. Hall's credits include *Cool Hand Luke* (Stuart Rosenberg, director, 1967); *Hell in the Pacific* (John Boorman, director, 1968); *Fat City* (John Huston, director, 1972); *Electra Glide in Blue* (James William Guercio, director, 1973), and *The Day of the Locust* (John Schlesinger, director, 1974).

Winton Hoch, a cinematographer since 1940, is best known for his work with John Ford. The Ford films he has photographed include *Three Godfathers* (shared credit, 1948); *She Wore a Yellow Ribbon* (1949), for which he won an Academy Award; *The Quiet Man* (1952), for which he shared credit and an Academy Award with Archie Stout); *Mister Roberts* (co-directed by Mervyn LeRoy, 1955), and *The Searchers* (1956). Hoch has shared credit as director of photography on *Joan of Arc* (Victor Fleming, director, 1948); *Halls of Montezuma* (Lewis Milestone, director, 1950), and *This Earth is Mine* (Henry King, director, 1959). He has a solo credit for *Jet Pilot* (Josef von Sternberg, director, 1957).

James Wong Howe has photographed more than one hundred feature films since 1923, including *The Criminal Code* (shared credit, 1931) and *Air Force* (shared credit, 1943) for director Howard Hawks; *Transatlantic* (1931), *Surrender* (1931), *The Power and the Glory* (1933) and *Fire Over England* (1936) for William K. Howard; *After Tomorrow* (1932) for Frank Borzage; *Yellow Ticket* (1931), *The Strawberry Blonde* (1940) and *Objective Burma* (1945) for Raoul Walsh; *The Thin Man* (1934) for W. S. Van

Dyke; *Mark of the Vampire* (1935) for Tod Browning; *The Prisoner of Zenda* (1937), *Algiers* (1938) and *Abe Lincoln in Illinois* (1939) for John Cromwell; *The Adventures of Tom Sawyer* (1937) for Norman Taurog; *Kings Row* (1941) for Sam Wood; *Yankee Doodle Dandy* (1942) for Michael Curtiz; *Hangmen Also Die* (1942) for Fritz Lang; *The North Star* (1943) for Lewis Milestone; *Body and Soul* (1947) and *The Brave Bulls* (shared credit, 1951) for Robert Rossen; *Come Back, Little Sheba* (1952) and *The Rose Tattoo* (1955) for Daniel Mann; *Picnic* (1955) for Joshua Logan; *Sweet Smell of Success* (1957) for Alexander Mackendrick; *The Old Man and the Sea* (1957) for John Sturges; *Bell, Book and Candle* (1958) for Richard Quine; *This Property Is Condemned* (1966) for Sydney Pollack; *Seconds* (1966) for John Frankenheimer, and *Funny Lady* (1974) for Herbert Ross. With *Hud* (1963), for which Howe won his second Academy Award (the first was for *The Rose Tattoo*), he began an association with director Martin Ritt, for whom he has also photographed *The Outrage* (1964), *Hombre* (1967) and *The Molly Maguires* (1970).

Laszlo Kovacs's early credits include *The Savage Seven* (1968) for director Richard Rush, *Targets* (1968) for Peter Bogdanovich and *That Cold Day in the Park* (1969) for Robert Altman. *Easy Rider* (Dennis Hopper, director, 1969) was a turning point in his career, and was followed in quick succession by such films as *Getting Straight* (Richard Rush, director, 1970); *Five Easy Pieces* (Bob Rafelson, director, 1970); *Alex in Wonderland* (Paul Mazursky, director, 1970); *The Last Movie* (Dennis Hopper, director, 1971); *The Marriage of a Young Stockbroker* (Larry Turman, director, 1971); *What's Up, Doc?* (Peter Bogdanovich, director, 1972); *The King of Marvin Gardens* (Bob Rafelson, director, 1972); *Slither* (Howard Zieff, director, 1973); *Paper Moon* (Peter Bogdanovich, director, 1973); *Freebie and the Bean* (Richard Rush, director, 1974); *Huckleberry Finn* (J. Lee Thompson, director, 1974); and *For Pete's Sake* (Peter Yates, director, 1974).

Hal Mohr began working as a cinematographer in 1913. Among the thirty-odd silent films he worked on is Erich von Stroheim's *The Wedding March* (1928) for which B. Sorenson and Ben Reynolds share photographic credit. Mohr shot *The Jazz Singer* (Alan Crosland, director, 1927), the first all-talking film, and early in the sound era he photographed a number of films for Henry King and Michael Curtiz, including the latter's *Captain Blood* (1935). Mohr won Academy Awards for his contributions to *A Midsummer Night's Dream* (Max Reinhardt and William Dieterle, directors, 1935) and *The Phantom of the Opera* (Arthur Lubin, director, 1943), a shared credit with W. Howard Greene. Other noteworthy credits include *Green Pastures* (William Keighley and Marc Connelly, directors, 1936); *Destry Rides Again* (George Marshall, director, 1939); *Another Part of the Forest* (Michael Gordon, director, 1948); *The Big Night* (Joseph Losey, director, 1951); *Rancho Notorious* (Fritz Lang, director, 1952); *The Member of the Wedding* (Fred Zinnemann, director, 1952); *The Wild One*

(Laslo Benedek, director, 1954), and *Underworld U.S.A.* (Samuel Fuller, director, 1961). In the late 1950s, Mohr photographed three films for Don Siegel, and in 1969 acted as special photographic consultant on Alfred Hitchcock's *Topaz*.

Joseph Ruttenberg's career spans six decades and includes over one hundred films. His list of credits includes *The Struggle* (D. W. Griffith, director, 1931); *Fury* (Fritz Lang, director, 1936); *A Day at the Races* (Sam Wood, director, 1937); *The Great Waltz* (Julien Duvivier, director, 1938); *Three Comrades* (Frank Borzage, director, 1938); *The Shopworn Angel* (H. C. Potter, director, 1938); *The Women* (George Cukor, director, 1939), for which Oliver T. Marsh shared credit; *Waterloo Bridge* (Mervyn LeRoy, director, 1940); *The Philadelphia Story* (George Cukor, director, 1940); *Dr. Jekyll and Mr. Hyde* (Victor Fleming, director, 1941); *Woman of the Year* (George Stevens, director, 1942); *Mrs. Miniver* (William Wyler, director, 1942); *Gaslight* (George Cukor, director, 1943); *The Prisoner of Zenda* (Richard Thorpe, director, 1952); *Julius Caesar* (Joseph L. Mankiewicz, director, 1953); *The Last Time I Saw Paris* (Richard Brooks, director, 1954); *Brigadoon* (Vincente Minnelli, director, 1954); *The Swan* (Charles Vidor, director, 1956), which Robert Surtees completed; *Somebody Up There Likes Me* (Robert Wise, director, 1956); *Gigi* and *The Reluctant Debutante* (Vincente Minnelli, director, 1958), and *Butterfield 8* (Daniel Mann, director, 1960), on which Charles Harten also worked. Ruttenberg's four Academy Awards were for *The Great Waltz, Mrs. Miniver, Somebody Up There Likes Me* and *Gigi*.

John Seitz photographed almost one hundred fifty films in his forty-seven-year career. His twelve films for director Rex Ingram (1920–1926) and King Vidor's *The Patsy* (1928) constitute his best known work during the silent era. After the advent of sound, Seitz shot a number of films for Henry King (with whom he had been associated on two silent projects), Sam Wood and John Farrow, but his most distinguished work during this period was for Preston Sturges (*Sullivan's Travels*, in 1941, and *The Miracle of Morgan's Creek* and *Hail the Conquering Hero*, both released in 1944) and Billy Wilder (*Five Graves to Cairo*, in 1943; *Double Indemnity*, in 1944; *The Lost Weekend*, in 1945, and *Sunset Boulevard*, in 1950).

Haskell Wexler's first feature film was *Stakeout on Dope Street* (1958), directed by Irvin Kershner. He worked with Kershner again on *The Hoodlum Priest* (1961) and *A Face in the Rain* (1963), and with Elia Kazan on *America, America* (1963), Franklin Schaffner on *The Best Man* (1964) and Tony Richardson on *The Loved One* (1965). He won an Academy Award for *Who's Afraid of Virginia Woolf?* (1966), which Mike Nichols directed. Wexler shot *In the Heat of the Night* (1967) and *The Thomas Crown Affair* (1968) for Norman Jewison, photographed and directed *Medium Cool* (1969) and has been involved, either as cinematographer or cinematographer-director, with a number of documentary films. He was photographic consultant on *American Graffiti* (1973), directed by George Lukas.

Gordon Willis has shot *End of the Road* (1970) for Aram Avakian, director; *The Landlord* (1970) for Hal Ashby; *Loving* (1970) and *Up the Sandbox* (1972) for Irvin Kershner; *Klute* (1971) and *The Parallax View* (1974) for Alan J. Pakula; *Little Murders* (1971) for Alan Arkin; *The Godfather* (1972) and *Godfather II* (1974) for Francis Ford Coppola; *Bad Company* (1972) for Robert Benton; and *The Paper Chase* (1973) for James Bridges.

# Composers

Elmer Bernstein has composed the scores for *The Man With the Golden Arm* (Otto Preminger, director, 1955); *Men in War* (Anthony Mann, director, 1959); *Some Came Running* (Vincente Minnelli, director, 1959); *The Magnificent Seven* (John Sturges, director, 1960); *Summer and Smoke* (Peter Glenville, director, 1961); *To Kill a Mockingbird* (Robert Mulligan, director, 1961); *Birdman of Alcatraz* (John Frankenheimer, director, 1962); *Hud* (Martin Ritt, director, 1963); *The Great Escape* (John Sturges, director, 1963); *The Carpetbaggers* (Edward Dmytryk, director, 1964); *The Scalphunters* (Sydney Pollack, director, 1968); *I Love You, Alice B. Toklas* (Hy Averback, director, 1968); and *True Grit* (Henry Hathaway, director, 1970). He provided music for three films directed by George Roy Hill, *The World of Henry Orient* (1964), *Hawaii* (1966) and *Thoroughly Modern Millie* (1967). *Millie* won Bernstein an Academy Award.

Jerry Goldsmith has provided the music for films directed by John Huston (*Freud*, 1962; *The List of Adrian Messenger*, 1963); Franklin Schaffner (*The Stripper*, 1963; *Planet of the Apes*, 1968; *Patton*, 1970, and *Papillon*, 1973); Mark Robson (*The Prize*, 1963); Otto Preminger (*In Harm's Way*, 1964); John Frankenheimer (*Seven Days in May*, 1964; *Seconds*, 1966); Robert Wise (*The Sand Pebbles*, 1966); George Cukor (*Justine*, 1966); Sam Peckinpah (*The Ballad of Cable Hogue*, 1970); Howard Hawks (*Rio Lobo*, 1970); and Roman Polanski (*Chinatown*, 1974). His credits also include *Lilies of the Field* (Ralph Nelson, director, 1963); *A Patch of Blue* (Guy Green, director, 1965); *The Blue Max* (John Guillermin, director, 1966); *The Detective* (Gordon Douglas, director, 1968), and *The Don Is Dead* (Richard Fleischer, director, 1973).

John Green composed the score for *Raintree County* (Edward Dmytryk, director, 1957) and, with Albert Woodbury, adapted the standards that comprised the score of *They Shoot Horses, Don't They?* (Sydney Pollack, director, 1969). He is especially skillful at adapting stage musicals for the screen, his credits in this area including *Bye Bye Birdie* (George Sidney, director, 1963), *West Side Story* (Robert Wise and Jerome Robbins, co-directors, 1961), for which he shared credit and an Academy Award, and *Oliver* (Sir Carol Reed, director, 1968), which brought him a second Academy Award.

Alex North has written the music for *A Streetcar Named Desire* (Elia Kazan, director, 1951); *Death of a Salesman* (Laslo Benedek, director, 1952); *Viva Zapata* (Elia Kazan, director, 1952); *The Member of the Wedding* (Fred Zinnemann, director, 1952); *The Rose Tattoo* (Daniel Mann, director, 1955); *The Rainmaker* (Joseph Anthony, director, 1956); *The Long, Hot Summer* (Martin Ritt, director, 1958); *Spartacus* (Stanley Kubrick, director, 1960); *The Misfits* (John Huston, director, 1961); *The Children's Hour* (William Wyler, director, 1962); *All Fall Down* (John Frankenheimer, director, 1962); *Cleopatra* (Joseph L. Mankiewicz, director, 1963); *The Outrage* (Martin Ritt, director, 1964); *Cheyenne Autumn* (John Ford, director, 1964); and *Who's Afraid of Virginia Woolf?* (Mike Nichols, director, 1966).

# Costume Designers

Edith Head has been a motion picture costume designer since 1923. Among her early credits is *She Done Him Wrong* (Lowell Sherman, director, 1932). She has made contributions to films directed by William Wyler (most notably, *The Heiress*, of 1949, and *Roman Holiday*, of 1953); Joseph L. Mankiewicz (*All About Eve*, 1950); George Stevens (*A Place in the Sun*, 1951); Billy Wilder (notably, *Sabrina*, 1954, and *Witness for the Prosecution*, 1958); Alfred Hitchcock (notably, *Rear Window*, 1954, and *To Catch a Thief*, 1955); Stanley Donen (*Funny Face*, 1957); Frank Capra (*A Hole in the Head*, 1959, and *Pocketful of Miracles*, 1961); John Ford (*The Man Who Shot Liberty Valance*, 1962); Robert Mulligan (*Love With the Proper Stranger*, 1963), and Martin Ritt (*Hud*, 1963, and *Pete 'n' Tillie*, 1972). Five of Head's seven individual or shared Academy Awards were for films listed above. Her costumes for *Samson and Delilah* (Cecil B. DeMille, director, 1950) and *The Facts of Life* (Melvin Frank, director, 1960) were also honored by the Academy.

Theadora Van Runkle has designed the costumes for *Bonnie and Clyde* (Arthur Penn, director, 1967); *I Love You, Alice B. Toklas* (Hy Averback, director, 1968); *The Thomas Crown Affair* (Norman Jewison, director, 1968); *The Arrangement* (Elia Kazan, director, 1969); *The Reivers* (Mark Rydell, director, 1969); *Myra Breckinridge* (Michael Sarne, director, 1970); *Kid Blue* (James Frawley, director, 1973); *Mame* (Gene Saks, director, 1974), and *Godfather II* (Francis Ford Coppola, director, 1974).

# Film Editors

Hal Ashby's credits as a film editor include *The Loved One* (Tony Richardson, director, 1965), and four films for Norman Jewison: *The Cincinnati Kid* (1965); *The Russians Are Coming, The Russians Are Coming* (1966); *In the Heat of the Night* (1967), and *The Thomas Crown Affair* (1968). Ashby won an Academy Award for *In the Heat of the Night*. As a director, he has made *The Landlord* (1970), *Harold and Maude* (1971), *The Last Detail* (1973) and *Shampoo* (1974).

David Bretherton has edited films directed by Mark Robson (*Peyton Place*, 1957); George Stevens (*The Diary of Anne Frank*, 1959); John Frankenheimer (*The Train*, 1965); Joseph L. Mankiewicz (*The Honey Pot*, 1967), and Vincente Minnelli (*On a Clear Day You Can See Forever*, 1970). His credits also include *Ten North Frederick* (Philip Dunne, director, 1958); *Cabaret* (Bob Fosse, director, 1972), for which he won an Academy Award; *Save the Tiger* (John Avildsen, director, 1973); *Slither* (Howard Zieff, director, 1973), and *Westworld* (Michael Crichton, director, 1973).

Frank Keller has been an editor on such films as *The Five Pennies* (Melville Shavelson, director, 1959); *Pocketful of Miracles* (Frank Capra, director, 1961); *Beach Red* (Cornel Wilde, director, 1967), and *Bullitt* (Peter Yates, director, 1968), for which he won an Academy Award. He has since been associated with Yates on four additional films, including *The Hot Rock* (1972) and *For Pete's Sake* (1974).

Daniel Mandell was involved in the editing of Erich von Stroheim's *Foolish Wives* (1922). In the sound era he has been identified with the films of William Wyler and Billy Wilder. For Wyler, he edited *Counsellor-at-Law* (1933); *The Good Fairy* (1935); *Dodsworth* (1936); *Dead End* (1937); *Wuthering Heights* (1939); *The Westerner* (1940), and *The Little Foxes* (1941). *Witness for the Prosecution* (1957), *One, Two, Three* (1961), *Irma La Douce* (1963) and *The Fortune Cookie* (1966) are among his assignments with Wilder. Mandell's four Academy Awards were for *Sergeant York* (Howard Hawks, director, 1941), *The Pride of the Yankees* (Sam Wood, director, 1942), *The Best Years of Our Lives* (William Wyler, director, 1946), and *The Apartment* (Billy Wilder, director, 1960). Other credits include *Meet John Doe* (Frank Capra, director, 1941); *Ball of Fire* (Howard Hawks, director, 1942); *Guys and Dolls* (Joseph L. Mankiewicz, director, 1955), and three comedies starring Danny Kaye: *Up in Arms* (Elliott Nugent, director, 1944), *Wonder Man* (Bruce Humberstone, director, 1945), and *The Kid from Brooklyn* (Norman Z. McLeod, director, 1946).

Fredric Steinkamp has made editorial contributions to *All Fall Down* (John Frankenheimer, director, 1962); *Period of Adjustment* (George Roy Hill, director, 1962); *The Unsinkable Molly Brown* (Charles Walters, director, 1964); *Charly* (Ralph Nelson, director, 1966); *Grand Prix* (John Frankenheimer, director, 1966), for which he and his coeditors were honored with Academy Awards; *They Shoot Horses, Don't They?* (Sydney Pollack, director, 1969); *A New Leaf* (Elaine May, director, 1971), and *Freebie and the Bean* (Richard Rush, director, 1974).

# Producers

Peter Bart has held positions as vice president in charge of creative affairs and vice president of production at Paramount Pictures. He recently relinquished the latter post to personally produce a series of films for Paramount. A *New York Times* reporter before entering motion pictures, Bart wrote the screenplay of *Making It* (John Erman, director, 1971), which Albert S. Ruddy produced.

Pandro S. Berman was associated with RKO as both a studio executive and a producer in the 1930s, with MGM as a producer from 1941 through 1965, and with Twentieth Century-Fox as a producer for a brief period in the late 1960s. Of the seven Astaire-Rogers movies he produced, William A. Seiter directed one (*Roberta*, 1935), George Stevens one (*Swing Time*, 1936) and Mark Sandrich five (*The Gay Divorcee*, 1934; *Top Hat*, 1935; *Follow the Fleet*, 1936; *Shall We Dance?* 1937; and *Carefree*, 1938). Berman was Stevens's producer on *Laddie* (1935), *Alice Adams* (1935), *Quality Street* (1937), *Damsel in Distress* (1937) and *Vivacious Lady* (1938), and was involved with the director on *Gunga Din* (1939), though Stevens himself is credited with the production. Berman was producer of John Ford's *Mary of Scotland* (1936) and, as a studio executive, was instrumental in Ford's making *The Informer* (1935). He produced films directed by Gregory LaCava (*Stage Door*, 1937); George Cukor (*Sylvia Scarlett*, 1936, *Bhowani Junction*, 1956, and *Justine*, 1969); Vincente Minnelli (*Undercurrent*, 1946; *Madame Bovary*, 1949; *Father of the Bride*, 1950, and its sequel, *Father's Little Dividend*, 1951; *Tea and Sympathy*, 1956, and *The Reluctant Debutante*, 1958); Elia Kazan (*Sea of Grass*, 1947), and Richard Brooks (*The Blackboard Jungle*, 1955; *Something of Value*, 1957, and *Sweet Bird of Youth*, 1962). In 1958 Brooks directed *The Brothers Karamazov* and *Cat on a Hot Tin Roof*, two films made by Berman's and Laurence Weingarten's independent production company. Also part of Berman's seventy-six-picture career are *National Velvet* (Clarence Brown, director, 1944); *Ivanhoe* (Richard Thorpe, director; 1952); *The Prisoner of Zenda* (Richard Thorpe, director, 1952); *Butterfield 8* (Daniel Mann, director, 1960); *The Prize* (Mark Robson, director, 1963), and *A Patch of Blue* (Guy Green, director, 1965).

Bob Christiansen and Rick Rosenberg produced the theatrical feature *Adam at Six A.M.* (Robert Scheerer, director, 1970), and such movies for television as *The Glass House* (Tom Gries, director, 1971), *A Brand New Life* (Sam O'Steen, director, 1972), and *The Autobiography of Miss Jane Pittman* (John Korty, director, 1973).

Merian C. Cooper is perhaps best known as the coauthor, coproducer and director of *King Kong* (1933). He was also an RKO executive in the 1930s, and in the period 1948–1956 was producer, executive producer, or co-producer with John Ford of five films directed by Ford: *Fort Apache* (1948); *Three Godfathers* (1949); *Rio Grande* (1950); *The Quiet Man* (1952), and *The Searchers* (1956).

Roger Corman produced a number of astonishingly inexpensive program pictures in the late 1950s. His films as a producer-director include *The House of Usher* (1960), *Tales of Terror* (1961), *The Pit and the Pendulum* (1962), *The Wild Angels* (1966), *The St. Valentine's Day Massacre* (1967) and *Bloody Mama* (1970), of which all but the second-to-last were modestly budgeted. Corman has backed the first films of directors Irvin Kershner (*Stakeout on Dope Street*, 1958); Francis Ford Coppola (*Dementia 13*, 1963); Peter Bogdanovich (*Targets*, 1968), and Monte Hellman (*The Shooting* and *Ride in the Whirlwind*, both shot in 1967). His company, New World Films, is involved in the making of modestly-budgeted genre films and the presentation of such distinguished fare as Ingmar Bergman's *Cries and Whispers* (1972).

Albert S. Ruddy produced *The Wild Seed* (Brian G. Hutton, director, 1965), *Little Fauss and Big Halsy* (Sidney J. Furie, director, 1970), and *Making It* (John Erman, director, 1971) prior to *The Godfather* (Francis Ford Coppola, director, 1972). More recently, he has produced *Coon Skin* (Ralph Bakshi, director, 1974) and *The Longest Yard* (Robert Aldrich, director, 1974).

# Production Designers

Gene Allen has worked on the following films directed by George Cukor: *A Star is Born* (1954); *Bhowani Junction* (1956); *Les Girls* (1957); *Heller in Pink Tights* (1960); *Let's Make Love* (1960); and *My Fair Lady* (1964). Allen shares design credit on all of these films. His contribution to *My Fair Lady* resulted in an Academy Award. For Cukor's *The Chapman Report* (1962), Allen receives solo design credit, in addition to a cocredit for the film's "adaptation."

Harry Horner won Academy Awards for *The Heiress* (William Wyler, director, 1949), on which he shares credit with John Meehan, and *The Hustler*

(Robert Rossen, director, 1961). He has also designed *Born Yesterday* (George Cukor, director, 1950); *Separate Tables* (Delbert Mann, director, 1958); *They Shoot Horses, Don't They?* (Sydney Pollack, director, 1969); *Who Is Harry Kellerman and Why Is He Saying All Those Terrible Things About Me?* (Ulu Grosbard, director, 1971); *Up the Sandbox* (Irvin Kershner, director, 1972).

Polly Platt's close identification with the films of Peter Bogdanovich began with *Targets,* the director's first feature. (Platt was also coauthor of the story of the 1968 film.) Subsequently, she was production designer on Bogdanovich's *The Last Picture Show* (1971); *What's Up, Doc?* (1972); and *Paper Moon* (1973). She designed *The Thief Who Came to Dinner* (Bud Yorkin, director, 1973) and *The Other Side of the Wind* (uncompleted; Orson Welles, director), and assisted Robert Altman in an unofficial capacity on *Thieves Like Us* (1974).

# Screenwriters

Leigh Brackett, a screenwriter since 1945, is cocredited with the scripts of three Howard Hawks films: *The Big Sleep* (1946); *Rio Bravo* (1959); and *Rio Lobo* (1970). She wrote the screenplays for two additional Hawks pictures, *Hatari!* (1962) and *El Dorado* (1967), and for Robert Altman's *The Long Goodbye* (1973).

Ray Bradbury's adaptation of *Moby Dick* (John Huston, director, 1956) is his only work for the screen, though his fiction has been the basis of four films. The most notable of these is *Fahrenheit 451* (Francois Truffaut, director, 1966).

Lonne Elder III is the author of the prize-winning play *Ceremonies in Dark Old Men,* and of the screenplays for *Melinda* (Hugh A. Robertson, director, 1972) and *Sounder* (Martin Ritt, director, 1972).

Howard Estabrook won an Academy Award for his screen adaptation of Edna Ferber's *Cimarron* (Wesley Ruggles, director, 1931). Active until 1959, his work includes *David Copperfield* (George Cukor, director, 1935) and *The Human Comedy* (Clarence Brown, director, 1944).

Nunnally Johnson, a screenwriter since the early 1930s, received solo screenplay credit for the great majority of the films with which he has been involved. Among these are *The House of Rothschild* (Alfred Werker, director, 1934); *The Prisoner of Shark Island* (John Ford, director, 1936); *Jesse James* (Henry King, director, 1939); *Wife, Husband and Friend* (Gregory Ratoff, director, 1939); *The Grapes of Wrath* (John Ford, director, 1940); *Chad Hanna* (Henry King, director, 1940); *Tobacco Road* (John Ford, director, 1941); *Roxie Hart* (William A. Wellman, director, 1942); *The Moon Is Down* (Irving Pichel, director, 1943); *Holy Matrimony* (John M. Stahl, director, 1943); *The Woman in the Window* (Fritz Lang, director, 1944); *The Dark Mirror* (Robert Siodmak, director, 1946); *Everybody Does It* (Edmund Goulding, director, 1949), a remake of *Husband, Wife and Friend; The Desert Fox* (Henry Hathaway, director, 1951); the "Ransom of Red Chief" episode of *O. Henry's Full House* (Howard Hawks, director, 1952); and *How to Marry a Millionaire* (Jean Negulesco, director, 1953). Johnson shared writing credit on *Flaming Star* (Don Siegel, director, 1960); *The World of Henry Orient* (George Roy Hill, director, 1964) and *The Dirty Dozen* (Robert Aldrich, director, 1967) and made an uncredited contribution to *The Gunfighter* (Henry King, director, 1950), which he also produced. He was associate producer or producer of many of the films which he wrote and, beginning in 1954, with *Night People*, wrote, produced and directed a number of films, including *Black Widow* (1954), *The Three Faces of Eve* (1957) and *The Man Who Understood Women* (1959). He wrote and directed but did not produce *The Man in the Gray Flannel Suit* (1956).

W. D. Richter has worked on essentially unutilized drafts of *Melinda* (Hugh A. Robertson, director, 1972), *Lady Ice* (Tom Gries, director, 1973), and *Deadly Honeymoon* (Elliott Silverstein, director, unreleased). Following *Slither* (Howard Zieff, director, 1973), he wrote the screenplay for *Fat Chance* (Peter Hyams, director, 1974).

Alvin Sargent's career as a screenwriter dates back to 1966, when he was cocredited with Sidney Carrol for the screenplay of *Gambit* (Ronald Neame, director). His subsequent credits include *The Stalking Moon* (Robert Mulligan, director, 1969); *The Sterile Cuckoo* (Alan J. Pakula, director, 1969); *I Walk the Line* (John Frankenheimer, director, 1970); *The Effect of Gamma Rays on Man-in-the-Moon Marigolds* (Paul Newman, director, 1972); *Paper Moon* (Peter Bogdanovich, director, 1973), and *Love and Pain and the Whole Damned Thing* (Alan J. Pakula, director, 1973).

Budd Schulberg collaborated on the screenplay of *Winter Carnival* (Charles F. Resiner, director, 1939), and received solo credit for *On The Waterfront* (Elia Kazan, director, 1954), which won him an Academy Award, *A Face in the Crowd* (Elia Kazan, director, 1957), and *Wind Across the Everglades* (Nicholas Ray, director, 1958). His novel *The Harder They Fall* was adapted for the screen by Philip Yordan and filmed by Mark Robson in 1956.

Leonard Spigelgass, a screenwriter since the 1930s, has made contributions to nineteen feature-length films. The best known of these are *All Through the Night* (Vincent Sherman, director, 1942), in which Humphrey Bogart starred, *I Was a Male War Bride* (Howard Hawks, director, 1949), *A Ma-*

*jority of One* (Mervyn LeRoy, director, 1962), which Spigelgass adapted from his own long-running play, and *Gypsy* (Mervyn LeRoy, director, 1962).

Donald Ogden Stewart has shared writing credit on a score of films, including *Laughter* (Harry D'Arrast, director, 1930); *Smilin' Through* (both the version directed by Sidney Franklin in 1932, and remake directed by Frank Borzage in 1941); *Dinner at Eight* (George Cukor, director, 1933); *The Barretts of Wimpole Street* (Sidney Franklin, director, 1934); *The Prisoner of Zenda* (John Cromwell, director, 1937); *Holiday* (George Cukor, director, 1938); *Love Affair* (Leo McCarey, director, 1939); *Kitty Foyle* (Sam Wood, director, 1940); and *Tales of Manhattan* (Julien Duvivier, director, 1942). Four of his solo screenplays have been filmed by George Cukor: *Tarnished Lady* (1931); *The Philadelphia Story* (1940); *Keeper of the Flame* (1942); and *Edward, My Son* (1949). Stewart also provided the scripts for *White Sister* (Victor Fleming, director, 1933); *Night of Nights* (Lewis Milestone, director, 1940); *That Uncertain Feeling* (Ernst Lubitsch, director, 1941); *Without Love* (Harold S. Bucquet, director, 1945); *Life with Father* (Michael Curtiz, director, 1947), and *Cass Timberlane* (George Sidney, director, 1947).

# Script Supervisors

Hannah Scheel has worked as a script supervisor on European and American feature films, as a writer-producer of documentary films made in Europe in the postwar era under Marshall Plan auspices, as assistant to producer-composer Arthur Schwartz, as "Gal Friday" to Orson Welles, and as a story editor and associate producer for Selmur Productions.

Karen Wookey's credits include *The Arrangement* (Elia Kazan, director, 1969); *Flap* (Sir Carol Reed, director, 1970); *Everything You Wanted to Know About Sex But Were Afraid to Ask* (Woody Allen, director, 1972); *Slither* (Howard Zieff, director, 1973); *Paper Moon* (Peter Bogdanovich, director, 1973); *The Iceman Cometh* (John Frankenheimer, director, 1973); *The Parallax View* (Alan J. Pakula, director, 1974), and *The Day of the Locust* (John Schlesinger, director, 1974).